CRE▲TIVE
HOMEOWNER®

Furniture

Repair & Restoration

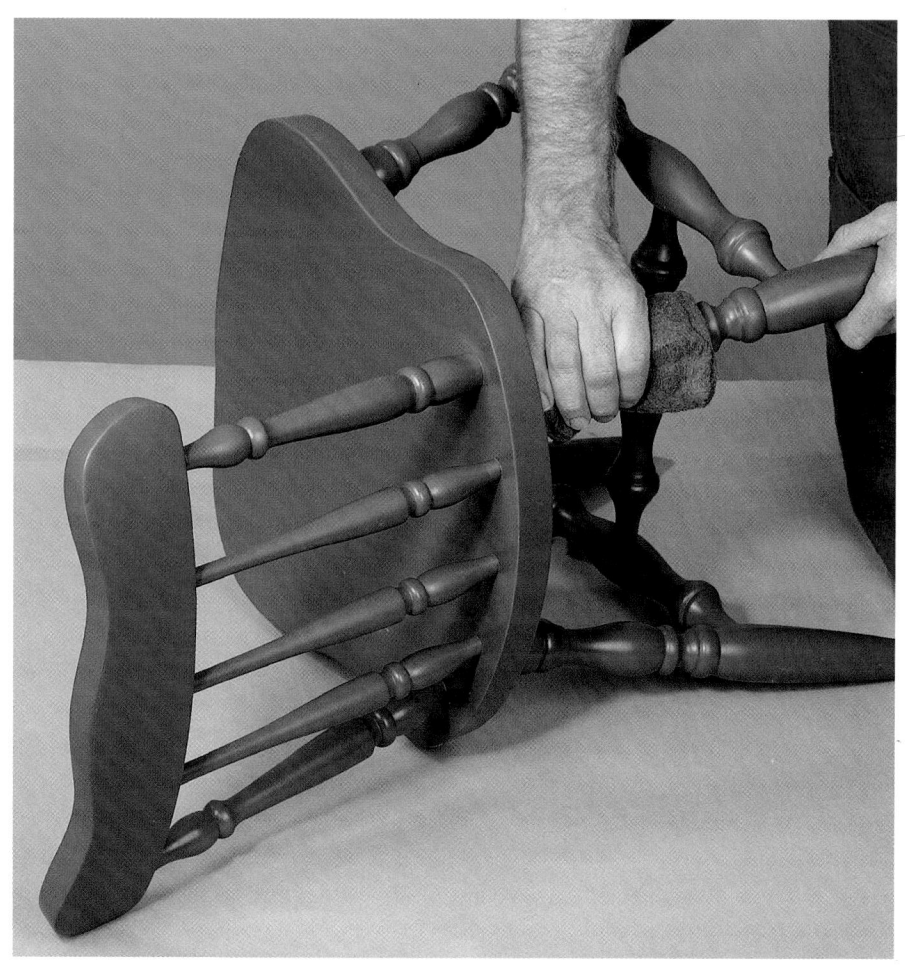

Brian D. Hingley

CREATIVE HOMEOWNER®, Upper Saddle River, New Jersey

FURNITURE REPAIR & RESTORATION

AUTHOR	Brian D. Hingley
MANAGING EDITOR	Fran Donegan
EDITOR	Lisa Kahn
GRAPHIC DESIGNER	Kathryn Wityk
PHOTO COORDINATOR	Mary Dolan
PROOFREADER	Sara M. Markowitz
DIGITAL IMAGING SPECIALIST	Frank Dyer
INDEXER	Schroeder Indexing Services
COVER DESIGN	Kathryn Wityk, David Geer
PHOTOGRAPHY	All photography by H. Howard Hudgins, Jr/CH, unless noted otherwise noted.
ADDITIONAL PHOTOGRAPHY	Lance Patterson/CH: pp. 8, 18, 34, 40, 58, 82, 92, 108, 116, 128, 136, 142, 148,160, 168
	Jim Roberson/CH: pp. 44, 45, 48, 49, 50, 53
	Marc Samu: p. 4
FRONT COVER	(table) Freeze Frame Studio/CH
BACK COVER	Left both Lance Patterson/CH
ILLUSTRATIONS	Rodney Stokes, Paul Schumm, Vincent Allessi

CREATIVE HOMEOWNER

VICE PRESIDENT AND PUBLISHER	Timothy O. Bakke
ART DIRECTOR	David Geer
MANAGING EDITOR	Fran J. Donegan
PRODUCTION COORDINATOR	Sara M. Markowitz

Current Printing (last digit)
10 9 8 7 6 5 4 3 2 1

Manufactured in the United States of America

Furniture Repair & Restoration
Library of Congress Control Number: 2009932395
ISBN-10: 1-58011-478-4
ISBN-13: 978-1-58011-478-3

CREATIVE HOMEOWNER®
A Division of Federal Marketing Corp.
24 Park Way
Upper Saddle River, NJ 07458
www.creativehomeowner.com

Planet Friendly Publishing
✓ Made in the United States
✓ Printed on Recycled Paper
Text: 10%   Cover: 10%
Learn more: www.greenedition.org

GREEN EDITION

At Creative Homeowner we're committed to producing books in an earth-friendly manner and to helping our customers make greener choices.

Manufacturing books in the United States ensures compliance with strict environmental laws and eliminates the need for international freight shipping, a major contributor to global air pollution.

And printing on recycled paper helps minimize our consumption of trees, water, and fossil fuels. *Furniture Repair & Restoration* was printed on paper made with 10% post-consumer waste. According to the Environmental Defense Fund Paper Calculator, by using this innovative paper instead of conventional papers we achieved the following environmental benefits:

Trees Saved: 20

Water Saved: 9,213 gallons

Solid Waste Eliminated: 559 pounds

Greenhouse Gas Emissions Eliminated: 1,913 pounds

For more information on our environmental practices, please visit us online at www.creativehomeowner.com/green

Safety First

Though all the methods in this book have been tested for safety, it is not possible to overstate the importance of using the safest procedures possible. What follows are reminders—some do's and don'ts of work safety. They are not substitutes for your own common sense.

■ Always use caution and good judgment when following the repair and refinishing procedures described in this book.

■ Always be sure that the electrical setup is safe; be sure that no circuit is overloaded and that all power tools and electrical outlets are properly grounded. Use GFCI-protected circuits whenever possible.

■ Always read container labels on paints, solvents, and other products; provide ventilation, and observe all other warnings.

■ Always read the tool maker's instructions for using a tool.

■ Always use hold-downs and push sticks whenever possible when working on a table saw. Avoid working short pieces if you can.

■ Always remove the key from any drill chuck (portable or press) before starting the drill.

■ Always know the limitations of your tools. Do not try to force them to do what they were not designed to do.

■ Always make sure that any power-tool adjustment is locked before proceeding.

■ Always clamp small pieces firmly to a bench or other work surface when using a power tool on them.

■ Always wear the appropriate rubber or work gloves when handling chemicals.

■ Always wear a disposable face mask when you create dust by sawing or sanding. Use a special filtering respirator when working with toxic substances and solvents.

■ Always wear eye protection when using power tools or striking metal on metal.

■ Always be aware that there is seldom enough time for your body's reflexes to save you from injury from a power tool in a dangerous situation; everything happens too fast. Be alert!

■ Always keep your hands away from the business ends of blades, cutters, and bits.

■ Always hold a circular saw firmly, usually with both hands so that you know where they are.

■ Never work with power tools when you are tired or under the influence of alcohol or drugs.

■ Never cut very small pieces of wood or pipe using a power saw. Cut small pieces off larger pieces.

■ Never change a saw blade or a drill or router bit unless the power cord is unplugged.

■ Never work in insufficient lighting.

■ Never work while wearing loose clothing, hanging hair, open cuffs, or jewelry.

■ Never work with dull tools. Have them sharpened, or learn how to sharpen them yourself.

Contents

Introduction

Furniture restoration has long been a popular pastime for do-it-yourself enthusiasts. During my years of working on furniture, I've discovered that people with all kinds of backgrounds, from students to homemakers to professional people, have either restored or tried to restore a piece of furniture.

There are myriad reasons for such wide appeal. The reason I hear most often is simply that furniture restoration is enjoyable. Retreating to the sanctuary of a home workshop to work on a furniture project provides not only satisfaction but relaxation and stress relief. Often your efforts will bring immediate, rewarding results. There's great personal satisfaction in taking a piece of furniture previously destined for the trash and transforming it into a useful, beautiful piece to grace your home for years to come.

People with artistic talent find that furniture projects offer opportunities for creative expression; while many repair techniques in furniture restoration are basic and standard, you can put your creativity to work in the later stages of refinishing as you strive to achieve just the right look for your piece. Others discover that the challenge of problem-solving—or just fixing something that's broken—can be satisfying.

One of the most obvious reasons to do anything yourself is to save money. Learning to restore furniture allows you to turn that yard sale or auction bargain into something of value for your home at a fraction of the cost of a comparable, fully-restored piece.

One of the first pieces of furniture I ever acquired and transformed was an old walnut Victorian rocker. The upholstery and springs were missing, but I knew the wood rocker and its frame were redeemable. The top of the rocker featured a beautiful hand-carved grape cluster, and I knew the chair could be a true thing of beauty once I refurbished it. I paid less than $20 for the chair, restored it, and had a professional upholsterer add springs and fabric. Even including the price I paid for a professional upholstery job, the antique rocker was a great bargain. Today that chair continues to occupy a place of honor in my living room more than 20 years after I first brought it home. Guests never fail to comment on its beauty and comfort.

Restored wood furniture usually has a value equal to—and in many cases greater than—a comparable new piece available in today's furniture stores. Much of today's manufactured furniture lacks quality construction, making wide use of plastics and other nonwood materials. Restoring old furniture that is not truly "antique," but all wood and built solidly, still makes sense in terms of practical use and value.

Another money-saving aspect of restoring furniture yourself is that when problems develop in your own household furniture, you can repair them. Keep in mind, however, that you need to know how to do the job correctly before attempting your own repairs. As a professional furniture restorer, I've had to salvage many botched repair attempts. Trying to fix a piece after it's been improperly repaired is more difficult and expensive than simply doing it right the first time.

Even though your piece may not be worth thousands, restoring it can produce a useful and beautiful addition to your home, as in this restored pine chest of drawers.

Working on a furniture project provides not only rewarding results but also relaxation and stress relief.

Yet another reason for furniture restoration is sentimental attachment. Your mother's china cabinet or foot-pedal sewing machine may not be a true antique or worth thousands, but you may never be able to replace its value as a family heirloom.

I once restored a customer's 40-year-old nightstand. It was in terrible shape, with water damage and a broken top. The piece was not technically valuable, but it had been part of the first bedroom suite of the customer's parents, and their daughter, my client, had it restored for them as a surprise Christmas present.

That client later wrote me a thank-you note, commenting, "You did a beautiful job on the nightstand. As you know, the restoration was a gift for my parents. The expression on their faces when they saw it was worth three times the money I spent on the restoration." Doing your own refurbishing projects on furniture with personal sentimental value can provide you with similar—or even stronger—feelings.

Restoring furniture is something you can do in the comfort and convenience of your own home, and you don't even need a workshop full of expensive tools and equipment. If you have a basement, a garage, an extra room, or even an enclosed porch, you can make space for a furniture project. And although many professional furniture shops accumulate expensive tools and equipment, often you can do the work required using only simple hand tools and a few small power tools.

If you have limited resources, you can buy your tools only as needed.

While it's true that some aspects of furniture repair and restoration require more ability than others—and there are projects best left to the hands of a skilled professional—don't allow this to discourage you from starting your own furniture projects. If you are patient and determined to learn, you can undertake the majority of restoration projects without having a high level of skill, as long as you have knowledgeable sources to which you can refer as you work.

Whether you want to lovingly restore a treasured antique or you just want to be able to solve practical furniture problems around the house, the following pages will provide a wealth of information to help you. Before you begin a project, read over the material. Then keep this book on hand for quick, easy reference while you work on your piece.

Each step-by-step project in the book begins with a suggested list of the tools and materials necessary to complete the work. Each task is rated by the level of difficulty of the work to be done on the furniture. This is indicated by one, two, or three hammers.

These difficulty ratings should help you gauge whether you want to tackle a project or not. This way, you won't be well into a project before discovering that you're in over your head.

It's important that—as a hobby—furniture restoration is enjoyable. It is my hope that this book will help you have many hours of pleasure as you set your hand to the task of furniture repair and restoration.

guide to skill level

Easy. Even for beginners.

Challenging. Can be done by beginners who have the patience and willingness to learn.

Difficult. Can be done by the do-it-yourselfer, but requires a serious investment of time, patience, and money in specialty tools. Consider consulting a specialist.

1
Getting Started

In this chapter you'll learn how to determine whether a piece of furniture is worth restoring. You'll also learn how to check for what exactly needs to be done to restore it. This examination involves not only the obvious things like the condition of the finish but also such items as loose joints and veneer, splits in wood, worn interior drawer runners, and even run-down hardware and mirrors. After you've learned what has to be done to restore the piece, you'll find out how to prioritize the work. Lastly, you'll learn about the kinds of wood (both hardwood and softwood) commonly used in furniture construction so that you can identify them as you work on your various furniture projects.

FURNITURE EXAMINATION

As a professional furniture restorer, I've examined thousands of pieces of furniture over the years to determine their condition and to provide repair cost estimates. After carefully inspecting a piece and presenting a cost estimate, it's not unusual for me to hear a customer exclaim, "I didn't pay that much when I bought it!"

Many times, after discovering that the customer had recently acquired the piece at a yard sale or flea market at a bargain price, I'm tempted to reply, "That explains why it needs so much work." In other cases, I might find out that the customer bought the piece 20, 30, or even 40 years ago—when it cost a fraction of what it would cost today.

If you're considering a piece of furniture for restoration, whether you're thinking about buying it or you already own it, you must know beforehand what to look for and how to inspect the piece. Some questions to consider before making the decision are listed in "Is It Worth Restoring?" on page 10. Once you know that you definitely want to restore the furniture, you must decide on your course of action.

Determining What Needs to be Done

What should you look for to determine the kind of work a piece needs? Some things, such as broken legs or missing veneers, are obvious. Other problems, however, such as previous bad repairs, missing or damaged drawer runners, or loose veneer, will show up only under careful examination. Look over the piece closely from top to bottom, and make a list, either on paper or in your mind, of what restoration work you'll have to do on the piece.

This Chippendale coffee table (above) shows extensive water damage to the finish and, to some degree, the wood. Restoration of the table (right) makes a significant difference in appearance.

This slant-top desk (right) is from the early nineteenth century. Any restoration work will require special care by a knowledgeable professional. The open lid reveals the detailed interior of the antique desk (below).

Finish Quality. First, consider the piece's finish condition: does it need refinishing—which involves totally stripping off the old finish, preparing the wood, and putting on a new finish—or can you clean, preserve, or rejuvenate the existing finish? Except for modern furniture, most pieces will hold their value better if they retain their original finish.

This rule is especially true for antiques—loosely defined as pieces that are at least 100 years old. The strict definition of antique furniture adhered to by many purists, however, includes only furniture made before 1830, which was the year that mass production of residential furniture began, making most furniture more affordable and plentiful. Unfortunately, many antique pieces of furniture have been significantly devalued by refinishing or restoration work.

If you think your piece fits this category, don't do anything to it until you consult with a professional furniture conservator or antique appraiser to determine its value and what, if anything, should be done to it. If something needs to be done, this type of work is best left to a knowledgeable professional. To find qualified furniture conservators or appraisers, call museums, historical societies, or The American Institute for Conservation of Historic and Artistic Works in Washington, D.C., and ask for recommendations. Check references carefully because not all furniture restorers are qualified to do this type of work.

is it worth restoring?

Ask yourself the following questions to help you decide whether you want to undertake a furniture-restoration project:

- Do you like the piece? You'll probably enjoy working on something only if you really like it or want it in your own home or if you're doing the work for someone else and you know he or she likes the piece.

- How much will the piece be worth once it's restored? To familiarize yourself with furniture values, visit antique furniture stores, used furniture shops, and even new furniture stores, and note the prices on furniture comparable with the piece you are considering restoring. Even if the piece won't have much monetary worth, you may still want to restore it for its sentimental value.

- Do you have a place or use for the piece? No matter how fine a piece that needs restoration may be, it will be of little or no use if you have no place to put it.

- Do you have the time to do the work? At a minimum, you'll need occasional weekends and perhaps one or two nights a week free to work on the furniture. Otherwise, you probably shouldn't consider restoring your own furniture.

- How much time will you need? If you've never restored furniture before, it may be difficult to estimate the amount of time a project will require. I've found that most projects require more work than is apparent at first glance. Sometimes even after a careful evaluation, a project will be more time consuming than you first realized. The important thing is not to rush; take as much time as necessary to do the job right; and enjoy the work. Even if you only have one night a week free or perhaps a weekend now and then, you can still complete a project by working step by step over a period of time.

- Is the piece worth restoring? This question immediately leads to several others, chief among them: How much work do you need to do? (See "Determining What Needs to Be Done," page 8.)

Though not extremely valuable, this old trundle sewing machine, when restored, would provide an interesting conversation piece for any room.

Most furniture, however, does not fall into this category, so you can approach it with less reverence. For example, the finish may look so bad that you're unwilling to live with it. If water or heat has damaged the furniture extensively, for example, it's likely that you'll have to remove the finish and apply a new one. Sometimes you can greatly improve a poorly finished (or refinished) piece by refinishing it yourself. If you can determine that the current finish is not original, and the color or shade is objectionable to you, consider refinishing it. An original finish will usually show natural wear and aging. This aging is called patina. Chair arms and rungs or stretchers, for example, may show wear in the finish; scratches and other damage will have affected the surface of the finish rather than just the wood underneath as in a refinished piece.

Structural and Other Repairs. Next, examine the furniture closely for any necessary repairs. Look at the structure or main joints of the chair, chest (and drawers), cabinet, bed, or table (legs). Sometimes loose joints aren't obvious; exert some firm pressure on a joint to see whether it moves. Check that drawers move smoothy and have drawer stops. Look for splits in chair and table legs, cabinet sides and tops, and tabletops. Also look for bad previous repairs (to fix) and missing parts such as stretchers or rungs on chairs or tables or missing pieces of a carving on a chest—always look inside, even under, drawers for these pieces. Don't forget to check for loose veneer. Test a veneer's integrity by lighly tapping it, using your fingernails. If the tapping sounds solid, it's OK. If it sounds hollow, it will need to be reglued. Lastly, examine all hardware and casters. Find a matching replacement for any missing pieces, or replace the entire set.

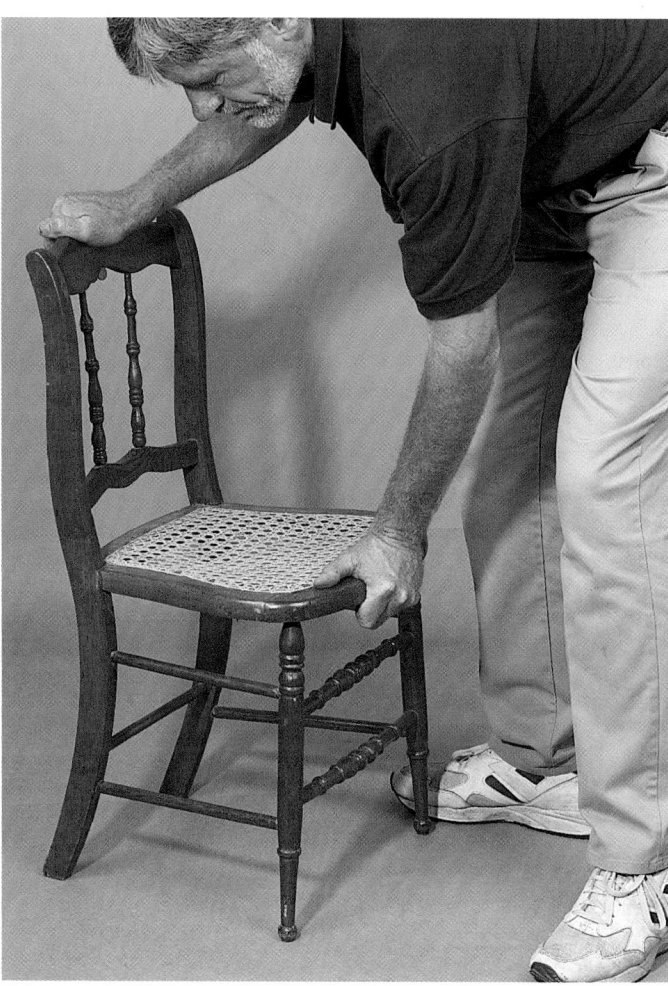

When checking for loose joints in chairs, grasp the top back rail with one hand and hold down on the front seat rail with the other while pushing back and forth on the back.

Water damage to the finish of the drop-leaf tabletop above makes it a candidate for refinishing. The damage is severe enough so that the finish cannot be saved.

This cabinet's drawer runner has been grooved by the drawer. The runner will have to be replaced or reinstalled upside down to provide a smooth surface.

planning the work

After examining the piece and determining what you need to do, schedule the work process. Make a list of everything that needs to be done, and put each item on your list in the order you'll follow when doing the work. If you neglect this step, you may end up redoing things you've already completed. If you complete the finishing part of the project, for example, and then go on with repairs, you may find that you've damaged the new finish while doing the repairs. You'll then have to go back and touch up the finish. The following is a general guideline you can use for work scheduling:

Repair Work. First you should complete the necessary structural work on the furniture.

■ Remove all hardware, glass, and mirrors. The glass in some kinds of furniture may have been installed using glazing compound, a hardened putty used around the edge of the glass to hold it in place. Unless the glazing compound is damaged extensively, you should leave the glass in place and mask it off using a low-stick adhesive masking tape. If any of the glass or hardware needs replacing, now's the time to find or order a replacement piece so it's ready to install when the restoration process is complete.

■ Make all the structural repairs. Reglue all loose joints, and repair all breaks, cracks, splits, and warps. Make or replace any missing large structural parts, such as chair stretchers.

■ Repair the drawers and doors. Fit all drawers and doors so they work smoothly. Repair or replace any drawer runners and drawer stops, if necessary.

■ Repair the veneer. Replace any missing veneer, and reglue any loose veneer. Replace any missing small parts, such as applied carvings.

Original Finish Restoration. At this point you will have completed the repair schedule and should have decided whether you want to restore the origi-

nal finish or refinish the piece. If you're restoring the finish, follow these steps:

■ Clean, touch up, and rejuvenate the existing finish.

■ Clean and polish all glass and hardware, and reinstall it.

Finish Removal and Replacement. If you decide to remove the old finish and refinish the furniture, follow these steps:

■ Remove the old finish by using a chemical stripper or some other stripping method.

■ Prepare the wood surface. Sand the wood, taking care of blemishes in preparation for the final finish. Fill, stain, or bleach the wood—you'll do one or more of these steps only when appropriate.

■ Finish the wood. Apply the finish you've chosen, following the step-by-step instructions.

■ Clean and polish all glass and hardware, and reinstall it.

An old wooden console radio (left) and coffee table (below) are examples of collectible furniture that can be well worth restoring.

WOOD IDENTIFICATION

Before restoring a piece of furniture, you'll want to know what kind of wood you're working on: solid or veneered, hardwood or softwood, open grained or closed grained. These factors can sometimes determine whether or not the furniture is worth restoring, as well as the type of repairs and finish the piece will require if you do restore it.

Identifying wood can be tricky because stains, finish, and aging can disguise wood by altering its original color and look. Light-color wood, such as poplar, birch, or pine, is often stained and finished to look like more-expensive walnut, cherry, or mahogany. Much modern manufactured furniture falls into this category. When you buy new furniture, read labels carefully to determine whether the wood is really what it seems. "Cherry finish" or "walnut finish" labels do not signify cherry and walnut wood—only that the piece is finished to look like those woods.

A painted piece of furniture, such as this kneehole desk, can take on a whole new look when it's stripped and refinished in a natural wood finish.

A variety of types of wood have been used in furniture construction. These woods (from left) can usually be identified by their color and grain pattern: heart pine, mahogany, walnut, cherry, pine, white oak, maple, red oak, poplar, birch, bird's-eye maple.

Older furniture can also fool you if you don't inspect it carefully. Certain parts of a piece, such as the top or drawer fronts, may be made from a hardwood such as mahogany or mahogany veneer, while hidden parts may be made of inferior wood stained and finished to match. Side rails on many beds, both old and new, may be constructed of a less-expensive wood like poplar or butternut, stained to match mahogany or walnut headboards and footboards.

Most wood exposed to sunlight for long periods will lose its characteristic color and become much lighter. Some woods, such as cherry, can darken with exposure to light or from treatment with oils, waxes, and polishes. In cases where a piece's original wood has been altered, you will have to rely on your ability to recognize the grain, texture, and figure (grain patterns and other markings) rather than color. The more you work with furniture and become familiar with commonly used wood species, the easier it will be for you to identify them.

Wood is generally categorized into two groups: hardwood and softwood. Hardwood comes from deciduous trees, which have broad leaves that shed during a certain season of the year. Softwood comes from coniferous, or cone-bearing, trees with narrow leaves or needles that remain on the tree year-round.

The terms "hardwood" and "softwood" can be misleading. Although many types of wood in the hardwood category are indeed hard and dense, such as maple, oak, or walnut, there are others, like poplar, that are not. Most quality furniture uses hardwood in either solid or veneer form as a primary wood; a softwood, such as pine is used as a secondary wood for the inside of cabinets, drawer sides, backs, or bottoms.

Probably because of its availability, pine was used to build many early American furniture pieces. As hardwoods have become more expensive, pine has once again increased in popularity as a primary wood in furniture building and manufacturing. The following woods are commonly used to make furniture.

Hardwoods

Birch. Common in the United States and Canada, birch is a strong, hard, even-textured hardwood. In its natural state the wood appears white or creamy yellow to light brown with a tinge of red. Often, birch is stained to match other kinds of wood in furniture. Much of the clear, cabinet-grade plywood is produced from birch, which takes stain nicely and finishes well. In addition to being used in furniture, birch is often chosen to make interior doors and cupboards.

Cherry. American black cherry is another popular furniture hardwood. Cherry grows primarily in the eastern United States and is a light reddish brown to brown color, which deepens into a rich color as it ages. Cherry has a closed grain and is softer than birch. Much cherry lumber is narrow and has been used to produce many beautiful traditional furniture pieces.

Mahogany. Furniture makers have used mahogany for centuries. A strong, relatively hard wood that works and finishes well, mahogany is also used for decorative woodwork and was widely used in shipbuilding. Found in Africa, Central and South America, the West

This antique Empire sideboard was constructed using several types of wood. The primary wood is mahogany (including crotch mahogany grain patterns for door and back panels) while bird's-eye maple is used on the columns and in several center panels. The cabinet's interior is constructed primarily of poplar, a practice common even in fine furniture.

Indies, and southern Florida, mahogany falls into three basic categories: American mahogany (West Indian), African mahogany, and Honduran mahogany. Lauan, which resembles mahogany and comes from the Philippines, is often referred to as Philippine mahogany, although it's not a true mahogany species.

In mahogany's natural state the open-grain wood has a light pink to reddish brown color with a fine texture. In addition to straight grain, mahogany can have interesting patterns, including the crotch grain pattern often used as a veneer face for cabinet doors and drawers. Many people think of a harsh red color when they think of mahogany, but this is a result of dyes or stains that have been applied to the wood. Although you may find true mahogany finished in various tones of red, it can also be finished in beautiful warm brown or even golden tones.

Maple (Sugar Maple, Rock Maple). Maple, an exceptionally hard, dense, close-grained wood, is abundant in the United States. In its natural state the wood has a white or off-white to amber color. The grain is tight and subtle, except in the case of burl, curly, fiddleback, and bird's-eye maple. These grain patterns offer a variety of interesting, beautiful configurations and are often used for decorative purposes in tabletops, drawer fronts, or door panels, in both solids and veneers.

Because of the absence of a grain pattern in most maple, however, sometimes it can be hard to tell whether a piece of furniture is made of this wood. If so, lift the piece and judge it by weight. Because it's so dense, maple is heavier than most other furniture-quality wood.

Oak. Common varieties of oak used in furniture include white oak, red oak, and English, or brown, oak. Oak has a pronounced open grain with a rough texture. It is quite hard, sometimes making it difficult to work. White oak has a slightly gray-brown color; red oak is similar except that it has a reddish brown tinge. English oak tends to be a deeper brown color.

During the late nineteenth and early twentieth centuries, oak furniture began to be mass-produced in America, making it popular and affordable. Many of the pieces manufactured at that time still exist today and have become even more popular as true antiques have become more expensive and difficult to find. Quartersawn oak is a distinctive and sometimes beautiful oak-grain pattern used for decorative purposes on much of the late nineteenth- and early twentieth-century manufactured furniture. Quartersawn oak is milled by cutting the oak log into quarters lengthwise and then slicing the quarters into boards.

This hall tree is an American piece that relies heavily on the use of quarter-sawn oak for its decorative beauty.

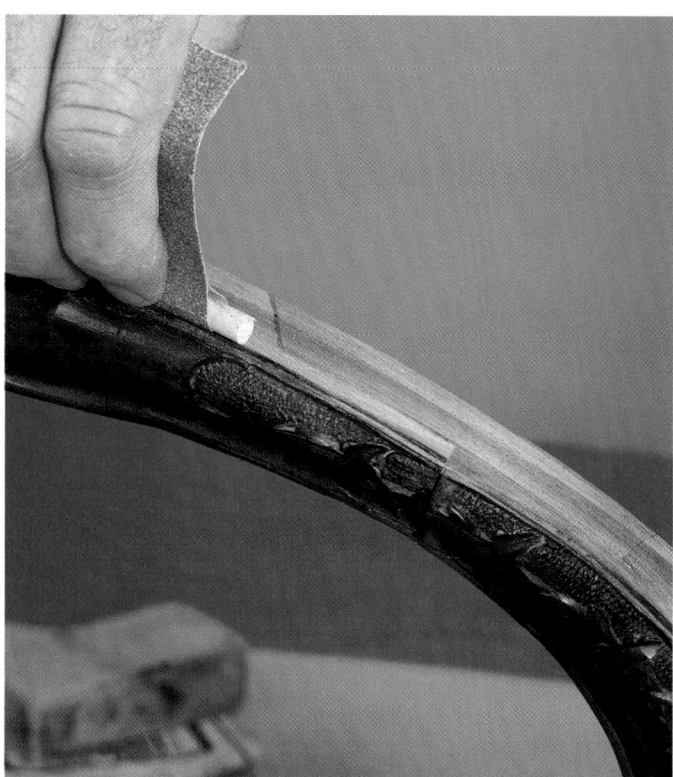

Walnut has been used in many American furniture pieces and has a gray to chocolate brown color.

Poplar. Another American hardwood, poplar has a straight, even, closed grain, but it is fairly soft, making it easy to work. Poplar is white or yellow, sometimes with a green cast and an occasional dark streak running through it. Poplar accepts stain and finish well and often is colored to resemble mahogany or walnut. It is widely used as a secondary wood for the insides of cabinets, chests, and drawers.

Rosewood. Grown in Brazil and India, rosewood is a distinctive-looking hardwood. The wood is naturally brown or reddish brown with dark or ebony grain figuring, but it can sometimes have a creamy color in it. Often used in musical instruments like pianos or guitars, rosewood, unlike most kinds of wood, is resistant to shrinking.

In furniture, rosewood appears primarily in veneer form and was used generously on Empire- and Victorian- style furniture during the nineteenth century. Because of its hardness and density, rosewood can easily be finished to a high luster.

Teak. A yellowish brown open-grain hardwood, teak comes from India, Burma, and Thailand. This naturally oily wood is popular for both interior and exterior woodwork, especially on boats. In the world of furniture, you're most likely to find teak in Scandinavian-style pieces, usually with a rubbed oil finish.

Walnut. Found in the eastern United States, American black walnut has been used extensively in furniture. The wood has a gray to chocolate brown color, sometimes with purple streaks or light-colored sapwood on the edges of its boards.

Not as hard as maple or oak but harder than mahogany, walnut works well in furniture building and can be finished in warm wood tones. Walnut usually has interesting and beautiful grain patterns ranging from straight grain to swirl patterns to distinctive burl grains, depending on the cut of the wood. Because it's an open-grain wood like oak, walnut must be treated with a grain filler to obtain a traditional smooth finish.

Another kind of walnut used in furniture construction, European walnut, is scarce and expensive. You'll find this wood most often in veneer form. While American walnut darkens with age, European walnut becomes lighter.

Other Hardwoods. Other kinds of hardwood used in furniture include ash, basswood, beech, butternut, and chestnut.

Ash and chestnut have a regular texture and open grain like oak. Ash is often used for garden tool handles and baseball bats but is occasionally used for furniture. Chestnut, valuable and well-known for its worm holes, has enjoyed some popularity in the form of wormy chestnut furniture.

Basswood and beech are both light-colored woods with tight, closed grains. These wood species can be stained to match other kinds of wood, such as cherry, mahogany, or walnut.

Similar in grain to walnut but light-colored, butternut may be stained to mimic walnut in furniture.

Softwoods

Familiar softwoods include pine, cedar, hemlock, fir, redwood, and spruce. Of these, pine, cedar, and redwood are most often used in furniture, including outdoor furniture.

Pine. Comprising a variety of species, pine may appear to have either a white-to-tan color or a yellow color with a brown grain figure. You'll also see knotty pine, known for prominent and abundant knots in its boards, which has enjoyed some popularity, particularly in Colonial-style reproduction furniture.

Found in abundance in America, pine has been widely used for many purposes besides furniture, including the construction of buildings and boats. Many early

American furniture makers used pine as a primary wood, and it can be found in some finer furniture as a secondary interior wood for drawer sides, bottoms, and runners. Pine, which can be finished attractively, continues to be a popular wood for some types of furniture today. You should note, however, that because pine has a tendency to accept liquid wood stain unevenly, producing a blotchy appearance, you should normally seal the wood before staining. (See "Washcoat," page 146.) This does not apply to gel stains.

Cedar. Cedar is a pink-to-brown close-grained wood used for exterior and interior woodwork, owing to its resistance to decay. Because cedar has a distinctive, pungent aroma that is disagreeable to insects such as moths, it's commonly used to line chests and closets.

Redwood. Like cedar, redwood is also used for exterior work because of its resistance to decay and insect infestation. As its name implies, this natural wood is red in color; manufacturers use it to produce exterior furniture, such as picnic tables or deck furniture.

Inlays and Veneers

There are many wood varieties that are not used as the primary wood in furniture construction but are frequently used as inlays and decorative pieces in the form of veneer. These wood species include satinwood, boxwood, holly, and ebony. While some are extremely distinctive in appearance, others are harder to identify. These exotic types of wood have been used for centuries to enhance the beauty of furniture.

Wood veneers have been used in furniture construction for centuries, and their beautiful distinctive colors and grain patterns can often beautify or accent an otherwise plain piece of furniture. Clockwise from left, the ones shown here are crotch mahogany, Honduran mahogany, Brazilian walnut, white oak, walnut, red oak, cherry, burl walnut, and rosewood.

2
Tools and Equipment

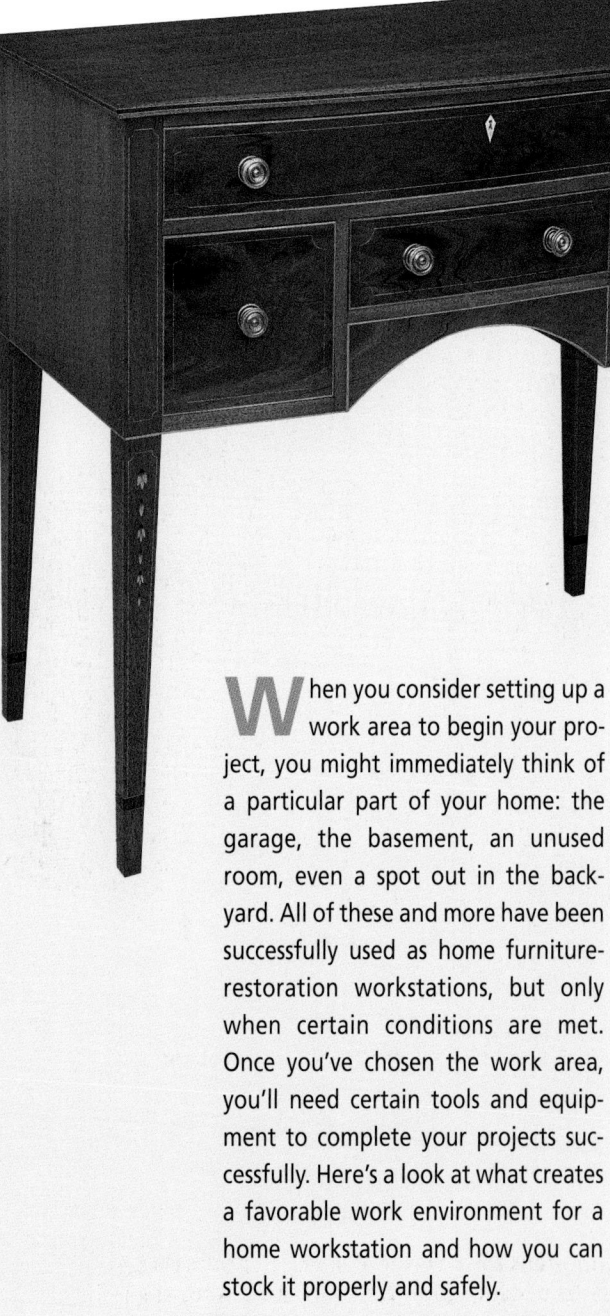

When you consider setting up a work area to begin your project, you might immediately think of a particular part of your home: the garage, the basement, an unused room, even a spot out in the backyard. All of these and more have been successfully used as home furniture-restoration workstations, but only when certain conditions are met. Once you've chosen the work area, you'll need certain tools and equipment to complete your projects successfully. Here's a look at what creates a favorable work environment for a home workstation and how you can stock it properly and safely.

THE WORK SPACE

For most furniture pieces, such as chairs, small tables, chests, or dressers, you'll need an area that measures about 100 square feet (10 x 10 feet, for example). If you plan to work on larger pieces such as wardrobes, large dressers, or banquet-type dining tables, however, you'll need to expand the work area accordingly to fit the piece. Keep in mind that you may have more than one piece in your work area at a time. The best work area is one you can isolate from other areas of activity so that it can be kept as dust-free as possible when doing finishing work. You'll also need both work space and storage space for tools and supplies.

Ventilation. Although you'll want to keep your work area closed off from other areas, you'll still need a fresh-air supply. Some furniture restoration work, such as repairs, can be done without concern for ventilation. Other phases of the work, such as stripping and finishing, which generate strong fumes, must have proper ventilation. To deal with hazardous fumes you'll need at least two windows or doors, one on each side of the work area.

Temperature. Temperature control in your work space is also important. Ideally, you should maintain a temperature range of 65 to 75 degrees F, with a low humidity level, particularly during the finishing process. Temperature considerations aren't as crucial while doing repairs, sanding, or stripping, although some glues may not work well or dry properly if temperatures are too cold.

Power. Don't forget electricity accessibility as you plan your home work space. Have at least two electric plug outlets, which will enable you to plug in a small power tool and an electric light source at the same time. For a permanent workshop, consider installing a dedicated electric circuit. You can run the wiring in surface-mounted raceways. You may also be able to run a heavy-duty extension cord with two outlets to your work area. If you're running a cord outdoors, use one rated for exterior use.

Lighting. Lighting is a crucial consideration for your work area. Basements and garages typically have just enough light to see but not enough to see well when performing detailed repair work or furniture finishing. During daylight hours, you may have enough windows to provide adequate light, but night work means you'll need as much light as possible. You can buy pre-wired fluorescent fixtures with a plug-in cord and mount them on the ceiling to provide additional lighting. You can also buy portable floodlights that hold standard light bulbs. These portable lights come equipped with spring clamps, so they can be easily moved and mounted wherever you need them while working.

Storage. Don't forget about your work-space storage needs. You'll need storage for tools, materials, and any parts or hardware disassembled from your furniture project. All solvents, chemicals, and finishes must be stored according to safety instructions that come with each product. Most, if not all, will need to be kept away from heat, sparks, and flame, so consider this as you plan your storage space.

You'll need tools and equipment to be as accessible to your work area as possible. You can tuck other items, like stripping materials, finishing materials, and hardware, which you'll use only from time to time, safely away in less convenient areas, even completely out of the work area.

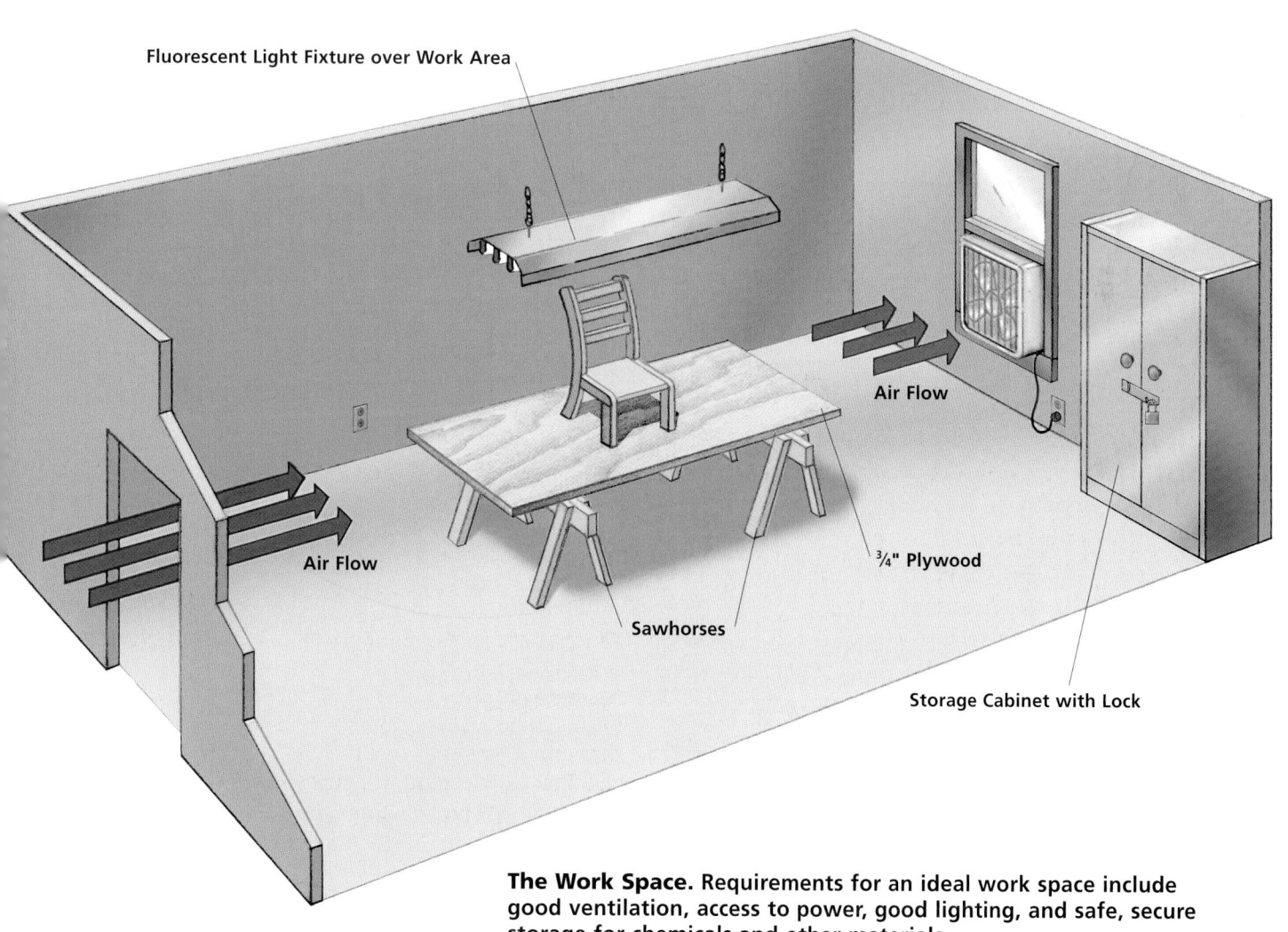

Fluorescent Light Fixture over Work Area

Air Flow

Air Flow

¾" Plywood

Sawhorses

Storage Cabinet with Lock

The Work Space. Requirements for an ideal work space include good ventilation, access to power, good lighting, and safe, secure storage for chemicals and other materials.

You can make a good workbench surface for working on smaller items, such as chairs, by using a 3 x 4-ft. sheet of ¾-in. plywood resting on a set of sawhorses. If necessary, you can use the sawhorses by themselves for larger pieces, or you can remove them, stack them, and set them aside to make room for freestanding furniture.

The Workbench

You can create a simple, compact work surface using a 3 x 4-foot sheet of ¾-inch plywood resting on a set of saw-horses. A setup like this provides an ideal work surface to tackle small pieces, such as chairs, drawers, and bed parts, because it brings them up to a convenient working height.

You can also set a larger piece of furniture, such as a chest of drawers, on the horses without using the plywood. When you need to work on tabletops or a large, freestanding item, you can quickly dismantle the workbench by leaning the plywood against a wall and then stacking the horses and setting them aside.

If you don't have a set of sawhorses or don't want to build them from scratch, you can buy a sawhorse kit at a hardware store, home center, or building supply center. Another possibility for a more permanent, table workbench is to use an old library table, buffet, or flat-top desk.

SAFETY

In my years as a furniture restorer I've witnessed many accidents—and even experienced a few myself. Most of the accidents I've seen resulted in only temporary injuries, although a few were more serious. You can avoid harm or injury by following some simple safety precautions. The tips listed here should help in making your home workshop a safe place, but remember that it's your responsibility to ensure your safety and the safety of those around you.

Preventing Fires

Fire prevention is a primary consideration. Many of the materials used in furniture restoration are either flammable or combustible. Even wood sanding dust is highly flammable.

Avoid Smoking. First and foremost, establish a "no smoking" rule in your work area. If you are a smoker, remember that even if you leave the work area to smoke, you may still have flammable chemicals or solvents on your hands or clothing that could easily ignite. This happened once to a co-worker who had been using paint stripper. He lit a cigarette, and his shirt, splattered with stripper where he had inadvertently wiped his hand, caught on fire. Fortunately he was able to put out the fire quickly without injury. He was, however, inducted into the furniture-repair shop's "Hall of Flame" as its first—and fortunately only—member.

There are other, more subtle, fire hazards. Check stoves and furnaces for open-flame pilot lights. Consider any electric motors or equipment that could produce sparks: If excessive levels of vapor, mist, or dust build up, these could be fire-ignition sources. Be careful not to create sparks with metal tools, or even static electricity.

Dispose of Used Rags Properly. Rags used for stripping, cleaning, staining, and finishing are ideal candidates for spontaneous combustion. Oil-soaked rags—especially those containing quick-drying oils—are particularly susceptible to this hazard. Spontaneous combustion occurs when heat generated by the chemical reaction of volatile materials in, say, rags containing finish builds to a point where it causes the rags to ignite and burn. This can occur in chemical-soaked rags that are simply left lying around, balled up or lying on top of one another. The safest way to get rid of used rags is to unfold and hang them to dry completely before discarding them in a closed metal container.

Buy a Fire Extinguisher. Invest in a good fire extinguisher that's rated for both type A (trash, wood, and paper) and type B (chemical) fires, either of which can occur in a workshop environment. Mount the extinguisher in an area that's easily accessible in case of an emergency, and check it annually to be sure it's charged and ready to use.

Assemble a First-Aid Kit. In case of a fire-related, chemical, or tool-handling accident, make sure you have a first-aid kit stocked with plastic bandages, gauze, scissors, first-aid cream, and eye-flushing solution.

Protecting against Chemicals

Wear Breathing Protection. Another important safety consideration is how to protect yourself from toxic fumes and dust. Besides making sure you have an ample fresh-air supply, wear a respirator around fumes and a dust or particle mask when doing heavy or prolonged sanding. When sanding a piece of wood that has been stripped or bleached, use a respirator because you may

be breathing not only wood dust into your lungs but also all the chemical residues left from the old stripper, the old finish, or the bleach. Ordinary dust masks don't protect you from dangerous chemicals and finish fumes. Respirators have special disposable organic cartridges for this purpose. When the cartridges need to be replaced, you'll begin to smell the fumes from solvents while wearing the mask.

Store respirator masks in sealed plastic bags to make the cartridges last longer. Respirator masks, although considerably more expensive than dust masks, are a worthwhile investment if you plan to do stripping or finishing work.

Protect Your Eyes, Skin, and Ears. When you're using solvents, chemicals, and finishes, eye and skin protection are also important. Protect your eyes by using safety goggles or glasses, preferably glasses with enclosed sides, whenever you do work that could pose any danger to your eyes. Keep an eye-flush bottle in your first-aid kit in case a chemical splashes into your eyes.

Important safety items for any furniture workshop include a closed metal container for used rags, an appropriate fire extinguisher, and a well-equipped first-aid kit.

You should use gloves whenever your hands will be in finish remover, or any solvents, such as mineral spirits, alcohol, lacquer thinner, and stain. Although failure to wear gloves may not be a health hazard, wearing them will keep your hands clean. Vinyl or latex gloves are fine for most jobs, and they're inexpensive and disposable. They are also thinner, so you can get more of a feel for what you are doing. If you want more protection for jobs like stripping finish, use industrial-type gloves made from neoprene, which resists virtually all chemicals. These gloves are available in long-length versions, which protect not only your hands but your wrists and forearms. Rubber gloves will protect your hands from most stripper stains and solvents. After prolonged use the gloves may weaken, so keep several pairs available in your workshop. Protect your clothes with a chemical-resistant bib apron.

You may need ear protection if you plan to use loud power tools, such as a circular saw or electric sander. Use industrial ear plugs or earmuff-type hearing protectors.

Store Chemicals Safely. Storage is also a safety issue. Many solvents, chemicals, and finishes need to be stored away from heat, sparks, and flames, in properly labeled, sealed containers. Caustic materials should be kept in their original containers with the original label.

Never store finishes, paints, or thinners in drink containers such as cups, soda bottles, and milk cartons. Children associate cups and bottles with food and drink. Keep all solvents, chemicals, and finishes locked away from the reach of children or pets. If you are unable to lock them in cabinets, lock up your entire work area when you're not present.

Check containers at least once a year for rust, corrosion, or swelling: if any of these things occur, discard the item properly or transfer contents into a new, properly labeled container.

Be Environmentally Responsible. Most home-workshop applications don't pose major environmental safety problems because of the small amounts of hazardous materials used. But keep in mind that finishes applied with spray guns or aerosol cans can affect air quality. Disposing of old thinners by pouring them down a sink drain or on the ground can pollute ground water. If possible, try to use up all chemicals. If you must dispose of leftover chemicals, consult your local waste management department or check the Environmental Protection Agency (EPA) Web site (www.epa.gov) to find out how to do so properly.

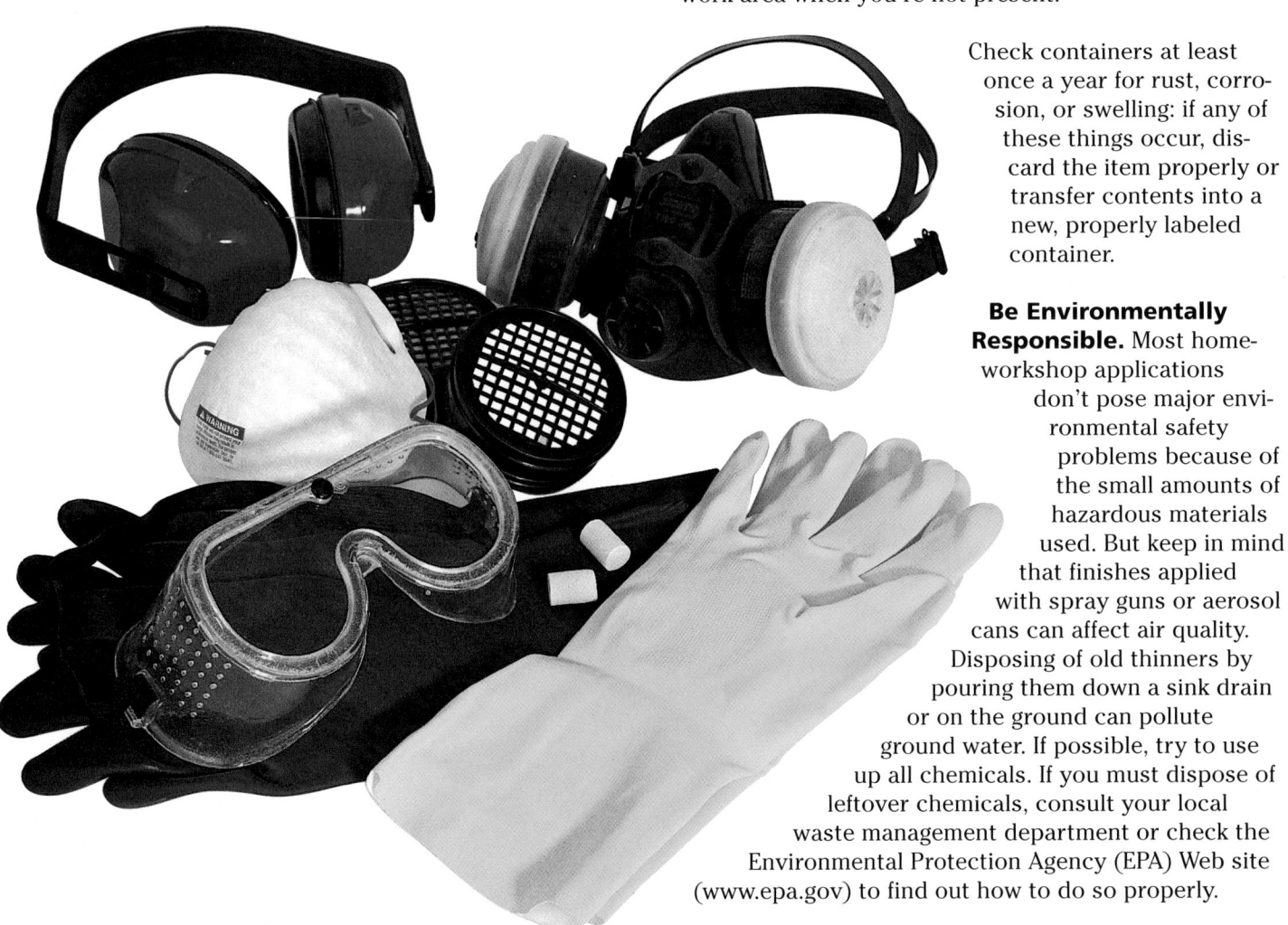

Safety equipment, such as gloves, safety glasses, hearing protectors, respirators, and dust masks, can provide you with appropriate protection during various phases of furniture restoration.

TOOLS AND EQUIPMENT

Before you begin a project, turn to the section of this book dealing with your particular project and read over the material to see what tools you'll need. If you don't have a particular tool, consider whether you can substitute something that will work just as well. (See "Improvising Tools," on page 24.) Before you buy a new tool, determine whether it will be something you can use frequently. If it's an expensive item that you'll rarely use after you complete your project, you might be able to borrow or rent it instead of buying it.

Hand Tools

Hammer. A claw hammer is essential for most furniture jobs. Claw hammers are designed not only for hammering and nailing, but also for extracting nails from wood. Unlike finish claw hammers, which usually weigh 16 ounces, and framing hammers, which weigh 20 ounces or more, furniture claw hammers range from 7 through 13 ounces. You may also use an upholstery tack hammer for replacing upholstery. Lightweight and narrow, upholstery tack hammers have a magnetic tip on one end of the head for picking up and starting tacks while using only one hand.

A rubber mallet is good for knocking loose furniture joints apart and banging them together when regluing. The rubber head minimizes damage to the furniture's finish and wood. Use a wooden mallet to tap a wood chisel when you need more force behind it. The wooden head doesn't damage wooden chisel handles.

Hammers used in furniture repair include (from top) an upholstery tack hammer, mallets (wooden and rubber), and a lightweight claw hammer.

Measuring Tools. You'll need to make accurate measurements when doing repair work on furniture. A steel measuring tape works well for this. You can also use a folding wooden carpenter's rule, although it's difficult to measure inside dimensions of drawers and cabinets with a wooden rule unless you get one that's equipped with a small sliding brass rule at one end.

Squares also come in handy for precise furniture work. You can use a large carpenter's framing square to check the squareness of drawers and cabinets or a sliding T-bevel to copy odd angles. Other kinds of squares you might want include try squares, adjust-able combination squares, and large T-squares, which are especially good for use as a straightedge.

Measuring tools such as these, including various types of squares for checking the accuracy of angles, are often required for furniture work.

PRO TIP: improvising tools

Start your furniture restoration "career" by buying only what you need, and increase your equipment collection piece by piece. If you have a limited budget, look for ways to improvise.

Make Do. Use a claw hammer and a piece of soft wood in place of a rubber mallet to knock loose joints apart or to tap them together when regluing. Sometimes you can use a large nail in place of a nail set or scratch awl. Use a ruler or yardstick instead of a measuring tape or folding ruler. You can substitute a clamp for a vise when you need to lock a workpiece to your bench. Try using a household grapefruit knife in place of a small spatula. Glue a piece of felt, cork, or leather to a block of wood as a sanding block for hand sanding.

Clamp Ingenuity. If you need a few small clamps but you have only one or two, use a pair of vise-type pliers as a small clamp. Create a tourniquet clamp for regluing joints using a piece of sturdy clothesline and a paint paddle or wooden dowel to replace a band or strap clamp. (See "Tourniquet Clamp," below.) Another inexpensive idea for some clamping jobs is to make a clamp using wedges and a wood block or two. (See "Wedge Clamp," above.) Because some glue-up jobs require extra long clamps—which can be quite expensive—you can sometimes hook two shorter clamps together to do the job. (See "Double Clamps," below right.)

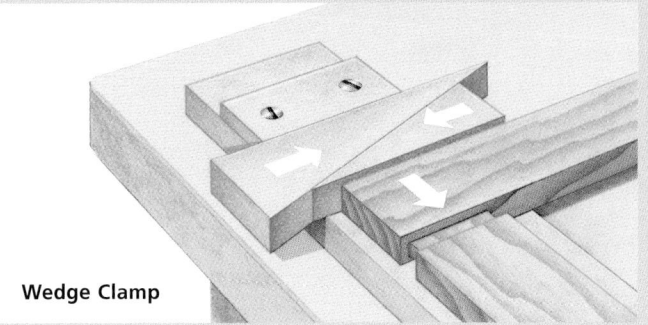
Wedge Clamp

No Substitutions, Please. Although you can improvise creative substitutions similar to the above examples, some aspects of furniture restoration require the right tool for the job to guarantee success. You'll need a good natural-bristle brush to apply solvent-based finishes like varnish or brushing lacquer, for example. Natural-fiber brushes apply these finishes more evenly than brushes with synthetic fiber, and they won't break down or melt when exposed to strong solvents such as those in lacquer. You'll also need a natural-bristle brush if you use a paint and varnish remover to strip an old finish, although for this purpose a cheap brush will do. Chemical removers can soften and melt synthetic bristles. Synthetic-fiber brushes such as nylon, polyester, or nylon/polyester blends work best when applying water-based finishes, however. Natural bristles tend to splay and lose their shape when exposed to water, making them awkward to use.

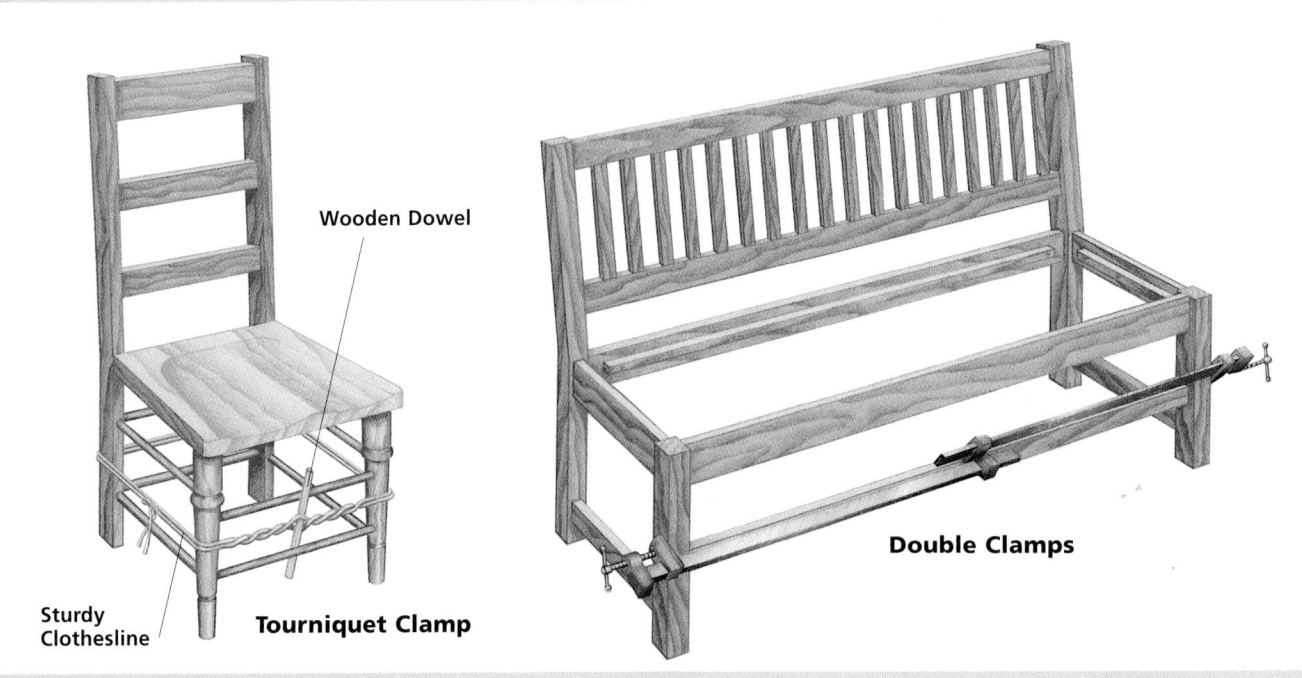
Wooden Dowel

Sturdy Clothesline

Tourniquet Clamp

Double Clamps

Handsaws. Handsaws are a must for cutting and shaping wood on the small scale needed for furniture work. A backsaw, a small square-ended handsaw with a rigid back and fine teeth designed to do precise cutting, is best for working on furniture.

If you have to make small scroll, or curved, cuts in thin wood, consider using a coping saw. The coping saw has a thin, narrow blade attached to a bowed metal frame with a wooden handle. You replace the blade much as you would a hacksaw blade.

When you need to cut veneer, use a sharp utility knife or, better yet, a veneer saw, a small, unusual-looking saw with an angled handle that's offset.

Although you'll rarely use a hacksaw, you should include one in your workshop. An occasion is likely to arise when at least the blade by itself can be used to cut through old nails or screws that must be cut close to the surface.

Chisels and Planes. The wood chisel is a vital tool for a furniture workshop. You'll find yourself reaching for it frequently, to do anything from installing mortise hinges on doors to cleaning old glue from joints. Remember to keep wood chisels sharp. A sharp chisel is easier to use and less likely to cause an accident. (See "Sharpening a Chisel or Plane Blade," page 26.) Dull cutting tools require more force and are more likely to slip. When a tool slips with a

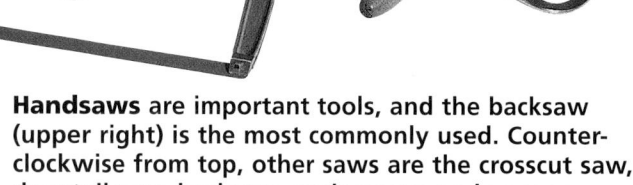

Handsaws are important tools, and the backsaw (upper right) is the most commonly used. Counterclockwise from top, other saws are the crosscut saw, dovetail saw, hacksaw, coping saw, and veneer saw.

lot of force behind it, the results can be disastrous. Chisels come in a number of blade widths. A common range of sizes is $\frac{1}{8}$-, $\frac{1}{4}$-, $\frac{3}{8}$-, $\frac{1}{2}$-, $\frac{3}{4}$- and 1-inch-wide blades. A $\frac{3}{4}$-inch chisel can handle most work, although you'll probably need smaller chisels from time to time.

For heavy-duty chiseling jobs, such as cutting out a mortise in a piece of wood, mortise chisels are available. Firmer chisels—a term given to certain chisels because of their sturdy build—can also be used for heavier chisel work, including cutting mortises. For lighter, more delicate hand chiseling work, paring chisels are available.

Another type of chisel, which is similar to the paring chisel except that it's built for heavier work, is the bevel-edge, or bench, chisel. If you're going to own only one type of chisel, bench chisels are the best, because they can be used for all-around work.

Although a hand plane is not essential, you'll find that at least a block plane can be helpful when doing small wood repairs like fitting a wood patch to repair a damaged corner. The plane lets you smooth the patch, as well as the edge of the top where the patch will be applied, allowing them to fit together precisely and accurately.

Another small but useful tool is the utility, or hobby, knife. You can use it in many ways, from cutting veneer patches to cleaning old glue from joints. A rasp is especially beneficial for roughly forming wood that needs to be shaped because it cuts away wood quickly. A wood file allows you to cut away wood, or shape it, with greater precision than a rasp provides.

Wood planes, bench chisels, paring chisels, wood rasps, wood files, and even a utility knife are commonly used in addition to handsaws to cut.

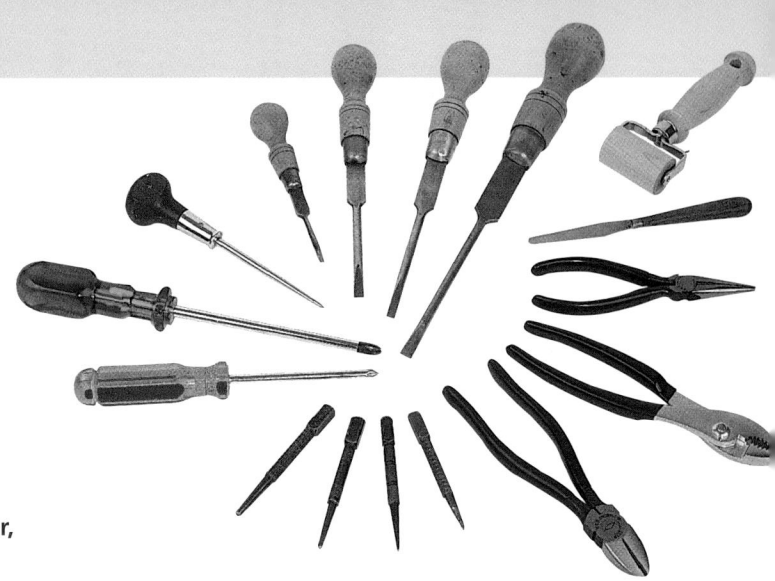

Screwdrivers. Sooner or later you'll need both flat-blade and Phillips screwdrivers. There are two important things to remember about screwdrivers: Have several sizes on hand so you can use the right-size blade or tip for the screw you're working on, and buy high-quality screwdrivers that won't wear out quickly. A good screwdriver will make your work easier and should last indefinitely—if you don't abuse it.

Small hand tools, such as (clockwise from right) a palette knife, pliers, nail sets, Phillips screwdrivers, a scratch awl, flat-blade screwdrivers, and a veneer roller, are indispensable when repairing furniture.

sharpening a chisel or plane blade

The secret to using a chisel or plane successfully is to keep the blade sharp. Although the steps below describe how to sharpen a chisel, the same steps apply to sharpening a hand-plane blade after removing it from the tool.

1. Grind the Bevel. If the blade is new or already has a clean and straight beveled tip, go on to Step 2. If there are chips on the edge or the edge is not consistent, start with this step.

You can use a bench grinder or a belt sander with an 80-grit sanding belt to grind the bevel. Lay the chisel on the tool rest of the bench grinder with the beveled side of the tip flat against the wheel. If you're using a belt sander, lay the beveled side of the tip flat against the platen area of the sander.

After you determine the bevel angle, maintain the angle while applying light pressure, holding the chisel on the grinding wheel or belt sander. If you think you need it, attach a grinding jig to the chisel to help maintain the proper bevel angle. Keep the tip edge squared with the side edge of the chisel blade. When you're grinding the bevel, keep a cup of water nearby into which you can dip the chisel tip every few seconds. This will keep the tip from burning, which will draw the temper from the steel.

If you have deep nicks in the tip, mark a line across the blade just below that nick or chip using a square and a marker pen. Put the tip straight into the grinding wheel at a right angle with the wheel until you grind back to the line. Then use the grinder to regrind the proper bevel.

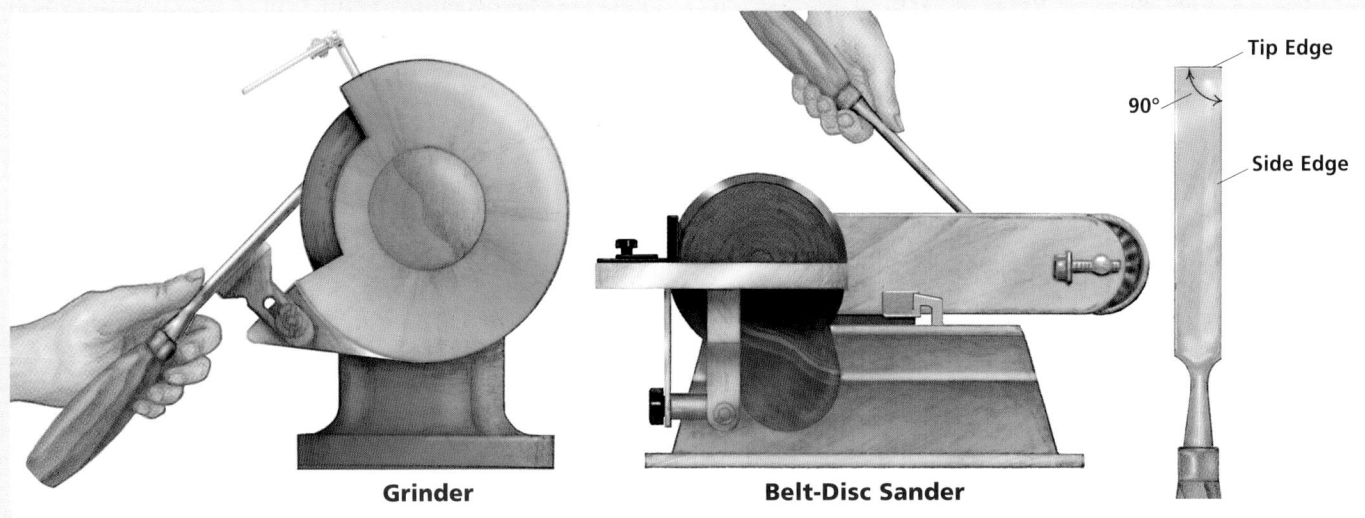

Grinder

Belt-Disc Sander

Tip Edge

90°

Side Edge

1 Hold the chisel at the correct angle when grinding a bevel. You can use a grinding wheel or a bench-top belt-disc sander. Keep the tip edge of the chisel square with the side edge when you grind it.

Pliers. Include three kinds of pliers in your toolbox: standard pliers, diagonal or straight cutting pliers (end nippers), and needle-nose pliers. You'll probably use the cutting pliers most often to pull out old nails embedded in wood and to cut off nailheads.

Other Hand Tools. Other tools you may need include a scratch awl, a small spatula or palette knife for patching holes and working with different kinds of wood putty, a nail set for setting finishing nails below the surface, and a small veneer roller for pressing freshly-glued veneer. You can also use a wallpaper seam roller to press newly-glued veneer.

Clamps

Clamps are among the most basic and useful tools in the furniture shop and are essential for any gluing or regluing job. You'll need several basic types for the majority of your furniture work. Using the right clamp for the job can make the difference between a permanent repair and a temporary one.

C-Clamp. Perhaps the best-known kind of clamp, the C-clamp is shaped like the letter "C" and works well for many purposes. Use C-clamps for small-size projects; switch to bar or pipe clamps for any work spanning more than four or five inches.

2. Hone the Edge. For this step you'll need a honing stone and oil. Buy a stone that has a coarse side and a fine side. Use the coarse side first; then turn the stone over and finish with the fine side.

Apply a small puddle of honing oil on the coarse side of the stone, and lay the flat side of the chisel across the face of the stone. Put your fingers on top of the blade to ensure that it stays completely flat while rubbing it back and forth on the stone. Next, turn the chisel over with the beveled side down, laying only the bevel flat against the surface of the stone. Keep the beveled edge flat against the surface of the stone while rubbing it back and forth.

Turn the stone over to its fine side and apply a small puddle of honing oil. Lay the face, or flat side, of the chisel blade flat against the stone, and draw it across with a few strokes. Then turn the chisel over with the beveled side against the stone, allowing the beveled surface to rest flat against the stone. Raise the handle

of the chisel slightly to increase—by a minute amount—the angle of the bevel at the tip, creating a micro-bevel. Rub the chisel back and forth on the stone as before.

3. Finish the Edge. For this step you need a piece of leather called a strop to touch up the sharpened edge. Some woodworkers mount the strop on a flat piece of wood and use a stropping compound on the leather.

Lay the face of the chisel flat on the surface of the leather, and pull the chisel toward you in a trailing, not a leading, stroke. After a few strokes, turn the chisel over, laying the beveled edge flat against the leather. Again draw the chisel toward you. When you're finished, you'll end up with a razor-sharp edge, so be careful. To touch up a chisel edge after use, repeat this last step or buff the beveled edge on a felt wheel installed on your bench grinder and charged with polishing compound.

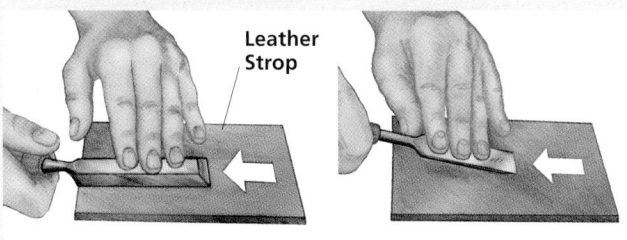

2 Using a honing stone that has a coarse and a fine side, apply honing oil to the stone. Rub the chisel back and forth on the coarse side as shown, first on the flat side and then on the bevel side. Repeat the procedure on the fine side of the stone, lifting the chisel slightly on the bevel side to create a micro-bevel.

Leather Strop

3 Touch up the sharpened edge on a piece of leather by moving the chisel in a trailing stroke, first on the flat side and then on the bevel.

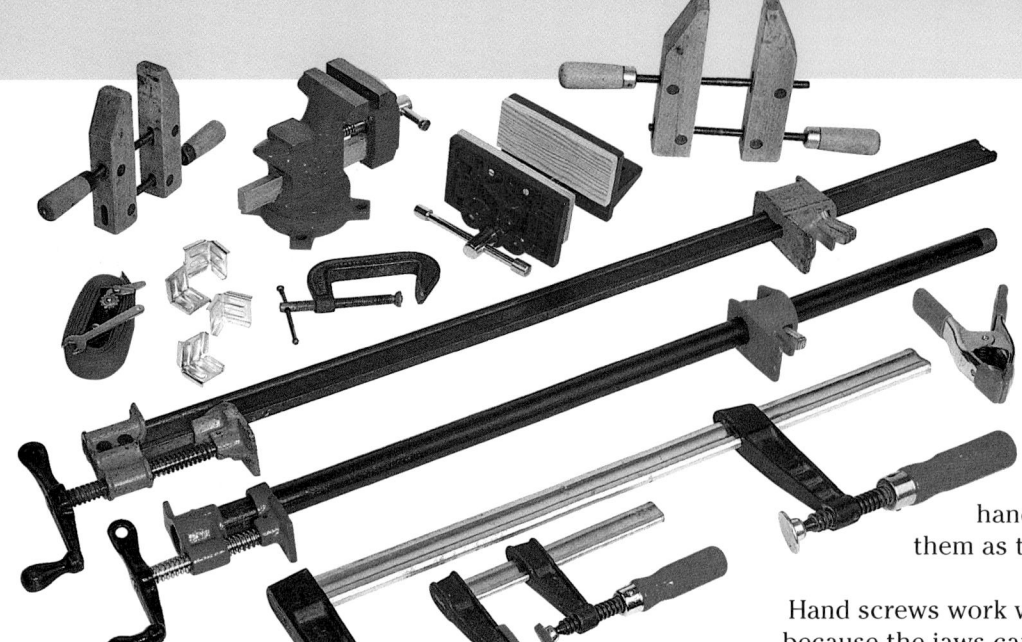

for jobs such as holding chair joints together after you've glued them.

Hand Screw. A hand-screw clamp has two wooden jaws with two threaded rods running through them. The rods have wooden handles that you use to tighten or loosen the jaws. The jaws can be adjusted quickly to fit a particular job by grasping both handles, one in each hand, and moving them as though you were peddling a bicycle.

Hand screws work well for certain gluing projects because the jaws can cover a large area, distributing even pressure over that area when adjusted properly. Because the jaws are made of wood, rather than metal, they minimize damage to the project.

When clamping with a hand screw, you can keep the jaws parallel with one another or angle them to accommodate the work. For most jobs you'll probably use a medium-size hand screw—about 8 to 10 inches—and possibly a smaller one for more delicate tasks such as gluing small veneer patches.

Several types of clamps will be required for gluing projects. Cushion the jaws with wood blocks (left). A bench vise (top center) is also useful to hold a small workpiece stationary, freeing your hands.

Bar and Pipe Clamps.

Particularly helpful for gluing large panels or for spanning distances of 6 inches or more, bar and pipe clamps consist of a bar or pipe fitted with two jaws. The jaw on one end has a crank or handle you use to screw the clamp down for final tightening. The other jaw is made for quick adjustment by sliding it up and down the length of the bar or pipe so it fits your particular work. These clamps come in lengths from 12 to 96 inches. You can also purchase pipe-clamp jaws and assemble your own clamps to create whatever length you need. Pipe is available from hardware stores or plumbing-supply centers. Just make sure to have the ends of the pipe threaded to accommodate the threaded jaw parts.

When considering the sizes you'll need, remember that long bar clamps can also be used to glue short jobs, but short clamps are limited and can't accommodate large projects. On the other hand, if your clamp is too large it can be awkward to operate. Begin with a few medium-size clamps (48 inches long) and if you can afford it, a few 12-inch-long clamps for small jobs.

Strap Clamp. Another basic clamp, the strap (or belt) clamp, consists of a strap that fits around the work to be glued. The strap has hardware that enables you to tighten it like a seat belt and then use a crank, wrench, or screwdriver to do the final tightening. Strap clamps work well

Spring Clamp. Used for jobs requiring firm holding power but not as much pressure as other clamps might provide, spring clamps work like a clothes pin. The clamps have protective plastic over the jaw tips to keep them from damaging wood, and they come in a number of sizes.

Bench Vise. A bench vise is an extremely useful piece of clamping equipment to have in your workshop. A vise will hold a small workpiece stationary, freeing your hands to work on it. Without a bench vise, you'll find many woodworking tasks frustrating, dangerous, and sometimes impossible. You can mount a bench vise to any workbench or table, as long as the surface is solid and stable. Depending on the vise type, you'll mount a bench vise to the top surface or to the side of a benchtop. Top-surface bench vises have a swivel, allowing the vise to turn in different directions.

Most bench vises have steel jaws, which can be damaging to wood, so it's a good idea to attach wooden pads to the inside of the jaws as a cushion and to prevent furniture damage. Cut softwood blocks to fit the inside of the vise joints, and use contact cement to attach the blocks to the jaws.

Woodworker's benches usually come equipped with special woodworking bench vises. These vises, which are also available separately to be mounted to an existing workbench, have wooden jaws.

Power Tools

Thinking of power tools for furniture work or woodworking may bring to mind a number of large, expensive pieces of equipment: table saws, wood lathes, radial-arm saws, band saws, shapers, planers, and jointers. To this list you could add drill presses and scroll saws.

Although some of these tools can be helpful, they are necessities only if you plan to construct your own furniture from scratch. You can do most furniture restoration and repair with just a few power tools. Remember, you may not need all the tools listed below for your particular project. Unless you're setting up a permanent repair shop, look ahead to the instructions for the project and check on what tools are required.

Electric Drill. Electric drills are available in corded and cordless models. Cordless models come with rechargeable power packs and a recharger. You can get a drill kit with two power packs, one of which you can recharge while you're using the other. If you don't get such a kit, buy a second power pack anyway—it will come in handy. Cordless drills have been greatly improved over the last few years and work well for just about any job, depending on the power level of the unit. You'll pay more for a cordless drill, but you won't need access to electricity in the immediate work area. Buy a minimum 12-volt model to ensure that you'll have enough power for your work.

Regular electric drills come in horsepower ratings from ⅓ hp to 1½ hp. Electric drills come in standard sizes of ¼-, ⅜-, and ½-inch models. These measurements refer to the size of the chuck opening, which is the part of the drill that tightens to hold the drill bit or attachment you're using. A ¼-inch drill will probably handle most furniture repair jobs, but occasionally you might need the larger ⅜-inch size. If you don't already own a drill, purchase a ⅜-inch-chuck model. For the majority of furniture-restoration projects—and most household uses for that matter—a drill with a ½-inch chuck generally will not be worth the extra expense. Look for a drill with these features:

• **Variable speeds.** Lets you control the speed of the drill, slowing it down or speeding it up while drilling or driving screws. This feature is necessary for screwdriving.

• **Reversing switch.** Enables you to reverse the direction of the bit or attachment you're using.

• **Double insulation.** Provides insulation between the wiring of the drill and the drill casing to protect against electrical shock without using a three-prong plug.

Most corded and cordless drills have an adjustable clutch system that enables you to adjust the torque so you don't drive screws too deeply into wood. This feature also lets you drive screws without stripping or breaking off the heads. Many drills also allow you to loosen and tighten the chuck without using a chuck key.

Electric drill accessories include drill bits, screwdriver bits (Phillips and flat-blade), sanding and grinding attachments, a wire brush wheel, and a lamb's-wool buffing and polishing attachment. Drill stands are also available that can turn your drill into a small drill press. Lastly, a doweling jig allows you to align dowels when joining two pieces of wood; you can also drill out broken dowels and install new ones in the same location. A doweling jig can be a useful addition to your home workshop.

An electric drill is often necessary for furniture repair. A large variety of accessories, including a doweling jig (top left), a portable drill stand (top center), and buffing, grinding, and sanding attachments (left), can make a drill an even more useful power tool.

Power Sander. Sanding by anyone's definition is a mundane, arduous task. Electric power sanders can save you many hours of monotonous labor.

There are many kinds of widely used electric sanders. Orbital sanders move the sandpaper in a circular motion. Oscillating sanders move the paper back and forth. Disc sanders spin the paper, and belt sanders turn a continuous-loop sanding belt. Most of these sanders are good for general-purpose work, but they must be followed up with hand sanding to remove the scratch marks they leave behind. In recent years two other sanders have been developed: the random-orbit sander and the detail, or triangle, sander. Random-orbit sanders are so named because of the random circular pattern of the sanding pad and thus the sandpaper. The sanding pad incorporates an orbital as well as a back-and-forth movement. When used correctly, random-orbit sanders are noted for removing and smoothing wood quickly with barely noticeable sanding marks.

Detail sanders, which usually have a small triangular pad, are good for sanding tight areas, including inside corners and edges. The pad moves in an orbital fashion, producing arc-shaped oscillations that in turn sand and smooth the wood.

You should invest in a random-orbit sander and a portable belt sander before investing in any other sanding equipment. You can use the random-orbit sander to prepare and smooth wood for finishing. Use the belt sander when you have to cut down an area of wood quickly. The belt sander is not used for most finish sanding work because it can leave deep sanding marks that are difficult to remove.

Because sanding marks often aren't visible until the wood is finished and it's too late to remove them, wipe the wood with mineral spirits before finishing to reveal the marks. You can then sand them out before you begin applying the finish.

Circular Saw. If you have straight cuts to make, you can use a regular handsaw or, for long or repetitive cuts, a circular power saw. A circular saw is also useful for cutting multiple kerfs when you need to notch wood or for cutting slots—in a side rail of a bed, for example. For cutting wood up to 2½ inches thick, buy a 7¼-inch circular saw with a minimum of 10 amps. If, however, you'll be using the saw for much heavy cutting, buy at least a 13-amp model.

Saber Saw. Another versatile saw you may want on hand is the saber saw, or portable jigsaw. You can use the saber saw to make rough cuts in wood up to 3 inches thick and smoother cuts up to 2 inches thick. Although saber saws are primarily designed for making curved cuts, including totally enclosed hole cuts of any shape, you can also use them to cut short straight-line cuts if necessary.

Saber saws are usually rated according to amperage, blade speed, and the stroke length of the blade. The more amps a saw has, the greater its power. Blade speed is measured by strokes per minute (spm). The stroke length is the distance the blade moves up and down while operating; it can range from ½ inch to 1 inch.

You can buy saber saws with a single speed, two speeds, or variable speeds. They are also available with a mechanism for rotating the blade while cutting. Called scrolling, this feature enables you to exercise more control when making small cuts. The base on most saber saws is adjustable for making angled cuts. You may also want to check out the cordless models now available.

If you think you'll be using the saw often, get a model with plenty of power and variable speeds. A 3.5-amp or greater saw should be sufficient. Also consider a saw with the scrolling mechanism.

Small power tools, such as (from left) a router, a circular saw, and a saber saw, can make cutting or shaping wood quick and easy when properly used.

Router. The router is an excellent, versatile tool for making quick work of cutting and shaping wood. A great variety of bits is available to suit almost any requirement you'd have. You can use a router to make groove cuts in wood, as well as furniture joint cuts such as dadoes, rabbets, mortise-and-tenons, and dovetails. (See "Types of Joints," page 56.) Router bits are also available for cutting rounded and molded edges in wood.

If you want to transform your router into a small shaper, you can buy a table to mount the router upside down, making it a stationary machine and allowing you to pass the wood through the router blade rather than move the router through the wood. This method gives you the added control needed to make delicate cuts.

You can buy routers in sizes from 1 to 3 horsepower (hp); a 1-hp model will more than suffice for most furniture repair work. If you're considering turning your router into a stationary shaper, consider getting a more powerful 2- or 3-hp model.

Because routers can cut and shape wood quickly, you should practice on scrap wood to master your technique. Make sure you've firmly clamped the piece you're cutting in place and you've tightened the router bit before beginning your cut.

Bench Grinder. Although you wouldn't classify bench grinders as strictly a woodworking tool, the vast majority of furniture builders and restorers have at least one permanently mounted somewhere in their shops. Bench grinders accommodate two wheels, usually a grinding wheel and a cloth buffing wheel, and include features like adjustable tool rests, wheel guards, spark deflectors, and eye shields.

Make sure you mount the bench grinder on a sturdy workbench or table. You can

A bench grinder can be outfitted with a cloth buffing wheel on one side and a grinding wheel on the other for shaping the bevel on a chisel tip. You'll use polishing and buffing compounds with the buffing wheel to clean and polish furniture hardware.

use the grinding wheel for shaping the bevel on a chisel or plane blade prior to honing, or whenever grinding metal is necessary in the furniture shop, such as when shaping a metal mending plate. The cloth buffing wheel is excellent for cleaning metal, particularly old brass hardware. Different grades of polishing and buffing compounds produce varying degrees of luster on the metal. (See "Cleaning and Polishing Hardware," page 000.) You can also substitute a wire wheel for those times when you need to remove heavy rust, scale, or paint from any kind of metal.

Electric Appliances. Even though electric irons and electric burn-in knives are not power tools, they appear here because of their usefulness in furniture repairs.

You might be tempted to use your household iron, but you'd be better off buying a separate one—perhaps a used model—for your furniture workshop. You can use a hot iron, along with a damp rag, to steam dents out of wood surfaces. (See "Steaming Out a Dent," page 138.)

Electric burn-in knives, which you can buy from furniture-restoration supply catalogs, have a metal tip that heats to a temperature hot enough to melt a hard lacquer or shellac resin stick. (See "Repairing Damage Using a Burn-in Knife," page 122.) You can also buy a plug-in rheostat control for an electric burn-in knife. The rheostat has a heat control knob that enables you to maintain a constant knife temperature for melting and smoothing the burn-in stick. The melted resin from the burn-in sticks fills scratches and dents in a finished surface without disturbing the surrounding finish. The resin hardens as it cools; then you sand and smooth it to blend in with the surrounding surface.

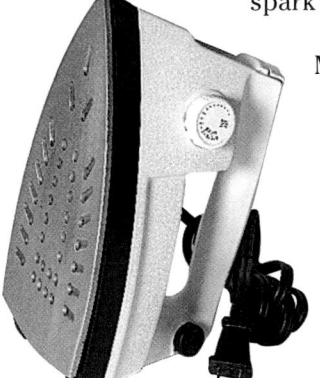
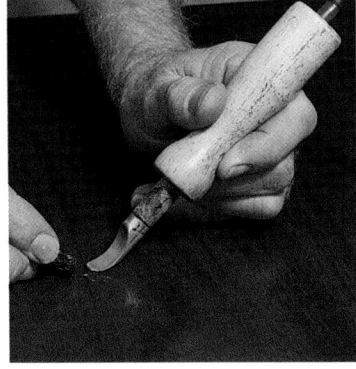

A household iron is useful for steaming dents out of wood and attaching heat-activated veneer to furniture surfaces. Use an electric burn-in knife (right) to melt lacquer and shellac sticks and smooth the material for repairing nicks in finished surfaces.

Stripping and Finishing Tools

Tools that are useful in the stripping process include square-tipped putty knives or paint scrapers and brass-bristled brushes. When using either tool, be careful, and use a light touch whenever possible to keep from damaging the wood.

It's best to use tools with wood or metal handles instead of plastic because remover can soften and dissolve plastic. Use a wide putty knife to scrape the finish off the piece's surface after the remover softens or dissolves it. For small areas, you'll need a narrow putty knife. Grind the sharp corners of the knife to keep it from accidentally gouging the wood surface as you scrape.

Use a brass-bristled brush to remove finish from carvings, cracks, and crevices after a chemical remover has dissolved the finish. Brass bristles are softer and easier on wood than steel, and they won't corrode. Other tools to help you pick stubborn finish out of nooks and crannies include an awl or ice pick, a knife with a sharp point, and a pointed wooden dowel.

Natural-Bristle Brushes. When you're ready to strip or finish, brushes are a necessity unless you're dipping furniture in a stripper vat or spraying the finish. There are numerous brushes available for these tasks, and they come in a variety of sizes and styles. For finishing with solvent-based finishes like varnish, alkyd urethane

Useful tools for stripping off old finishes include a natural bristle brush (for applying the remover), nylon abrasive pads and a spatula-type putty knife (for scrubbing and scraping the old finish from the surface), a brass-bristled brush and sharpened wooden dowel (for removing old finish or paint from crevices), and a cloth for wiping up residue.

(polyurethane), or shellac, use a natural-bristle brush, which is made from animal hair. The bristles are finer than synthetic bristles, and they hold solvent-based finishes well so that the finish material flows evenly. Unlike the synthetic types, natural bristles also stand up to any strong solvents that are used in some solvent-based finishes like brushing lacquer.

A common, readily available natural bristle is called china bristle. Bristles are identified on the brush handle. China bristle is made from hog hair. Other natural-bristle brushes use horse, sable, badger, or ox hair. The finer the hair, the better the brush. A fine badger-hair brush, for example, is an excellent tool for applying shellac or an oil-based finish such as varnish.

Synthetic-Bristle Brushes. If you're using water-based finishes, buy a brush with bristles made of synthetic fiber, such as nylon or polyester. Nylon bristles are good for thin, water-based coating; polyester bristles are better for heavy-bodied latex finishes. Natural bristles do not work well with water-based finishes because the bristles splay and lose their shape when exposed to water. Although synthetic-bristle brushes work well with water-based coatings, they usually aren't good to use with strippers because the strong chemicals in some finish removers can dissolve the bristles. For applying finish removers, use an inexpensive natural-bristle brush. When using wood bleach, however, a natural-bristle brush won't hold up, and you can substitute an inexpensive synthetic-bristle brush instead.

Artists' Brushes. Excellent tools for touch-up work when refinishing or for touching up an existing finish, artists' brushes are available with various types of tips and bristle materials in a variety of sizes. For touch-up work using artists' brushes, use a natural-bristle material. As for size, it's usually a good idea to have on hand small, medium, and large brushes. The brushes are sized according to number: #2 (fine) through #10 (broad).

Brush Buying Tips. When buying a brush for finishing work, get the best one you can find. Although it's not true with everything, brush quality usually has a direct correlation with price.

The brush should have a tapered tip, rather than a squared-off tip. When you look at a cross section of the tip, the bristles should come to a point, similar to the A-shape of a roof. Known as a chisel trim brush, it works well for the final tipping-off process, which you do to remove brush marks and bubbles while the finish is wet.

Brushes vary greatly in size. A good brush for finishing is 2 to 2½ inches wide. You can go larger than this, but if you encounter any tight areas, larger brushes can be awkward

PRO TIP: maintaining brushes

To get the longest life from your brush, here are some recommendations.

• **Soak the brush before each use** just beyond the top of the bristles at the bottom of the metal ferrule in the appropriate thinning solvent for the finish you are using. After soaking for a few minutes, remove the brush from the solvent and shake out any excess. The brush is now ready for use. Soaking the brush like this will protect the bristles and make the brush easier to clean after you use it.

• **To clean the brush,** wipe any excess finish from the bristles into the container or brush the finish out onto a scrap surface until the brush is as dry as possible. Clean the bristles well in the appropriate solvent, and shake out any excess. Then wash the entire brush with warm water and a sudsy soap, and rinse out all the soap with water.

• **To store the brush,** shake out any excess water, and wrap the brush in kraft paper or paper-bag paper. When you wrap the brush, make sure the paper extends well beyond the top of the bristles onto the metal ferrule. Next, fold the paper over, several inches below the tip of the brush and back up onto the brush above the bristles. Use a rubber band to hold the paper in place until your next use. Hang the brush or lay it flat so you don't put pressure on the bristles and cause them to lose their original shape.

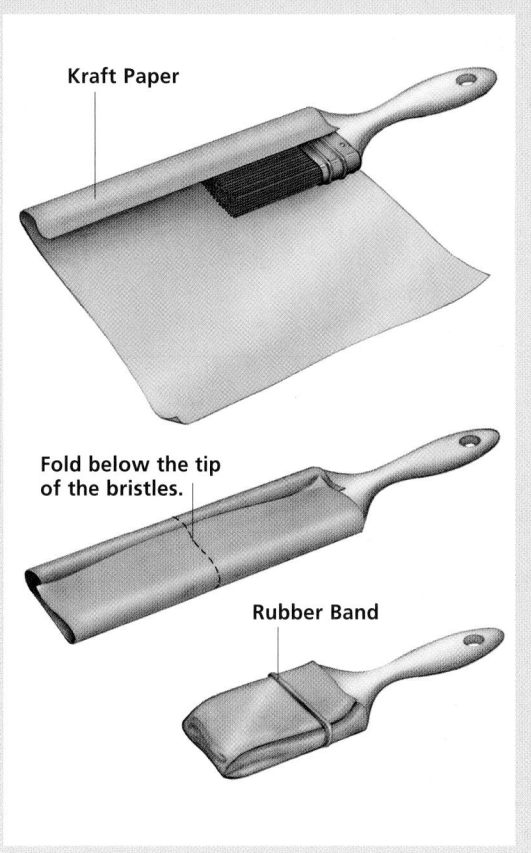

Kraft Paper

Fold below the tip of the bristles.

Rubber Band

to use. You can also finish a large surface well with this size brush and maintain good control in the process.

Another thing to look for when judging general brush quality is long bristle length. This does not mean that all short-bristle brushes are inferior. There are some natural-bristle brushes, such as those made from badger hair, that have relatively short bristles because the hair is so flexible. These fine-haired, flexible brushes are good for applying thin, solvent-based finishes.

Check the thickness or density of the bristles by wrapping your thumb and forefinger around them to bunch them together. The amount of bristles on the brush should not be too sparse; otherwise, the brush won't hold much material. Also, check the tip to make sure it's trimmed evenly. Check the straightness and uniformity of the bristles, and push them against the palm of your hand to make sure they will spring back and that no bristles come loose. One more sign of a quality brush is that the individual bristle tips will be flagged or split, much like the split ends on hair that's been damaged. These flagged ends help hold and spread the finish.

Brushes are important for finishing work. These brushes include artists' brushes used in touch-up work, natural-bristle brushes, and synthetic-bristle brushes.

3
Repair Materials

This chapter covers the materials needed for repairing furniture, including instructions on the selection and use of wood screws, nails, dowels, and various types of wood glue. You'll find valuable tips to make your regluing projects easier and to ensure their success. We'll also look at what's necessary for the repair shop with regard to solid wood and veneer.

The materials you'll need for repairing specific pieces of furniture will depend on the project you're preparing to tackle. If you're dealing with a one-time project, follow the instructions and buy only the materials required for that piece. If you plan to collect old furniture and do most of the repairs yourself, however, you may eventually need all or most of the materials mentioned in this chapter.

MECHANICAL FASTENERS

Most good wood furniture is held together by joinery and glue. When that furniture breaks and you're faced with repairing it, you sometimes need the help of fasteners such as dowels, nails, and screws to strengthen weak areas.

Wood Screws

There are many ways to join wood in making furniture, such as mortise-and-tenon joints, dowel joints, and dovetail joints. Wood screws are not a substitute for this kind of joinery, but they still have many applications in furniture and its repair. Corner glue blocks on many chairs and table frames are attached with wood screws to reinforce leg joints and make them strong and stable. In pieces such as tables or chests of drawers, the tops are often attached to the bases using wood screws. Some dining room chairs use wood screws to attach arms to the frame and back.

Other uses of wood screws in furniture include attaching hinges for doors, desk drop lids, and table leaves. In some cases, wood screws may even be useful when repairing splits and breaks in wood.

Selecting Screws. Wood screws are categorized according to head shape (flathead, ovalhead, roundhead); diameter, indicated by the gauge numbers 0 through 24; and length, indicated by the distance from the top of the screwhead to the tip of the shank, usually ¼ to 6 inches. You'll most commonly use #6 through #14 flathead screws in furniture repair, from ¾ inch to 2 inches in length. You might sometimes use oval- or roundhead wood screws when the head is to remain visible rather than countersunk and covered.

A good rule for determining the length of screw neces-

When installing a screw, make your job easier by matching the screwdriver tip size to the screwhead and slot size.

Small brads, used with glue, are helpful for fastening blocks or other attachments to furniture in inconspicuous spots.

sary for a job is to choose a screw that will sink about two-thirds of its length into the base, or primary, piece of wood. When you use large screws, rub a little hard wax or soap into the threads to make driving the screw easier. Other lubricants may stain wood.

Using Screws. It's important to match the correct size screwdriver with the screw. Make sure the screwdriver tip fits the thickness of the screw slot and the width of the screwhead. The better the fit, the easier your job will be and the less chance you have of damaging the screw, the surrounding wood, or even yourself.

When applying pressure to drive or remove a screw, make sure the screwdriver tip is aimed away from you in case it slips from the screwhead. If you're installing a screw in wood that has not been previously drilled for the screw, be sure to drill a pilot hole. The hole must be large enough to allow the screw to go into the wood without splitting it, but not so large that the screw won't tighten securely. When you install screws for hinges, make the pilot hole the same diameter as the screw shaft minus the threads. In softwood, drill the hole to about one-half to two-thirds the length of the screw; in hardwood, drill to the full depth.

When you use a wood screw to attach one piece of wood to another, drill a pilot hole in the bottom piece of wood so that the screw will tighten in the hole. Next, drill an oversize hole in the top piece of wood so that the screw shank moves freely in it. This allows the screw to tighten in the bottom without tightening in the top piece. In this way, the screw acts as if it were a clamp, pulling the two pieces of wood tightly together.

Nails and Brads

Contrary to the many "repairs" I've had to fix, the answer for most structural problems in furniture is not to drive a large nail into it. This approach to repair usually just complicates matters at best. Nails do, however, have some appropriate uses in furniture restoration.

Common nails have a head and can be used to secure backs to cabinets, chests of drawers, or dressers. They can also attach a drawer bottom where it joins the drawer back. Finishing nails and brads have virtually no head and can be countersunk, or set, with a nail set, thus hiding the nail. You can use finishing nails for attaching molding around a drawer front, to hold glass in a cabinet door frame, or for attaching drawer stops.

Mechanical fasteners such as mending plates, screws, nails, and dowels are not the primary methods of holding furniture together, but they can be useful for some aspects of furniture repair.

Nail Sizes. Nails are denominated by the term penny, which is abbreviated d. The d stands for denarius, an ancient Roman silver coin, the penny of the New Testament. In a system developed in England many years ago, the penny number of a nail referred to the cost of 100 nails of that size, but today it indicates the nail's length. A 2d nail, for example, is 1 inch long, and for each increase in penny size the nail length increases by ¼ inch. Therefore a 3d nail is 1¼ inches long, a 4d nail is 1½ inches long, and so on.

Wire brads come in lengths of up to 3 inches. Small wire brads (less than 1 inch) are particularly useful for doing delicate work such as attaching small moldings.

Using Nails. When using nails in wood that is exceptionally hard, such as maple or oak, drill a pilot hole to keep from splitting the wood or bending the nail. Sometimes you can snip the head from the nail and use the nail as a drill bit for the pilot hole. Drill the hole a little less than the full length of the nail so that when you drive the nail into the wood, it will tighten securely.

Another simple method that sometimes works to keep wood from splitting when driving a nail is to clip off the sharp pointed tip. This allows the nail to enter the wood and crush wood fibers without pushing them apart at the grain line, causing a split. This method works well when using tiny nails or brads to attach small, delicate pieces of wood.

Dowels

Dowels are cylindrical rods that are used to attach pieces of wood to one another and to strengthen furniture joints. Although you may see plastic or metal dowels, the vast majority of furniture joints have wooden dowels. You can also use dowels to add strength and support when repairing splits and breaks in wood.

Dowel Sizes. Dowels are readily available at home centers and hardware stores in 36-inch lengths and in diameters from ⅛ to 1 inch. The most common diameter sizes for dowels used in furniture applications are ¼, ⁵⁄₁₆, ⅜, and ½ inch.

Using Dowels. To use a dowel in a joint you must cut it to size, chamfer the ends, and cut a groove in its side before installing it. The chamfer makes the dowel easier to insert into a hole, and the groove allows excess glue to escape from the hole and prevents wood around the hole from splitting as a result of pressure. To groove a dowel, clamp it lengthwise in a vise and cut the groove with a backsaw. Some stores stock pre-cut, ready-to-use grooved dowels in an assortment of diameters and sizes. Some general rules about using dowels include the following:

Before installing a dowel, chamfer the end that will be inserted and cut a groove in its side lengthwise to allow excess glue and air to escape as the dowel is being forced into the hole.

• **If possible,** use a dowel with a diameter no larger than one-half the thickness of the wood it is entering. A large dowel could weaken the wood. In a ¾-inch piece of wood, for example, the dowel should measure ⅜ inch in diameter or less.

• **When using dowels** in a joint for strength, use at least two dowels if you can.

• **Cut dowels** about ⅛ inch shorter than the length of the hole they're meant for in order to leave room for glue and to allow you to pull the joint tight.

Mending Plates and Corner Braces

Mending plates and corner braces are flat metal plates and angles, usually with countersunk holes so they can be attached with screws. You'll rarely, if ever, find these plates on old handmade furniture; if so, they've been added as a repair. Some antique furniture employed the use of wrought-iron plates where necessary to add strength not provided by the wood itself; an example is the use of a spider-shaped plate on the underside of a pedestal table base to reinforce and lock leg joints at the central column. As long as the iron plate remains attached, these old pedestal base legs seldom become loose.

Try not to use metal plates. Professionals and purists oppose their use, but in some instances they are the only means of providing strength to an otherwise weak repair. If you must use mending plates, install them where they won't show.

ADHESIVES

There are many kinds of adhesives on the market with just as many claims for their abilities. Glues used for furniture repairs are not as varied and fall into one of the following categories.

Polyvinyl Glue

Probably the most popular and useful general-purpose wood glue available, polyvinyl glue is sold in plastic jugs or squeeze bottles in liquid form. It is colored either white or creamy yellow and is often called carpenter's glue. Solvents include vinegar and warm water.

When using polyvinyl glue, clamp the work tightly after gluing for at least an hour but preferably overnight. You can clean up any excess with plain water while the glue is still wet. It's important to clean excess glue from unfinished wood thoroughly—otherwise, the glue spots will show up as white or light splotches when you stain and finish the wood. If the piece you're gluing is a finished piece, you can usually let the excess glue set up for 30 minutes to an hour, then peel or lift it off the finished surface. Be careful not to allow the excess glue to dry too long if the finished surface is at all porous; the glue may become difficult to remove or may even lift the finish off with it.

Polyvinyl glues were originally developed as non-waterproof glues, and because most furniture is not subject to water, these glues work well. If you need to glue up an outside piece, such as a porch rocker or garden bench, you can get polyvinyl glues in a waterproof version.

Hide Glue

Hide glue dates back to early Egyptian times and is so-named because it's made from the hides and hoofs of animals.

The glue of choice for furniture makers before 1900, hide glue is reversible, meaning that joints glued with it can be

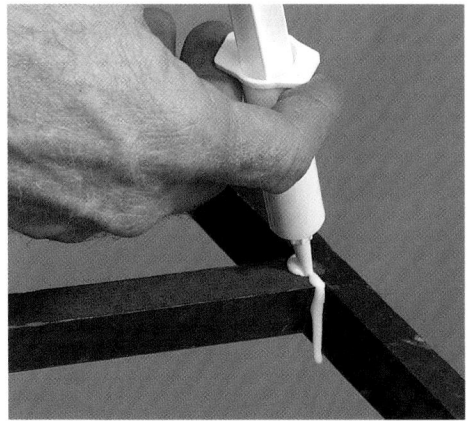

If it's impractical to disassemble the piece, use a plunger to inject glue into a small hole drilled into the joint.

undone by applying heat and water. This reversibility makes the glue ideal for use on genuine antiques.

Originally, hide glue came in dry form, and heat was required to liquefy it. Although a dry form is still available, today you can buy a ready-to-use liquid. While also made from natural animal proteins and reversible, liquid offers the advantage of a longer open working time.

When you use hide glue, make sure the joints are clean, dry, well-fitting, and under clamp pressure for about five hours. After you remove the clamps, allow the glue to cure overnight before using the piece of furniture.

Epoxy

Epoxy is expensive, and you may have to work quickly when using it, but it's an excellent glue for certain jobs. Epoxy works well on nonporous material such as metal or glass. It's waterproof, solvent-proof, and heat resistant. Epoxy remains somewhat flexible over time and fills gaps well when you don't have tight-fitting joints.

Epoxy consists of a resin and a hardener, which must be mixed together according to label directions. Many manufacturers sell epoxy in a dual-cylinder plunger that doles out just enough of each ingredient. It's important to mix the two parts thoroughly to ensure that the epoxy will set up and dry completely.

Epoxy is convenient for small repair jobs. Clamp the parts together until the epoxy sets. One way to be sure the epoxy has set is to save some excess from your original mixture and check to make sure it's hard before you remove your clamps. When clamping, don't squeeze all the adhesive out of the joint. Once epoxy cures, solvents won't affect it.

There are a variety of glues available for furniture work, each with different properties. The glue you choose will depend on your project.

PRO TIP: doing glue repairs

Working with glue can sometimes be more challenging than it first appears. I learned this quickly when I made my first solo attempt at furniture repair by regluing a dining room chair, a job I envisioned as quite simple.

Everyone in the furniture shop had gone home, and I stayed late to do the job. After disassembling the chair and cleaning each joint, I applied glue and began to reassemble the parts. The difficulty arose when I discovered that many parts of the old, handmade Hitchcock chair I was working on wouldn't fit properly unless I fitted them into their original holes. I had interchanged several stretchers, so I couldn't get the chair back together properly. After much frantic trial and error—and having to revive the glue by reapplication in several joints after it had become stiff—I finally got the chair back together and in clamps.

The following are some tips that may help you avoid some of the same trials in your gluing projects:

• Read and follow the directions for the glue you are using. Some glues emit fumes, which require adequate ventilation or the use of a respirator. Don't ignore directives about temperature; most glues require normal room temperature to dry properly.

• Clean all mating surfaces of old glue, finish, and the like. If you disassemble joints, label them with masking tape and a marker to ensure proper reassembly.

• Assemble all joints on a flat surface without glue using the clamps you'll use when gluing the piece. Check for fit and alignment of all joints before removing the clamps, and then remove all the clamps and place them out of the way but within reach.

• Disassemble the joints and apply glue, reassembling them one by one.

• Reapply the clamps, check for fit and alignment of the joints again, clean off any excess glue, and leave the clamps on for the specified time.

One final note about gluing projects: It's sometimes easier to do the job in stages rather than all at once. Some styles of chairs, for example, can be glued up by first gluing and assembling the legs and seat. After this part of the chair is dry, you can remove the clamps, and then glue and assemble the chair back to the chair base. You can determine whether this method is best after test-fitting the joints.

Contact Adhesive

Although contact cement is used most commonly to apply sheets of plastic laminate to tables or countertops, you can also use this adhesive to apply wood veneer to solid wood surfaces. You apply contact cement evenly to both surfaces and allow them to become dry to the touch, usually within 10 to 15 minutes. You then put the two surfaces together, starting at one edge and working across the piece, lowering and pressing the veneer or laminate to the solid surface it's joining.

Once the two surfaces make contact, they become instantly bonded and cannot be separated, so you'll need to align them exactly right the first time using a slip sheet or wooden dowels as spacers for the surfaces until you have them lined up. Contact adhesive is available in both solvent- and water-based formulas.

Resorcinol

Resorcinol glue has excellent resistance to moisture and has even been used by boat builders. The adhesive contains two parts: a powder and a liquid catalyst that are mixed according to label directions. Apply pressure for about two hours to the pieces being joined by the glue.

One consideration when using resorcinol is that it dries to a dark reddish-brown color and could possibly stain light-colored wood.

Other Kinds of Glues

There are several other kinds of glues that are not as popular for furniture repair as those mentioned, but may still come in handy.

Cyanoacrylate. Perhaps better known by the trade name Super Glue, this adhesive does not have wide application in woodworking and furniture repairs. However, because it's strong and quick (albeit expensive), it's good for small-application jobs such as accidental splinters or splits that can occur while working on furniture. Cyanoacrylate adhesives cure by chemical reaction rather than by water or solvent evaporation, so they set in a matter of seconds or minutes.

The glue I've used and recommend for furniture applications comes with a bottle of spray accelerator. You simply apply the glue, hold the pieces together, and spray on the accelerator, which follows the glue into the crack with a chemical reaction that results in almost instantaneous bonding.

A word of caution about using cyanoacrylates: Your fingers can be glued together as quickly as wood can, so be careful any time you use this kind of glue. And because cyanoacrylates can have a shelf life as low as 6 to 12 months, buy only the quantity you believe you can use in that time period.

Polyurethane Glue. The word polyurethane probably conjures up images of a durable finish for wood. But recently several polyurethane glues have been developed and made available for use by woodworkers.

Polyurethane glue is a one-part, ready-to-use formula that you apply to one surface of the two surfaces you want to join. After you assemble the parts, use clamps to apply pressure until the glue sets—from 1 to 4 hours, depending on temperature and humidity. The glue usually takes about 24 hours to become fully cured.

An advantage of polyurethane glues is that they are waterproof and fairly ease to use. A disadvantage is that cleanup can be messy and requires a solvent.

Urea-Formaldehyde Glue. This glue is made by mixing a powder with water according to label directions. It is a strong, highly moisture-resistant glue and can be used for joints that will be under high stress. Joints should be clean and well-fitting. Because this type of glue contains formaldehyde, which has been shown to cause cancer in laboratory animals, be sure to read and follow individual label precautionary measures for use, handling, storage,

and disposal of the product. Mix only what you need immediately, and clamp the joint for 5 to 12 hours. Allow a minimum of 24 hours before you use the piece.

SOLID WOOD AND VENEERS

Unlike furniture making, furniture repair does not require large stockpiles of expensive lumber. Many times you can get by with small sections of veneer and scraps of wood that a furniture maker would use as kindling to start a fire in a wood stove.

Solid Wood. Small pieces of solid wood, such as scraps and cutoffs, work fine for replacing glue blocks, doing small patch repairs, and replacing small pieces of molding. Other repair tasks, such as replacing a rocker runner, will require larger pieces of wood. You can usually buy what you need from specialty lumberyards in whatever size and quantity you require. Eventually you'll end up with an ample supply of small pieces useful for many repairs.

Wood Veneer. You'll need to keep only small amounts of veneer for furniture repair. Buy what you need from a local wood specialty store or through a woodworking catalog. Sometimes veneer suppliers will offer sample sets of veneer. These sets, which contain a variety of veneers in small quantities, can be useful for repairs. Also, check with woodworkers in your area; they may sell you small amounts of what you need.

Some of the more commonly used wood veneers you might want on hand include two types of mahogany (straight grain and crotch-cut grain), some walnut (straight-grain and burl-cut grain), a few varieties of oak (regular and quartersawn), rosewood, and some maple (regular and bird's eye).

Small pieces of wood such as this one, which is being prepared as a patch for a crushed corner on a desk top, come in handy in the furniture-repair shop.

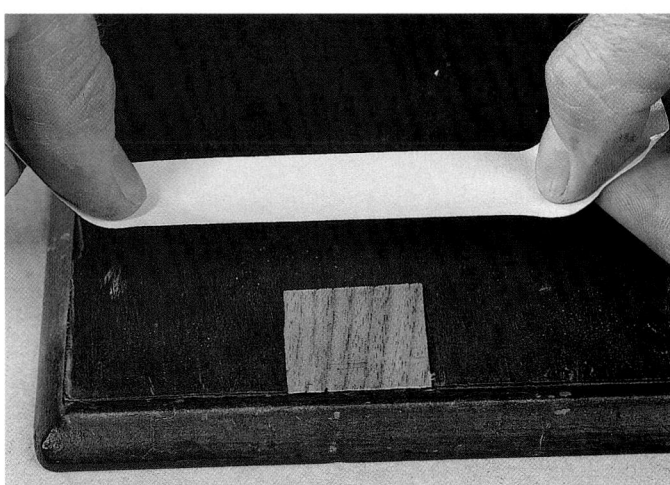

Small veneer pieces that a furniture builder may throw away can often be put to good use in repair work. You can also buy sample sets of different varieties of veneer.

4
Refinishing Supplies and Materials

Restoring a piece of furniture may mean trying to repair and revive the original finish in some way. More often it means removing the original finish and preparing the bare wood for a new finish. This chapter covers materials for removing finishes and sanding, preparing, and finishing the bare wood. If you're planning to stock your home furniture shop with supplies, consider the shelf life of any volatile liquid materials you buy. Strippers, stains, and finishes don't last indefinitely and can sometimes go bad before you have a chance to use the entire amount. Always check labels carefully to see whether they contain information regarding shelf life, and only buy what you can use in the prescribed amount of time. Because there are so many different products and brands available with varying degrees of shelf life, it is difficult to give guidelines on individual materials. If shelf life is going to be an issue when you buy a particular product and it's not mentioned on the label, consult your supplier or call the manufacturer for additional information, and label your own products.

MATERIALS FOR REMOVING FINISHES

Old-timers used a caustic solution of lye and water to strip paint from furniture. Because this solution is so strong and effective in removing hard-to-strip paints and finishes, it can still be found in some strippers' dip tanks today. The problem with this method is that because the solution is so strong, it can also loosen glue joints, discolor wood, and burn the user's skin and eyes. The water-based solution also raises wood grain, creating a fuzzy texture.

Other, easier-to-use strippers have become available in the past 30 to 40 years, most of which contain an effective solvent called methylene chloride. These strippers are fast-acting on most finishes and should be relatively safe to use as long as you read and follow all directions. Note, however, that methylene chloride is a suspected carcinogen. Also, anyone with a history of heart problems should not use methylene chloride. Keep in mind that you'll need to work in a well-ventilated area and wear protective clothing, gloves, an apron, and safety glasses.

Methylene Chloride Strippers

You can buy methylene chloride-based paint and varnish removers in liquid or semi-paste form in various strengths, depending on other solvents used. The solvents in both forms evaporate quickly, which is why they have such strong fumes, so manufacturers add paraffin wax to slow down the evaporation somewhat. Because the strippers contain wax, it's important to rinse or wash the piece down after stripping, better preparing the piece for the next step in the refinishing process. Lacquer thinners work best for this cleaning,

Using a chemical stripper (at top right in photo) is the easiest way for a do-it-yourselfer to remove a finish. You'll also need a brush, a scraper, an abrasive (steel wool, abrasive pads, and/or a brass brush), and rags. Lacquer thinner cleans the wood surface when you've finished stripping.

but you can also use mineral spirits or denatured alcohol.

Liquid Remover. Liquid remover is thinner than semi-paste and begins to act immediately on the old finish. Because the liquid is thin and runny, it doesn't cling and therefore works better on horizontal surfaces. Liquid removers are available in a water-wash or no-wash form. After you've removed the finish with a water-wash remover, you're supposed to wash or rinse the piece with water to remove any residue. Washing with water raises the wood grain, however. The no-wash variety claims it doesn't need washing. I prefer using lacquer thinner to clean up the piece after stripping, even with no-wash removers.

Semi-Paste Remover. Semi-paste has a thicker consistency than liquid remover, allowing it to cling to vertical surfaces much better than liquid products. The thicker coat that results also allows the remover to work a bit longer.

Reduced-Hazard "Safe" Strippers

Of course, no stripper is completely safe. However, a number of strippers have recently been developed without the use of methylene chloride or other harsh chemicals. Some of these strippers are nonflammable and can be used without gloves.

Because of the safety claims of these products, it may be worthwhile to check into them for your particular project. Check the label to make sure the one you buy is formulated to strip the kind of finish you're removing. You'll find that there are trade-offs with most, if not all, of the reduced-hazard strippers: They tend to be more expensive and much slower-working than standard chemical strippers.

Solvent Wood Refinishers

Another kind of stripping product is a wood refinisher. Refinishers are made up of solvents consisting of a mixture of chemicals much like those used in lacquer thinner. These solvents dissolve finishes from the top down, enabling you to soften the finish, taking it off a little at a time or even redistributing it on the wood without totally removing it. Sometimes this can be useful, as in the case of an old cracked or crazed finish that you just want to rejuvenate rather than totally strip.

Because refinishers are basically pure solvent, they will work only on evaporative finishes such as shellac and lacquer, which form a film simply by the evaporation of the solvent and can be redissolved by the same solvent. Other finishes, such as oil-based varnishes, are called reactive finishes. These finishes, which form a film as the resin goes through a chemical change, require conventional strippers to be removed.

If you're stripping a shellac or lacquer finish and you want to remove it completely, remember that although refinishers do a good job, they're slower and more expensive than paint and varnish removers. Refinishers are also flammable and tend to create strong fumes during use, and they require adequate ventilation, protective clothing, and gloves.

To lighten wood (left side of wood sample), you need bleach. Use regular household bleach (left) or two-part wood bleach, followed by a neutralizing solution of vinegar and water.

Bleach and Vinegar

It is rarely a problem to darken wood color, which you can easily do by using wood stains. Reversing the process and lightening wood, however, usually requires bleach.

You'll find wood bleach in paint or hardware stores. Wood bleach comes in two parts; when the two parts combine, a chemical reaction takes place and bleaches the wood. You combine some two-part bleaches in equal parts prior to applying it to the wood, and some you apply separately in sequence to the wood. Pay close attention to label directions when using wood bleach.

Household, or chlorine, bleach is a less potent form of bleach. You can use chlorine bleach, but it may require several applications to lighten the wood sufficiently. When you use bleach, remember that you must remove all finish, oil, and wax from the wood to allow the bleach to penetrate and work.

Let your first application work overnight before you decide to do any more. After the final bleaching application is dry, wash the wood with a water and white vinegar solution to neutralize the bleach. Once the wood is dry, sand it with fine sandpaper (220 to 280 grit) to smooth the wood. Don't apply too much pressure, or you'll cut through the bleached surface of the wood. The wood is now ready to be stained or otherwise prepared for finishing.

Steel Wool

For nonprofessionals, the most available form of steel wool is the fist-size or smaller pad, which comes in seven different grades, from #0000 (the finest) to #3 (the coarsest). You'll use several grades for furniture work. The #3, #2, and #1 steel-wool pads work well for removing old finish after you've softened or dissolved it using finish remover. Dip the pad in the solvent, and scrub with the grain of the wood to remove the old, softened finish.

Use #000 or #0000 pads to rub out dust particles from finish coats before applying the next coat. You can also use

them to rub down the final finish coat to achieve a satin, hand-rubbed look. Sometimes you can do this final rub using oil or wax to give the finish even more luster. These fine steel-wool pads are also useful for cleaning dirt, grime, oil, or old wax from existing finishes. You can do this on most finishes by dipping the wool in mineral spirits and rubbing down the old finish, followed by a wash-down and then a wipe-down using a clean rag. After the piece dries, apply a new coat of wax. The #0 and #00 pads are rarely used because they tend to be too fine for removing a finish and too coarse for rubbing one out.

Abrasive Pads. In some applications you can use a modern substitute for steel wool: the nylon abrasive pad, which is not as hard on wood but is as durable and can accomplish the same results. If you're stripping old finish from wood, for example, and are concerned about unnecessary scratches, nylon abrasive pads work well. Use them just as you would steel wool.

Rags

Whether you're stripping, cleaning, or waxing an old finish, regluing a loose joint, or staining, filling, or finishing wood, rags are a necessity in the furniture shop.

For some purposes, such as stripping old finish or cleaning excess filler from wood, almost any old rag will do, as long as it doesn't contain any oils or silicones that can get into the wood. But for staining and finishing, it's important to use clean, soft, lint-free rags, such as those torn from an old white cotton T-shirt. White rags ensure that no fabric dyes or color will stain the wood, and cotton, unlike synthetic fabrics, tends to absorb stains or finishes well. Using a smooth, rather than ribbed or textured, fabric is also important in preventing streaks in your stain or finish during application.

If you have problems finding enough rags for your projects, try locating rag suppliers in your area, or even diaper services that will sell you old laundered diapers. Use caution when you get rid of old oily rags. (See "Dispose of Used Rags Properly," page 21.)

SANDPAPER

Sandpaper, which is basically nothing more than sand or another abrasive glued to a paper backing, is essential in furniture work. Sandpaper is used not only to prepare the wood's surface but also in the finishing process itself to give you superior results.

Today most sandpaper is made from abrasives other than sand, which may be attached to cloth or even polyester film instead of paper. These coated abrasive sheets come in a variety of grits, or grades, which refer to the size of the abrasive particles. The sheets also come in a variety of types, which refer to the kind of abrasive material used. The type and grit of sandpaper you need will vary, depending on the project you're undertaking.

"Open Coat" or "Closed Coat." These terms refer to the amount of abrasive material applied to the sandpaper's backing. "Open coat" means the abrasive grit is spread out on the backing sheet, covering only about 40 to 70 percent of the area, to prevent friction-generated heat while sanding and to keep the abrasive surface from clogging. "Closed coat" means 100 percent of the backing surface is covered with abrasive, providing more cutting ability but causing the paper to clog more easily.

Weight. Weight classes of sandpaper are determined by the thickness of the backing paper. The weights are rated by the letters A, C, D, E, and F, with A representing the lightest weight and F the heaviest. For furniture woodworking purposes, A, C, or D are appropriate weights; E and F papers usually have extremely coarse grit, such as that used on a belt sander or on a power sander, (the type used to remove finish on old wood floors). The thicker woodworking papers (C and D weights) are better for power sanders and handheld sanding blocks because they will last longer. They are not as good for hand sanding without a block in tight spots or rounded surfaces such as turnings or spindles because they are stiff and tend to crack more easily. An A-weight paper can be folded or even crumpled easily and works well in tight areas.

Sandpaper is essential both in preparing wood for finishing and in the finishing process itself. Use sanding blocks for any large, flat surfaces.

masking tape

Masking tape works well for some aspects of furniture restoration, such as protecting a portion of furniture during the stripping or finishing process. If you want to refinish the top of a table but not the legs or base, for example, use masking tape and paper (doubled or tripled old newspaper) to protect the area you're not finishing. Masking tape is also useful for taping off glass areas that can't be removed during the refinishing process. When doing repairs, you can also use masking tape to hold small pieces of veneer or wood in place while regluing.

If you've ever applied masking tape to a surface and left it on for more than a day or two, I'm sure you know that removing it can be tedious and difficult. To make such removals easier when the job is done, manufacturers have developed a masking tape with less adhesion. Called painter's tape, this product

Masking tape is useful for covering areas that need to be protected during refinishing. The blue tape is a special quick-release type.

often comes in a color that's different from regular masking tape—usually blue. You can find it where painting supplies are sold.

Automotive paint-supply stores usually stock a thicker, better grade of masking tape in a variety of widths. Although this automotive-grade tape is more expensive, it's a superior tape that works much better than the average grade of masking tape.

Make your own cork sanding block by gluing ⅛-in.-thick gasket cork to a softwood block measuring 2¾ x 3⅞ in. Chamfer the top of the block.

Sanding Blocks. You can buy various kinds of sanding blocks at paint and hardware stores, or you can make your own. (See "Improvising Tools," page 24.) You can also buy solid felt or cork sanding blocks, which work especially well, from finishing-supply catalogs. The size of your block should enable you to wrap one-quarter or one-half of a sheet of sandpaper around the sides firmly enough to grip and hold it in position while sanding. When the paper becomes worn in one area, shift and reposition it on the block so you can use a fresh area.

Types of Sandpaper

Garnet. This paper uses the natural mineral garnet as an abrasive. It's usually reddish-brown in color and sands just about any type of wood well. Since the development of aluminum oxide, a synthetic abrasive with excellent cutting ability, garnet paper has become less popular among woodworkers, but it still does an excellent job.

Aluminum Oxide. This synthetic abrasive is usually brown, white, or pale gray in color. It's tough and durable and has excellent cutting ability. Often called production paper, aluminum oxide is widely used to smooth and prepare wood but can also be used for sanding during the finishing process.

Silicon Carbide. Silicon carbide, another synthetic abrasive, is waterproof and extremely hard. This paper is dark gray, brown, or black and is used for wet sanding with a lubricant such as water or oil. Silicon carbide works well for sanding finishes between coats or for sanding the final finish to produce a desired sheen.

Stearated silicon carbide paper comes in a grayish-white color, which indicates it's been manufactured with a lubricant (stearate) included in its abrasive surface. The lubricant minimizes "gumming up" of the paper while sanding between coats of finish. Excellent for finish sanding, silicon carbide paper can also be used to sand wood.

Grits and Grades

The standard method for grading sandpaper is to label the back of each sheet according to grit size. The lower the number, the coarser the grit. There are other ways to grade sandpaper, though, one of which is simply to label it with a description such as fine, medium, or coarse. Another method identifies the grit size by using zeros or numbers. The more zeros, the finer the paper; the higher the number (up to 4½), the coarser the grade. (See "Choosing the Right Sandpaper," below.)

Choosing the Right Sandpaper

Grit	No.	Description	Purpose and Comments
12	4½	Extra Coarse	Rough sanding and shaping; rust and
16	4		paint removal; not recommended for
20	3½		furniture
24	3		
30	2½		
36	2		
40	1½	Coarse	Rough sanding and paint removal;
50	1		shaping wood; rarely used on furniture
60	½	Medium	Rough sanding to remove deep scratches;
80	0		shaping wood; must be followed by finer grit before finishing wood
100	00	Fine	Preliminary sanding and preparation of
120	000		wood before applying finish
150	0000		
180	5/0	Very fine	Preparation of hardwoods for finishing
220	6/0		and occasionally sanding between coats
240	7/0		
280	8/0	Extra fine	Sanding and smoothing finishes between
320	9/0		coats
360	*	Superfine	Sanding and smoothing finishes between
400	10/0		coats
500	*	Ultrafine	Sanding final finish coats, usually with
600	*		water or another lubricant such as oil, to
and above			produce various sheens

WOOD-PREPARATION MATERIALS

Once you've stripped and rough-sanded a piece of furniture, you need to prepare it for final finishing. You may see that the wood has imperfections, such as nicks and cracks, that need to be fixed with wood putty. Or you may notice that the wood has an open grain that must be filled. When you've done those tasks, you'll probably want to stain the furniture before putting on a clear-coat finish.

Wood Fillers

Wood Putty. Wood putty is available in a variety of forms and under a number of names, including wood dough, plastic wood, wood patch, water putty, and the like. Basically, there are three kinds of putty: nitrocellulose-based wood putties, which clean up with lacquer thinner; acrylic-based putties, which clean up with water; and gypsum-based putties, which come as a powder.

Apply wood putty by pressing it into a hole with a putty knife or dull screwdriver (top). Any excess can be sanded flush when the putty dries. When stained, putty takes on a solid color without grain or figure.

PRO TIP: sanding secrets

- Divide sandpaper into quarters, cutting it with scissors or tearing it on the edge of a shop table or bench.

- Use a sanding block (preferably cork, felt, or rubber) for sanding flat surfaces. Use straight strokes and even pressure.

- You can make a shaped block to get into the contours of molding and other shaped wood. Sometimes a piece of dowel will work.

- Use folded paper to get into cracks, corners, and crevices.

- Sand with the direction of the wood's grain to prevent cross-grain scratches. When sanding burl, swirl, or crotch-grained woods, use the finest paper available. Use masking tape to protect an adjacent piece of wood with the grain running in a different direction. (See the photo above right.)

- Never use a grade that's coarser than necessary.

- Work progressively through coarser to finer grades. When using coarse paper, your next step should be

under 100 points. For medium grade paper, you can step up to 100 or more points, and for finer papers, 200 or more.

- When hand sanding without a sanding block, you can trifold a quarter-sheet of paper (use a half-sheet for larger areas), which will give you a better grip while sanding. When one side of the paper is worn, fold out a new section of paper, and continue until all three sides are used up.

- If the paper is stiff (C and D weights) and you are not using a sanding block, you can make the paper more flexible by pulling the back side over a bench-top edge.

- Clean your paper when it starts to clog by using a stiff bristled brush or by tapping the paper on a hard surface.

You can patch wood defects with standard wood putty (center), available in a variety of colors, or with two-part fillers (right), including auto-body filler (left). Two-part fillers need to be tinted before application, using dry powdered stains, or touched up to match the surrounding wood during the finishing process.

Because there are so many brands and types from which to choose, it's important that you read labels to see how various kinds of wood putty work. Factors to consider include drying time of the putty, whether it shrinks when dried, whether it is stainable, and how it sands. As you work on furniture, you'll probably find yourself experimenting with different brands until you find the one that best suits you.

Wood putty works best when used to fill smaller blemishes such as nailholes, nicks, or cracks. If possible, small scratches and dents should either be sanded or steamed out and large problem areas patched with matching wood, but there are certainly times when wood putty becomes necessary in furniture restoration.

You can buy wood putty in such generic wood-tone colors as mahogany, walnut, or maple, but the only accurate way to match it with your project is by direct sight comparison. Wipe raw wood with mineral spirits and match the wet wood putty to this color as closely as possible. You can mix dry powdered stain with the wood dough if needed to adjust the color for a closer match. Dry powdered stains are available in small quantities from finish touch-up supply houses or woodworkers' supply catalogues; they are dry, concentrated colors that will go a long way.

If the wood putty you use shrinks as it dries, you may need to make a second application to build it up so that you can sand it even with the wood's surface. If you're not satisfied with the way the putty looks after you've applied it and sanded it smooth, you can fine-tune the color match using an artist's brush and artist's colors or pigment from wiping stains. You can even paint in grain lines to continue the grain pattern of the wood through the patched area.

Two-Part Fillers. Another handy item for patching or repairing wood is two-part auto-body filler; there is a variation of this product developed (and colored) especially for use on wood. Fillers are thick, creamy substances to which you add a catalyst that causes them to heat up and harden in minutes. The cured filler can then be cut, shaped, or sanded to any form you need. The two-part filler materials adhere well as long as the wood has been cleaned of other materials such as finish or wax; they become extremely hard, making it easy to shape large areas such as corners and edges; they dry fast; and they do not shrink. You shouldn't use these materials for some pieces—particularly antiques—but for many applications they can yield wonderful results. These fillers work well, for example, if you have an area on a piece of furniture that your dog has chewed.

To match wood putty with the finished color of natural wood, wet the raw wood with paint thinner, and then compare it with the color of the wet putty.

To change the color of wood, you can choose from among many available products, including dyes (left half of photo), which come in both dry powdered and premixed liquid form, and pigmented wiping and penetrating stains. Some woods require grain filler (far right) before staining.

Paste wood filler is a creamy substance that's used to fill the pores of open-grained woods before finishing. The material helps produce a smooth, closed-grained look.

Two-part fillers don't absorb stain readily, so you'll need to add color to come close to the desired finished wood color. You can color the filler by using dry powdered stain and then touching it up with an artist's brush. Use artist's colors or pigment from wiping stains to match the wood tones and the surrounding grain lines.

Paste Wood Filler. When wood filler is mentioned, the first thing that comes to mind for most people is the kind of wood putty mentioned above. Paste wood filler, also known as grain filler or pore filler, is not the same as wood putty or two-part filler. Paste wood filler is a creamy product used for packing into the pores of open-grain woods such as oak, walnut, or mahogany. It provides a smooth, even surface on which a finish can be built. If you don't want a glassy-smooth, closed-grain look to your finish, paste wood filler is not necessary.

The paste comes in both water- and oil-based forms, and either will work well provided you follow label directions. Water-based filler dries considerably faster than oil-based. The quick drying time gives you less time in which to work, but it also means less waiting time before the next step in the finishing process. Available in neutral or tinted wood colors, paste filler can be further tinted with a tinting colorant such as Japan colors, artist's oil colors, or universal tinting colors. You should be able to get tinting colorants at a good paint, hardware, or art-supply store. Use Japan or artist's oil colors to tint oil-based filler; use universal tinting colors (UTCs) to tint water-based filler.

Wood Stains

You may be surprised to learn that you won't need wood stain for some refinishing projects—for example, those pieces that have the natural wood color showing through. If you want to match a particular color, give inferior wood an expensive look, or bring out otherwise subtle grain patterns in wood, however, wood stain is a necessity. Generally speaking, wood stains fall into two broad categories: pigmented stain, made up of finely ground color particles suspended in a solvent, and dye stain, made up of color particles dissolved in a solvent. There are also some stains that combine both pigment and dye.

Pigmented Stain. The most common form of pigmented stain, called a wiping stain, is available in both oil-based and water-based forms. One of the biggest advantages of pigmented wiping stains is that they're easy to use and readily available in paint or hardware stores. They come in wood tones as well as white or light pastel colors for giving wood a pickled effect. Wood-tone stains work well when you're staining inferior woods such as poplar or birch to make them look like more expensive species. These stains also help to provide uniform color to otherwise uneven wood tones. Some woods, such as pine, however, tend to result in a blotchy appearance when they are stained. Uneven wood density causes uneven color penetration.

Pigmented stains color wood by depositing pigment in the grain of open-grained woods (and on the surface of any wood). These pigments tend to settle to the bottom of the container unless they are agitated by stirring or shaking. The stains contain a solvent and a binder. The binder serves to hold the pigment in place so that it adheres to the wood surface. Because of the thick color pigments, pigmented stains tend to be opaque, which allows them to resist fading as a result of sunlight exposure. This opacity also makes them good for staining an

otherwise unattractive wood to improve its appearance. On some woods that are naturally attractive, however, the opacity can mask their beauty. A better choice for such woods might be a dye stain.

Dye Stain (Aniline). While pigmented stains tend to be opaque, dye stains are translucent. This is true because the color materials are completely dissolved in the stain solution, allowing the stain color to penetrate into the wood rather than staying on the surface like pigment. Because of this, you can change the color of an attractive wood without masking its natural beauty. These stains aren't as readily available as other types; you may have to order them through woodworkers' or finishers' supply catalogs.

Dye stains are made from aniline, a derivative of petroleum and other related hydrocarbon compounds, and are often called aniline stains. The medium used for these dyes may be water, alcohol, or oil (mineral spirits or lacquer thinner).

Water-soluble dye stain comes in a powdered form to be mixed in warm water. Because water stain will raise wood grain, you need to prepare the wood surface by wetting it with plain water. After the wood dries, sand it with extra-fine paper to smooth the raised grain and prepare it for staining. This will keep you from having to sand the raised grain after staining, thus cutting through the stain color. If you use water stain, allow the piece to dry overnight before finishing it.

Alcohol-soluble stain is much like water stain but uses alcohol as the solvent and does not raise the wood's grain. Alcohol stain can be bought premixed and is fast-drying, a disadvantage if you try to apply it any other way than with a spray gun. You can use alcohol stain for shading, tinting, or touch-up work.

Oil-soluble dye stains are also available in premixed form, although you can get them in powered form, too. The stains dissolve in mineral spirits or lacquer thinner; they are slower drying than alcohol-soluble dye stains and can be applied with a brush and rag much like a pigmented stain. Color penetration of oil-soluble dye stain is not as good as that of water-soluble dye, and the colors are susceptible to fading in sunlight. Oil-soluble dye stain also tends to lack the clarity of water stain.

Another kind of dye stain that is a substitute for water stain is NGR (non-grain-raising) stain. NGR stains are water-soluble, but they don't contain water. The dye is first dissolved in a glycol ether solvent, then thinned with alcohol or lacquer thinner. You can clean up NGR stains with water and add them to water-based finishes. As the name states, NGR stains do not raise the

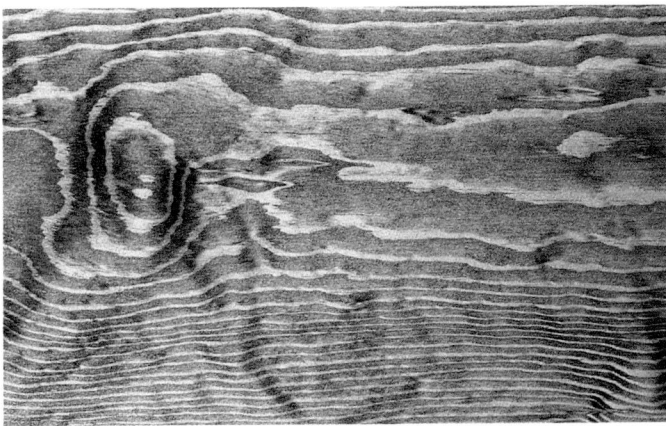

Stain blotching is caused by swirly grain or uneven density in wood. Pine (above) is among the woods that commonly blotch when you apply stain.

grain of wood as water stains do. NGR stains usually come in premixed form, and although they can be applied like water stain, they don't penetrate the wood as well. They also tend to lack the clarity of water stain.

Gel Stains. Gel stains have become invaluable in furniture work, and they're particularly well-suited to the novice because they're so easy to use. Gel stains are drip- and run-free, don't make a mess, and provide even, consistent color without showing overlap marks or blotchiness. Because of their thicker consistency, gel stains work well on vertical surfaces, whereas thinner stains present application problems. Gel stains come in an oil-based pigmented and in a water-soluble dye-stain form, which offers a user-friendly alternative to other dye stains. This type of dye gel is an excellent alternative to mixing up your own water stain, and it makes for easy application. You'll find gel stains in home centers, hardware, paint stores, and woodworkers' or finishers' supply catalogs.

The same color stain may look different, depending on the wood to which it's applied. Here the same stain was applied to maple (top), mahogany (upper middle), poplar (lower middle), and oak (bottom).

tack cloth

The tack cloth is a rag used to pick up dust and other materials from the surface of bare or finished wood before applying a new coat of finish. You can buy tack cloths at hardware or paint stores; they are relatively inexpensive. Store-bought tack cloths contain a varnish-like substance to make them sticky so that they will attract and pick up dust and other loose particles that could otherwise get trapped in the finish. They've also been chemically treated to keep them from drying out. Using a tack cloth will give you a smooth, more professional-looking finish.

If you want to make your own tack cloth, use a 12-inch square of lint-free cotton rag or cheesecloth. Dip the rag in warm water, wring it out, and then dip it in turpentine or mineral spirits and wring it out again. Drip varnish over the rag's surface, and squeeze the rag into a ball until varnish is distributed throughout the rag, making it tacky enough to pick up dust but not so wet that it will leave varnish on your surface.

To keep your tack cloth from drying out, keep it in a sealed container—a jar or self-sealing plastic bag. If it does dry out, repeat the above process to rejuvenate it.

Stain Controllers. Stain controllers can be used before applying a liquid stain to keep the stain from penetrating unevenly. Stain controllers (also called wood conditioner, pre-stain, and grain tamer) are composed primarily of slow-evaporating, petroleum distillate solvents. They work by filling up the pores and less-dense parts of the wood so the stain can't penetrate. The stain just mixes with the solvent near the surface.

To use a stain controller successfully, apply it to the wood with a brush or rag until all parts of the wood stay wet and no more of the liquid is absorbed into the wood. This usually takes successive applications for 5 or 10 minutes, but the number of applications needed will vary depending on the wood and the ingredients used in the stain controller.

When no more dry spots appear on the wood, wipe off all the excess stain controller and apply the stain as quickly as possible—within 30 minutes is best. If you wait too long, enough of the stain controller will have evaporated or been absorbed deeper into the wood so that the stain will again penetrate and blotch the wood.

FINISHES

In furniture restoration, "finish" refers to the material that coats the wood for the purpose of protecting and beautifying it. Although a finish can be tinted or colored, usually it's clear or almost clear. Except for painted finishes, the wood is usually colored using wood stains, wood fillers, or bleaching prior to applying the finish. In furniture restoration, shellac, lacquer, varnish, polyurethane, oil, wax, and paint are commonly used.

Stains, paint, and clear finishes (left to right) are made of just three ingredients: Stains and paints contain colorant (usually pigment), binder, and solvent or thinner; finishes are simply binder and solvent or thinner.

solvents

There are three basic solvents important in preparing finishes and in general furniture restoration: lacquer thinner, denatured alcohol, and mineral spirits. Keep in mind that these solvents can be dangerous if you don't follow the label directions concerning the use of protective clothing and equipment and safety practices for fire and explosion prevention.

Lacquer Thinner. Lacquer thinner is the strongest of the three solvents; it is so strong that it will quickly dissolve both shellac and lacquer finishes. As its name suggests, its primary use is for thinning lacquer. Lacquer thinners are also good solvents for cleaning up a piece of furniture after stripping off the old finish. Because it's a strong solvent and will dissolve or soften most finishes, it's handy to have in your shop for cleaning out spray guns and brushes.

Lacquer thinners can be formulated differently, and some cheap types that are good for cleanup work may not work well for finishing. Evaporation time may also vary for different lacquer thinners, which will affect lacquer-drying time. If the lacquer dries too slowly, it can slow down the finishing process and allow dust to settle in the finish. If the lacquer dries too fast, other problems, such as blushing, can arise. Moisture becomes trapped in the finish, causing it to "blush," or appear milky or cloudy. Thinner problems are usually associated with spray lacquer finishes because brush lacquers are already formulated for brushing and don't have to be thinned.

If you're using the thinner to thin a lacquer finish, check the label of the lacquer material to see whether a particular thinner is recommended. If no thinner is recommended, it's usually best to begin with a standard lacquer thinner ("medium" or "normal" evaporation speed). Then add lacquer retarder (a slow-drying thinner) to slow the evaporation rate to suit the prevailing temperature or humidity conditions.

Alcohol. Like lacquer thinner, alcohol can dissolve shellac and lacquer finishes, but it is weaker, making it a much slower-working solvent. Denatured alcohol is used primarily for thinning shellac. If you're applying a shellac finish or homemade French polish, you'll need to have denatured alcohol on hand. Sometimes this solvent is also useful for rejuvenating an old shellac finish by dissolving and redistributing the old finish and then reapplying a coat or two of new shellac. This process is called reamalgamation, and it sometimes requires the addition of some lacquer thinner to the solvent mix.

Mineral Spirits. Mineral spirits, or paint thinner, is used for thinning and cleaning up oil-based paint and varnish, but it has additional uses in furniture restoration. It's a good cleaning solvent for washing down old finishes to remove wax, silicone, and oil. Mineral spirits alone will dissolve and remove old waxes and oils, but it will only dissolve silicone, not remove it. To remove the dissolved silicone, follow the thinner by washing the surface using a solution of 1 cup of ammonia mixed in 1 gallon of warm water. You can sometimes then rewax or recoat the old finish to revive it. Mineral spirits also helps remove silicones from raw wood (following the procedure above), preventing problems when applying a finish. Other uses of mineral spirits include cleaning brushes, thinning pigmented oil stains and wood filler, and using it as a lubricant when wet-sanding finishes such as shellac or lacquer.

Shellac

The granddaddy of modern "film" finishes, shellac is manufactured much as it was decades ago from a resin secreted by the tiny lac insect in India and Southeast Asia. Shellac was originally sold in dry form as flakes, granules, or buttons, which were dissolved in denatured alcohol to produce liquid shellac. Although you can still buy shellac flakes, you'll most likely find it in premixed form in various "cuts": 1-pound, 2-pound, 3-pound. The pound measurement indicates the amount of dry material that has been dissolved in one gallon of thinner, thus a 1-pound mix would be thinner than a 3-pound mix.

Advantages. Shellac is one of the best finishes for bringing out the beauty of a good piece of furniture. If the wood is attractive to begin with, shellac will enhance that quality and give it a charm hard to achieve with other finishes. This is probably due to several factors. Shellac has no synthetic ingredients or added plasticizers, which can create an artificial look. Each successive coat of shellac melts into the previous coat, bonding with it to form a single layer of finish on the wood's surface. A good shellac finish can be built on most woods in about three or four coats with a scuff sanding between coats. The last finish coat can be waxed by rubbing it down with paste wax on a #0000 steel wool pad, followed by a buffing with a soft cotton rag. This allows for great clarity and depth, and because of its flexibility, the finish is non-chipping. Also, the natural orange tint of shellac imparts a warm

glow to the finish. Shellac was used to produce the classic French polish finish representative of many eighteenth-century European pieces. Modern shellac results in a nice Old World look and is appropriate on many older or antique pieces. Although this time-honored material may be outdone in some ways by synthetic finishes that are more durable, it's difficult to surpass the natural beauty of shellac.

As mentioned, natural shellac has a distinctive orange tint, which helps achieve a warm depth in the finish. White shellac, which is just bleached orange shellac and is actually clear, is also available. White shellac is a good alternative if you're finishing a light-colored or bleached wood and want to maintain the wood's original color.

Shellac was originally applied with a soft pad, or "rubber," as it is called in the method known as French polishing, but shellac can also be sprayed or brushed on, drying quickly for sanding and recoating. Shellac is often used as a sealer coat to prepare wood for other finishes. This sealer coat acts as a barrier, locking and sealing contaminants in so that they do not produce adverse reactions such as fish eye in lacquer, small areas where the finish separates on the surface, resembling the eyes of a fish. To use shellac as a sealer, you apply what's called a "wash coat" of shellac to raw wood and then scuff-sand the surface before applying the other finish.

Disadvantages. After considering the many good characteristics of shellac you might think, "Why use any other finish?" But shellac, like all finishes, has some drawbacks, including a short shelf life—about six months—after it's mixed. Once its shelf life has expired, "old" shellac won't dry after application, and you'll have to strip the finish from the wood. Because old shellac doesn't look any different, you won't know whether a questionable finish is bad until you apply it to the wood and wait to see whether it dries. If you have time, you could coat a sample piece of wood before applying shellac to your furniture.

The best way to make sure the shellac is still good is to mix it from flakes, granules, or buttons, or to buy liquid-form shellac in amounts corresponding only to your current project. This may seem troublesome, but it will save you extra work in the long run. Shellac finishes get scratch marks more easily and are not as durable as some other finishes, such as lacquer and varnish. White water rings, stains, and other blemishes are also a common problem because shellac is not as resistant to water or alcohol as lacquer and varnish.

Lacquer

If you talk to a furniture professional about finishes, before long lacquer will come up, and with good reason. Lacquer dries quickly, picks up few dust particles between coats, can be recoated quickly, penetrates wood well, adheres to previous coats by melting into them, is more durable than shellac, and can produce any number of sheens from matte to high gloss. Lacquer is a good, practical, attractive finish that can be built up to many coats in a short amount of time.

Since the 1920s, lacquer has been the most widely-used furniture finish. Most new furniture has a lacquer finish. Two common types of lacquer for woodwork are nitro-cellulose and cellulose acetate butyrate (CAB). There's not much difference between these formulations, except that CAB lacquer is more resistant to chipping and does not yellow with age, making it a good choice as a clear coating over white finishes.

Another type of lacquer, available in several forms, is called catalyzed lacquer. One kind of catalyzed lacquer contains a catalyst that is premixed during manufacture; another kind is a two-part version that has a catalyst you add just prior to applying the finish. This type should be mixed only as needed because it has a short shelf life once mixed.

Catalyzed lacquer produces a tough, durable finish. The secret to its toughness is the catalyst. After the finish dries through solvent evaporation, the catalyst causes a chemical reaction to take place that continues to harden, or cure, the lacquer for up to a few days. The following information applies to all lacquer; however, catalyzed lacquer is harder and considerably more resistant to scratching, heat, water, and solvents.

Advantages. Although conventional lacquer is not highly resistant to either solvents or heat, it offers more water resistance than shellac. A lacquer finish also offers good clarity and depth as long as you apply it properly and the finish doesn't blush. (See "Lacquer Thinner," page 50, for a description of the blushing problem.) You can rub out or polish lacquer to produce just about any type of sheen.

An evaporative finish, lacquer requires only about 15 to 30 minutes to dry. Because lacquer is quick-drying, you can apply several coats in the time it takes to apply one coat of a finish such as varnish. Fast drying also helps prevent dust and other particles from settling into the finish surface. Lacquer is similar to shellac in that each coat softens and bonds with the previous coat, forming a single layer of finish on the wood's surface.

Fish eye will occur in a lacquer finish if any wax, oil, or silicone is left on the surface when finishing. The effect is exaggerated here by applying a dark finish over a white substrate.

Sanding sealer contains a lubricant that causes the finish to powder easily when you sand it.

Problems. Despite all its pluses, lacquer still has some negatives. Because it dries so fast, lacquer is considered a spray-on finish. To spray a lacquer finish you'll need a professional spray system including spray gun, air compressor, air lines, and filter, not to mention a safety-approved exhaust system that can run into thousands of dollars in expense. This is an investment for the professional finisher that pays for itself over time, but for most do-it-yourselfers it's impractical.

Lacquer dries so fast because it requires a high percentage of volatile thinner to maintain the solids in its solution. The large amounts of thinner evaporate quickly, and that causes the main problem with lacquer: air pollution. Many parts of the country restrict the use of lacquer. Lacquer is also highly flammable and toxic. You need to be careful when you use lacquer, and you should use a respirator.

Spray lacquer's quick-dry feature can sometimes cause blushing. You can control blushing by using a slower-drying lacquer thinner in the lacquer mix and by adding a retardant. The retardant further slows the drying time and allows moisture to escape from the surface before the finish dries. It also allows the lacquer to flow out better.

Fish eye is another problem associated with lacquer. If the wood surface has any wax, silicone, or oils left on it when you apply the finish, these areas will appear as crater-like fish eyes. Rather than use shellac as a sealer coat to prevent fish eye, as mentioned earlier, you can add fish-eye eliminator to the lacquer mix (according to label directions) to solve the problem. Once you add fish-eye eliminator to the lacquer, each successive lacquer coat must also include it.

Variations. Lacquer sanding sealer can be used as the first coat or two when finishing with lacquer. The use of a sealer can improve adhesion between the finish and the wood. It also provides a barrier coat to seal in any contaminates that may remain on the wood's surface. Lacquer vinyl sealer is recommended for this purpose, but a wash coat of shellac will accomplish the same thing. Sanding sealer also works well to build up a smooth, even surface in preparation for the lacquer top coats. To aid in this, sanding sealer contains stearates. These stearates are soft, powdery soap-like substances that act as a lubricant for ease in sanding and add body to the finish, enabling it to build more quickly.

Although most lacquer finishing is done with a spray gun, lacquer is also available as a brushable finish. Because lacquer dries so rapidly, brushable lacquer contains special solvents to slow down drying so you have time to brush it on, although you have to work quickly. Even with these added solvents, brushable lacquer still dries fast and requires a little more practice than some other brush-on finishes. Once you get the hang of it, though, you can produce a good-looking, durable brush finish.

Because the solvents in lacquer are so strong, brushing can disturb some stains, particularly pigmented stains. To avoid this, seal the stain first with a coat of shellac. Some brush-on lacquers are self-leveling, meaning you can apply them generously to horizontal surfaces and brush marks will all but disappear. Two or three coats of brush lacquer will provide a good water- and alcohol-resistant finish.

Lacquer is also sold in aerosol cans. Don't try to do a total refinishing job with aerosol cans of lacquer, but you can use them with excellent results for touch-up work or spot finishing. You can also use them for spraying a finish that has been cleaned to revive it, particularly on smaller items such as chairs. The important thing about aerosol lacquer is to make sure to get a brand that has a good spray nozzle, as this will affect how the finish goes on the piece, which determines the final look. Finding the best spray nozzle is a matter of trial and error through trying several different brands.

Lastly, aerosol lacquers release a lot of material into the air. This produces a lot of overspray (a dry, rough, powdery form of lacquer), so you'll need good ventilation for safe use of any spray lacquer.

varnish

Varnish is one of the toughest, most durable wood finishes, standing up well to heat, moisture, alcohol, and wear. The biggest drawback to finishing with varnish is its slowness in drying. This makes varnish a good brushable finish but also allows it to collect dust particles while drying. You'll need to sand between coats, with rubbing and polishing on the last coat to remove these particles. It also means your finishing schedule will have to last two or three days or more, depending on the varnish type and the number of coats desired.

Oil-based varnishes have been used for centuries. They are made up of resins, drying agents, oils, and thinner solvents such as turpentine or mineral spirits. Before the twentieth century, varnishes used natural resins, usually fossilized pine sap. Since then, synthetic resins have been developed that are cheaper, more available, more consistent in quality, and more durable than natural resin varnishes. Alkyd, phenolic, and polyurethane are three types of synthetic resin varnishes.

Alkyd Varnish. Alkyd resin varnish, although slow-drying, produces a highly durable, attractive interior finish. It's available in gloss or satin sheen, and can be sanded and rubbed out on the last coat. Alkyd varnish is flexible and not as hard as polyurethane, so it's less brittle and will not chip as easily.

Phenolic Varnish. Phenolic resin varnish is usually called spar varnish and is excellent for exterior finishing work such as boat woodwork. Phenolic varnish is usually only available in a gloss sheen. It's flexible, allowing wood to expand and contract in exterior conditions without cracking the finish, and it also resists the sun's ultraviolet rays. The finish sometimes contains ultraviolet absorbers to help prevent it from yellowing or darkening with age. Because of its flexibility, phenolic varnish is not as resistant to abrasions as some finishes and can sometimes show worn areas with time and use.

Polyurethane Varnish. Polyurethane is highly resistant to water, alcohol, abrasions, and heat; it is available in gloss, semigloss, satin, or flat versions. It can be applied by spraying or brushing. It's the clearest of the varnishes and rubs out well on the last coat. It also tends to be faster-drying than other varnishes, thus eliminating some of the problem of dust particles settling into the final finish.

Because polyurethane will not dissolve or melt into previous coats as will lacquer or shellac, it's important to scuff-sand the finish between coats to provide for proper adhesion. Polyurethane is a tough, durable, practical finish, but you may want to consider its appropriateness for your piece, especially if it has historic or collectible value. Some furniture experts and collectors consider the look of polyurethane, especially waterborne formulations, to be too artificial or plastic. In truth, all modern film finishes contain plastic; it's just that polyurethane tends to be a little more cloudy in appearance, giving it a slightly more artificial look. Film finishes without plastic would include those used prior to the twentieth century, including shellac and natural resin varnishes.

Advantages. Varnish is especially good as a furniture finish. It has excellent water and alcohol resistance, and it's more solvent-, heat-, and abrasion-resistant than lacquer or shellac. It also brushes well, so it's easier for a nonprofessional to use.

Disadvantages. Varnish brushes well because it cures slowly, and this presents a quality-control problem: The surface can collect dust before it dries, resulting in a poor finish. It has a short shelf life because it easily skins over. The finish is hard to rub out to an even sheen, and it doesn't repair well, owing to its solvent resistance.

Oil Finishes

Oil finishes are reliable and well-tested products. They have been used by generations of furniture restorers and work well to enhance the natural beauty of wood. They are some of the easiest finishes to apply; it's hard to make a mistake. Oil finishes can even be applied without using a brush or any special equipment: you just wipe them on, let them soak in, and wipe them off. All you need for the work are a few rags. Be sure to dispose of all oily rags properly. (See "Dispose of Used Rags Properly," on page 21.)

Oil finishes are usually extremely thin, so they don't offer much protection for the wood surface. Because oil finishes penetrate deep into the wood, they tend to darken and intensify the wood's natural colors. Also, oil finishes can be extremely difficult—or impossible—to totally remove from wood if this ever becomes necessary.

If you plan to stain the piece, keep in mind that highly pigmented stain may restrict the penetration of an oil finish into wood. Basic types of oil finishes include linseed oil, tung oil, and penetrating resin, also known as Danish oil.

An oil finish is one of the easiest finishes to apply: You just wipe it onto the wood surface and then wipe it off. Some oils take a long time to dry completely, however.

Linseed Oil. Linseed oil was the oil finish used by many old-time wood finishers and is still used by some people today. It's exceptionally slow to dry and never really gets completely hard. Because raw linseed oil is so slow-drying, manufacturers add dryers to speed up the process. This form of linseed oil, known as boiled linseed oil, is best for finishing work.

Although linseed oil is easy to apply, it must be applied in multiple coats, with rubbing between them, to build up the finish to any degree. Some finishers say you must apply the oil twice a day for a week, twice a week for a month, twice a month for a year, and twice a year for life. Others say the schedule should be once a day for a week, once a week for a month, and so on. Although this kind of diligence in the finishing process can provide beautiful results, it still doesn't offer the wood much protection because of the softness of the oil and its inability to resist heat, wear, and moisture. Linseed oil, then, can make a fine finish for wood not subjected to any of these conditions, but more modern oils and finishes may still be a better choice for most furniture.

Tung Oil. Tung oil is derived from the nuts of the tung tree, which is native to China, and dries faster than raw linseed oil but slower than boiled linseed oil. It also produces a finish slightly more durable than linseed oil. Tung oil usually comes in a thinned-down form for ease of finishing. The finishing process is similar to that of linseed oil, in that it requires multiple coats to produce a satisfactory finish. The number of coats needed depends on the type of wood and the look you're trying to achieve.

Unlike linseed oil, tung oil does not necessarily require continued year-after-year coating; but if the finish begins to wear or dull, a new coat of tung oil will always renew it.

Oil-Varnish Finishes. These penetrating resin finishes are more-modern versions of oil finishes, producing excellent results with less time and effort. Often sold under names such as Danish oil and Teak oil, these finishes are essentially a mixture of oil and varnish. Manufacturers claim that the finishes "toughen the fiber of the wood," but because this type of finish tends to be relatively soft when dry, it's doubtful that it adds any real strength to a substance that is already as hard as wood. With multiple coats, the finish will eventually build above the wood's surface and produce a thin film. You can rub the surface down with #0000 steel wool between coats and after the last coat to produce a good-looking satin finish.

Penetrating resin finishes are available in clear or in various stain colors with the idea of accomplishing the staining and finishing processes in one step. In addition to the standard liquid variety, penetrating resin finishes are available in a gel form. Still an oil-varnish combination, sometimes using polyurethane as the resin, the gel is also a wipe-on finish, making for easy application.

water-based finishes

Finish manufacturers developed water-based finishes primarily to address air-pollution problems created by solvent-based finishes such as lacquer. Water-based lacquer, for example, has a much lower volatile organic compound (VOC) level and is less toxic and much less combustible than solvent-based lacquer. Its higher solids content allows the finish to build more quickly, too.

Even with all this going for it, many finishers are reluctant to switch from solvent- to water-based spray materials simply because it tends to present more problems: water-based finishes don't flow on as smoothly, get runs more often, are more susceptible to fish eye, take longer to dry, and cannot be polished to a high-gloss sheen. Finish manufacturers are working hard to improve water-based finishes in anticipation of future demand produced by stricter EPA standards regarding air pollution.

Water-based polyurethane can be applied much such as an oil finish by generously brushing it onto the wood, allowing it to penetrate, and then wiping off the excess. After several coats, with light sanding between coats, you can paste-wax the finish, producing a thin oil-finish look.

paint

Some people may consider paint an unacceptable option for furniture finishing. I agree that many beautiful woods have been hidden under the stroke of a paint-laden brush, all in the name of giving the piece a new look. When you finish—or refinish—a piece with wood originally meant to be seen, you should always use a transparent finish. Some pieces were created to be painted, however, such as many of the old Hoosier kitchen cabinets. Many different types of wood were often used in one cabinet, with the idea that they would be covered by paint.

Opaque, or solid-colored, finishes are available in pigmented shellacs and lacquers, pigmented oil varnishes or oil paints, and pigmented water-based finishes or latex paint. These opaque finishes basically work like their transparent counterparts, with the same preparation, application techniques, and drying times.

When applying paint to raw wood or over a previously painted or finished surface, follow label directions for undercoating and sealing prior to the final top coats. Just as clear finishes reveal and amplify surface imperfections, a painted finish will do the same, sometimes more so. Be sure to give preparatory work necessary attention to produce a professional-looking finish.

Paints are basically opaque versions of the clear finishes already discussed, with corresponding applications and characteristics. Opaque lacquer, for example, is a spray-on rather than a brush-on finish. If you have a spray system set up for refinishing, it works great and produces a tough, durable furniture finish. A wide variety of colors are available from auto paint supply stores. Lacquer paints are also available in spray cans for small finishing jobs.

If you don't have the necessary equipment to spray a lacquer, you can use one of the brushable paints available. The most common ones are either oil-based paints (alkyd resin enamels) or latex paints (latex enamels). Oil-based paints are considered pigmented varnishes, and they handle basically the same. As with varnish, thinning can be done with mineral spirits. Latex paints are like water-based varnishes, with thinning and clean-up done with water. These paints come in flat, satin, semi-gloss, or high-gloss sheens in an almost unlimited variety of colors. Some paints are designed for interior use and some are designed for either interior or exterior. This will be indicated on the label, and of course the finish surface characteristics will vary accordingly. Interior-exterior rated paints are formulated to withstand moisture and sunlight much better than coatings designed only for interior use.

When using paints to finish wood, you'll usually need to use an undercoat (primer) before applying the paint. This will provide a good foundation for the final finish coats. The primer coat can usually be tinted to more closely match the final paint color, making it easier to cover with the paint coats.

An alternative to using a primer coat is to use a thinned-down version of the paint itself as an undercoating. As with primer, sand this coat with very fine sandpaper when it dries in preparation for the top coats. Usually you can do a painted finish with three coats, one primer coat, and two top coats. Shellac can also be used as a sealer when painting raw wood or when painting over other finishes or paints left on the wood. Shellac works as a good barrier coat, sealing in resins from woods such as knotty pine, which would otherwise bleed into the paint. It also forms a barrier between the paint and otherwise incompatible finishes which may already be on the wood.

When choosing paint for furniture, keep in mind that the higher the sheen, the greater the reflectivity of the surface and the more it will show any surface imperfections. Although a flat sheen may not be appropriate for most furniture, a satin or semigloss can offer excellent protection and hide many surface blemishes.

Paint can be a beautiful furniture finish for chairs, tabletops, and cabinets. It's a good idea to seal the wood and use a primer when applying paint.

FINISHING TOUCHES

Once you've applied the finish to a piece of furniture, you're almost done restoring it. All that's left to do is to put some finishing touches on the piece.

Wax

You can add protection and sheen to many film finishes, especially glossy ones, using wax. A good furniture wax contains at least some percentage of carnauba wax, the hardest furniture wax available. Furniture paste wax is available in amber, dark, and clear shades.

Because it offers so little protection for the wood, wax is normally used only as a top coating for other finishes such as shellac. It's a good idea to replace wax every year or two by washing the surface down with mineral spirits using a nylon abrasive pad or #0000 steel wool and then reapplying the wax.

For pieces that will receive little or no wear, paste wax alone can provide a good, thin, natural-looking finish. Once you apply wax directly to raw unfinished wood, however, it can be extremely difficult to remove later.

Pumice and Rottenstone

Pumice and rottenstone are finely ground mineral materials that can be used as fine abrasives, along with an oil or water lubricant, to rub out the final finish coat.

Rottenstone. Rottenstone is a very fine gray powder, used with either oil or soapy water and a felt pad or soft cloth to rub it out. Rottenstone produces a satin to semigloss sheen.

Pumice. Pumice, a white powder, is the coarser of the two, and is usually used with an oil, sometimes thinned with mineral spirits, to produce a dull to satin sheen. A felt pad or soft rag is used for the rubbing process.

Rubbing Compounds

Rubbing compounds are similar to pumice and rotten-stone, in that they are abrasives used to rub out the final coat of finish to get a particular sheen. The difference is that they are premixed in liquid or paste form and you do not need to add additional oils or lubricants.

To clean and polish hardware, use an electric buffing wheel with polishing compound, premixed brass polish (right), or a homemade solution of ammonia and baking soda.

You can coat furniture with paste wax (far left) or liquid wax (far right rear) for a high-gloss sheen once you've applied the finish. You can also give the finish a satin or semigloss look by rubbing it with a pre-mixed rubbing compound (left and center rear, right front) or an abrasive such as pumice or rottenstone (center), followed by a coat of wax.

If you want to achieve a gloss or high-gloss finish, you'll probably have to sand the surface with a very fine wet-or-dry sandpaper (400- to 600-grit) before polishing out the surface with compound. When you use compound to polish a table top to a gloss sheen, a power buffer with a lamb's-wool pad makes the job go faster.

Burn-in Sticks. Also called shellac or lacquer sticks, burn-in sticks fill dents and scratches on finished surfaces without damaging the existing finish. These hard, solid sticks of finish come in a variety of solid, clear, amber, and translucent colors. They are available from finish, repair, and touch-up supply companies.

Brass Cleaner and Polish

The furniture restoration process often includes cleaning and polishing of brass or brass-plated hardware. You can clean and polish some hardware with an electric buffing wheel, using various buffing and polishing compounds. You can also use ordinary ready-mixed liquid brass polish available at most hardware stores and simply follow the label directions.

5
Structural Repairs I: Loose Joints

A basic knowledge of joints is important in furniture repair for a number of reasons. If joints are loose on a piece of furniture, you'll probably have to disassemble the piece to reglue it. When you look at the exterior surface of a joint, you may only see a line where the two pieces of wood meet. Your knowledge of joints can give you an understanding of what's hidden below the surface of that line, enabling you to work the joint loose without breaking it. If you have a broken joint or pieces are missing, knowing the type of joint you're working with allows you to repair it properly.

Recognizing different kinds of furniture joints can also help you determine the quality of a piece. If you discover that a chair is constructed using mortise-and-tenon joints as opposed to dowels, for example, you can be sure it's a high-quality construction. The same is true about furniture with dovetail construction on the drawers as opposed to rabbet-joint drawers. Dovetails are better joints and will last indefinitely.

TYPES OF JOINTS

There are a number of ways to join two pieces of wood, but most are variations of the following basic joints:

Butt Joint. This joint is made when two pieces of wood are butted together and glued. Boards are commonly joined end grain to edge grain, edge grain to edge grain, or edge grain to face grain, although other configurations are possible. When you glue an end-grain surface of one board to another wood surface, the joint won't hold unless it's strengthened with dowel pins or some other reinforcement. The reason for the reinforcement is that the end grain of wood doesn't provide enough solid surface for the bonding process to take place. When magnified, end grain looks much like the end of a group of drinking straws bunched together. Consequently, the open end of the grain fibers absorbs most of the glue you apply to the joint and doesn't leave enough on the surface to provide a good bond.

When you use the butt joint to glue two or more boards side by side, or edge grain to edge grain, as when making a wide top for a table, the joint can be quite strong. However, you must make sure that the joining edges are planed smooth to form a perfect fit, and that the joint is glued and clamped sufficiently.

Lap Joint. This joint is created when two pieces of wood overlap one another at a right angle. Usually, at least one piece of wood is notched out, allowing the other piece to fit down into it. This kind of lap joint is called a *full-lap joint*. Both pieces may also be notched to half of their thickness, allowing them to fit into each other. This joint is known as a *half-lap joint*.

Miter Joint. The *miter joint* is formed by cutting corresponding angles, usually at 45 degrees, on the ends of two pieces of wood and then joining them together. The most common use of the miter joint in furniture is in mirror and picture frames. The miter joint may be reinforced with pins or dowels or with the installation of a wooden back panel. A material that is frequently used for this is ¼-inch plywood.

Rabbet Joint. When you notch the end or the edge of a piece of wood and use that notch to join two boards, you've created a *rabbet joint*. You can also make a rabbet joint by notching both pieces of wood. The rabbet joint is not a strong joint in itself and is usually secured with fasteners such as nails or screws. Sometimes drawer sides are joined to the fronts with rabbet joints. Rabbet joints are used in casework furniture such as chests, or in some drawers to join the sides to the front and/or back. Cabinet backs can also be joined to the case with rabbet joints.

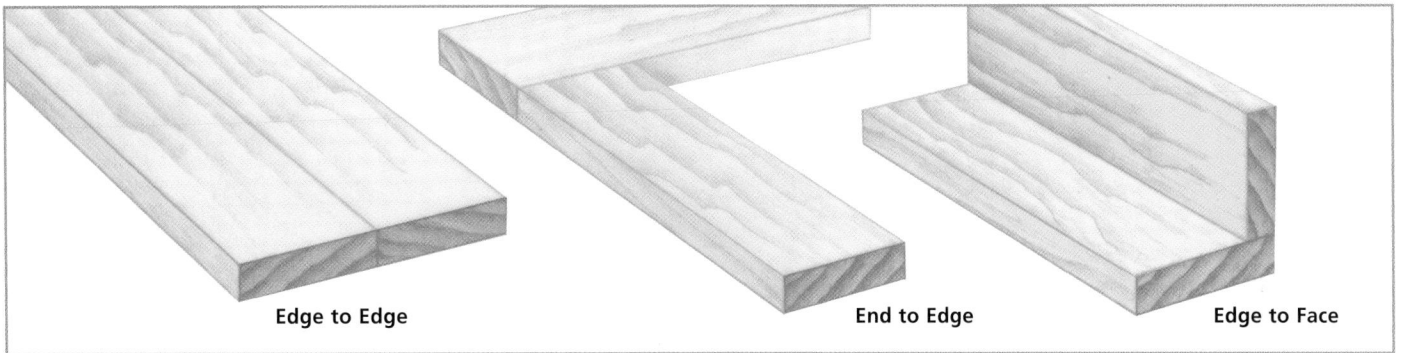

Edge to Edge   End to Edge   Edge to Face

Butt Joint. A butt joint occurs when two pieces of wood are butted together and joined. The most common—and strongest—butt joint in furniture is edge to edge.

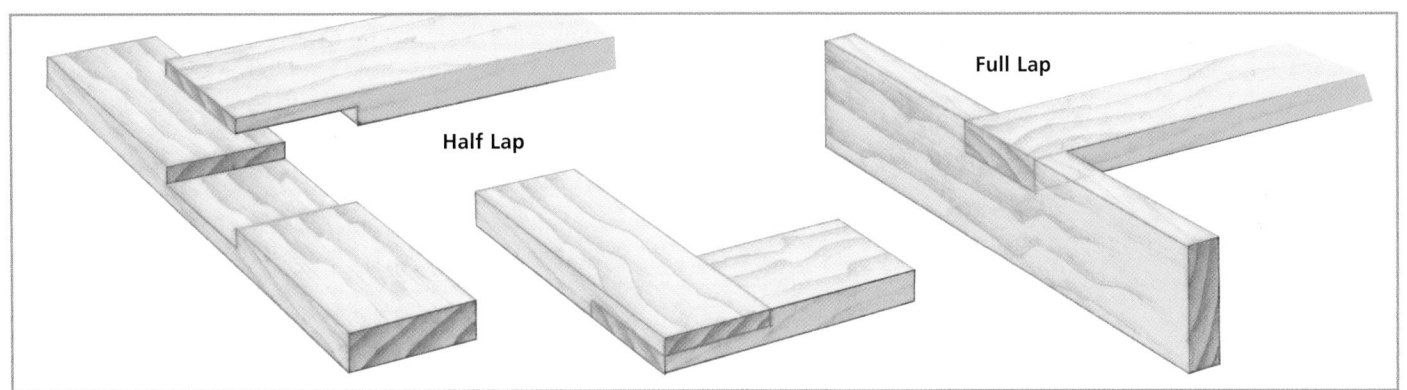

Full Lap

Half Lap

Lap Joint. When two pieces of wood overlap one another at a right angle, they form a lap joint.

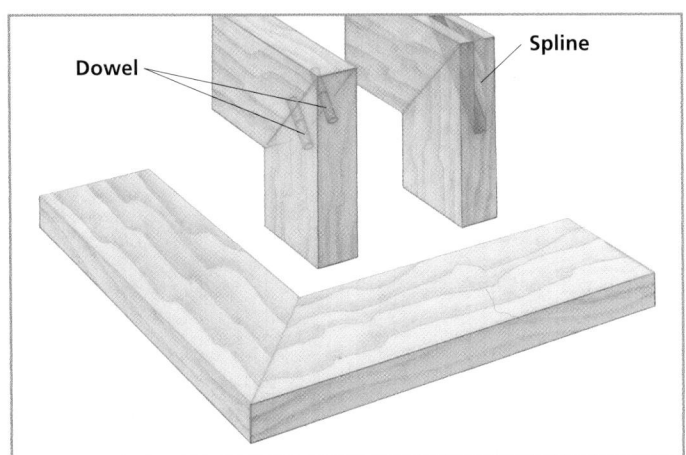

Dowel   Spline

Miter Joint. Cut corresponding angles in two pieces of wood and join them, and you've formed a miter joint. Miter joints are often reinforced using dowels or a spline.

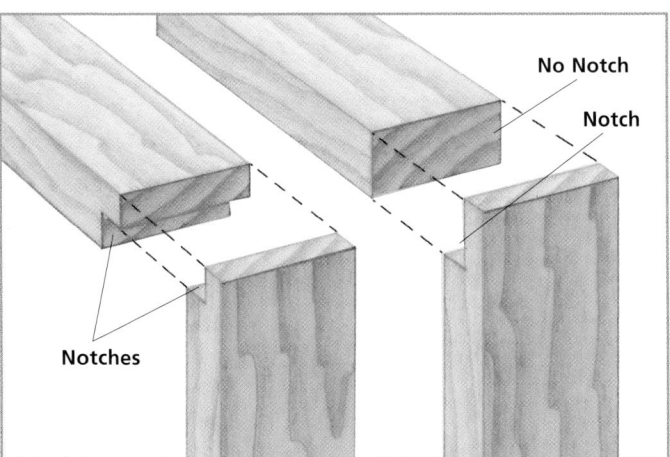

No Notch

Notch

Notches

Rabbet Joint. Joining two pieces of wood, one or both of which are notched, creates a rabbet joint.

Dado Joint. A *dado joint* is formed by cutting a groove across the grain in one piece of wood the exact size as the square-cut edge of another piece. The square-cut edge of the second piece is then inserted into the groove of the first piece to form a tight, secure joint. Dado joints are commonly used to join wood at right angles, as in bookcase shelves. Sometimes the dado is hidden because the groove is not cut all the way across the board to the front of the bookcase. This kind of dado joint is called a *blind dado*.

Mortise-and-Tenon Joint. The *mortise-and-tenon* is one of the strongest furniture joints, and its use usually signifies quality furniture. This joint is normally formed by cutting a square tongue—the tenon—on the end of one piece of wood and an equal-size square hole or slot—the mortise—in another. The tongue of the first piece is then inserted into the slot of the second. Although not necessary, sometimes a pin or peg is also inserted through the joint, perpendicular to the tenon, locking the joint together.

Dowel Joint. *Dowel joints* are basically substitutes for mortise-and-tenon joints, although they usually aren't as strong. Many modern pieces, particularly chairs, are constructed using dowel joints. A dowel joint is made by fitting a butt joint, drilling corresponding holes in the two pieces of wood to be joined, and then inserting the dowel pins before joining the pieces. Glue is used in this type of joint, and the dowel pins serve as round tenons, holding the two pieces together.

Dovetail Joint. The *dovetail joint* is one of the best joints used to join wood at a right angle. Easily distinguishable by its multiple flared tenons, which interlock like fingers and look like doves' tails, the dovetail forms a strong, durable joint. Most commonly used to attach drawer sides to drawer fronts, dovetail joints almost always indicate quality furniture. Hand-cut dovetail joints, most often seen in antique furniture, usually have tails that differ slightly in size and may vary in spacing. Machine-cut dovetails are excellent, strong joints, but the old hand-cut variety is still hard to beat.

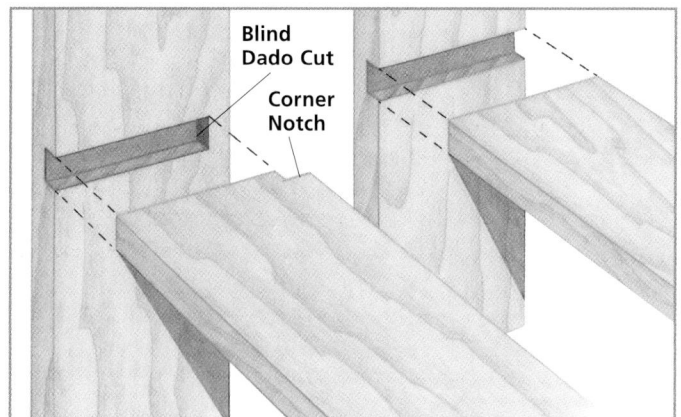

Dado Joint. Cut a cross-grain groove large enough to accept a second piece of wood (above). Cutting the dado short creates a blind joint.

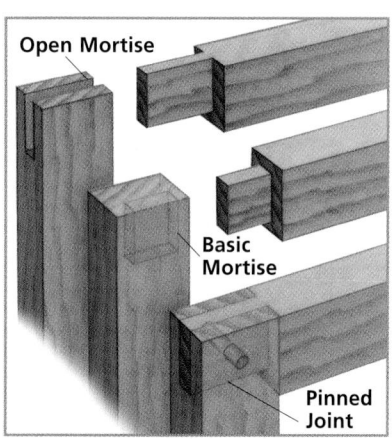

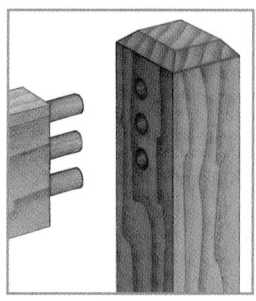

A dowel joint is basically a butt joint reinforced with dowels (below).

Mortise-and-Tenon Joint. A mortise-and-tenon joint is formed by cutting a tongue (the tenon) in one piece of wood and a matching hole or slot (the mortise) in the joining piece (left).

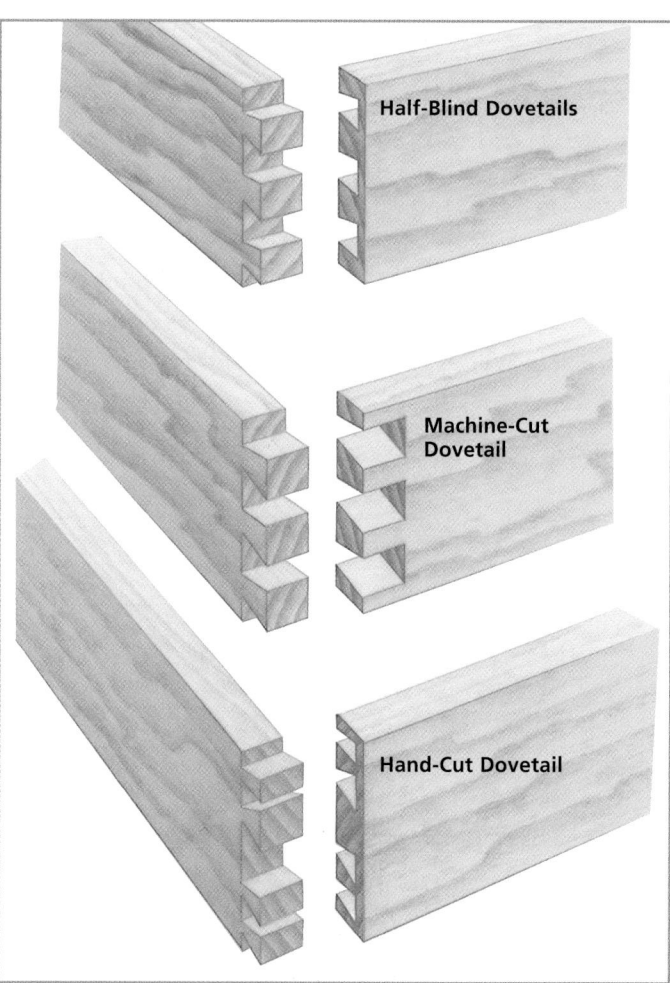

Dovetail Joint. Dovetail joints are formed by cutting alternating dovetail-shaped tenons, called tails, in two pieces of wood and joining the pieces by interlocking the tails. The cuts may be made by hand or machine.

Dovetail joints can be constructed using either "through" dovetails or "half-blind" dovetails. Through dovetails are cut all the way through the thickness of both joining pieces of wood, with the "fingers" visible from two sides. Half-blind dovetails are cut so that the dovetails are visible only from one side. See page 60 for illustrations of various types of dovetail joints.

REPAIRING LOOSE JOINTS

Loose joints are among the first problems you'll likely encounter as you begin to repair furniture, and they can be a problem on virtually every type of furniture. As you reglue loose joints on your piece using the step-by-step instructions included in this section, you may encounter other problems. If so, incorporate the repair into the regluing process. Because all regluing projects are not as simple as they might appear, I've included some problem areas to look for when regluing joints.

To fix a loose joint, in most cases you'll have to disassemble, clean, glue, reassemble, and clamp it. To take a joint apart, first make sure it isn't pegged or pinned. (See "Removing Pegs from Joints," page 62.)

Taking Joints Apart. Tap the joint with a rubber mallet or a hammer and a softwood or cork block. Begin tapping softly at first, and strike it only as hard as is necessary to break the joint loose but not hard enough to damage or split the wood. If the joint is too tight to break apart, it may not need regluing. If it's still neces-sary to separate the joint, drill a small hole into the joint and inject a 50-percent warm water and 50-percent vinegar solution into the joint, allowing it to soak for a while to loosen the glue. Tap the joint occasionally to see whether the glue has softened, loosening the joint.

Wooden buttons are decorative covers for countersunk wood screws. You can remove them by prying them out.

Regluing in Subassemblies. When regluing furniture, some pieces may have too many joints or may be too awkward to reglue all at once. In such cases you can often reglue components of the piece in subassemblies. On frame chairs with the main back post or stile continuing down in one piece to form the back leg, for example, you can reglue the chair's entire back section independently as one component.

With armchairs, sometimes you can add the arms after you've glued the rest of the chair, as long as you check to be sure they fit properly before the rest of the chair is dry. Some platform chairs, such as Windsor chairs, have back support posts that fit directly into the seat, where the base of the chair (consisting of seat, legs, and stretchers or foot rails) can be glued independently. You can then glue and attach the back later.

joint reinforcements

In addition to the pegs and pins mentioned earlier, other items to look for when disassembling loose joints are corner blocks, glue blocks, wooden buttons, wood screws, and metal braces.

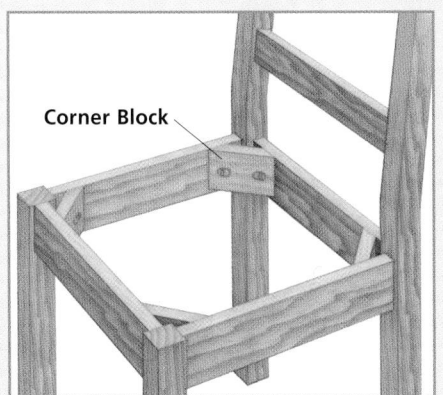

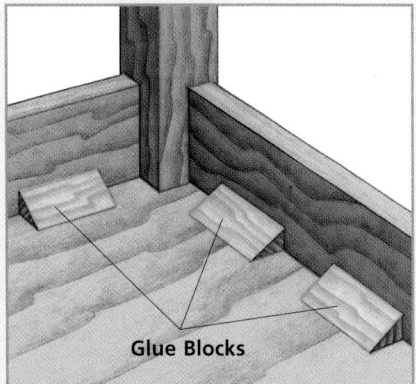

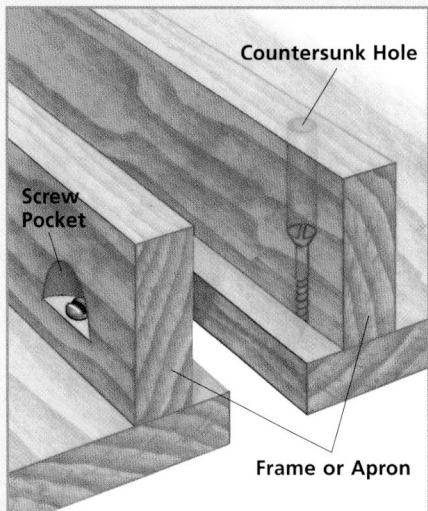

Corner Blocks. Often used in chairs and table frames, corner blocks are pieces of wood cut to fit into and reinforce corner joints.

Glue Blocks. Table and chest tops sometimes need extra gluing surface to hold them in place. That's where small glue blocks come in.

Screws. Wood screws are often used to reinforce a joint. The screws are attached through countersunk holes or screw pockets.

Removing Pegs from Joints

When you begin to disassemble a joint, look closely for pegs (small dowels) and pins (tiny brads or nails) that may be inserted through the joint to lock it together, and remove them before taking the joint apart.

Difficulty Level:

TOOLS AND MATERIALS
- Scratch awl
- ¼-inch chisel
- Needle-nose pliers
- Backsaw
- Drill and assorted bits
- Mallet
- Appropriate size dowel

1 Drill the peg. If a wooden peg or dowel is inserted through the joint to lock it together, hammer it out with a same-size dowel. If the peg won't move, make a center point in the end of the peg with a scratch awl. Choose a drill bit just smaller than the diameter of the peg, and drill out the peg using an electric drill.

2 Remove the peg. After drilling, loosen the remaining bits of the peg by gently tapping a ¼-inch chisel around its perimeter. Grasp the peg shards with needle-nose pliers and remove them. After regluing the joint, replace the peg with a new dowel of the appropriate diameter, and cut it flush with the wood surface using a backsaw.

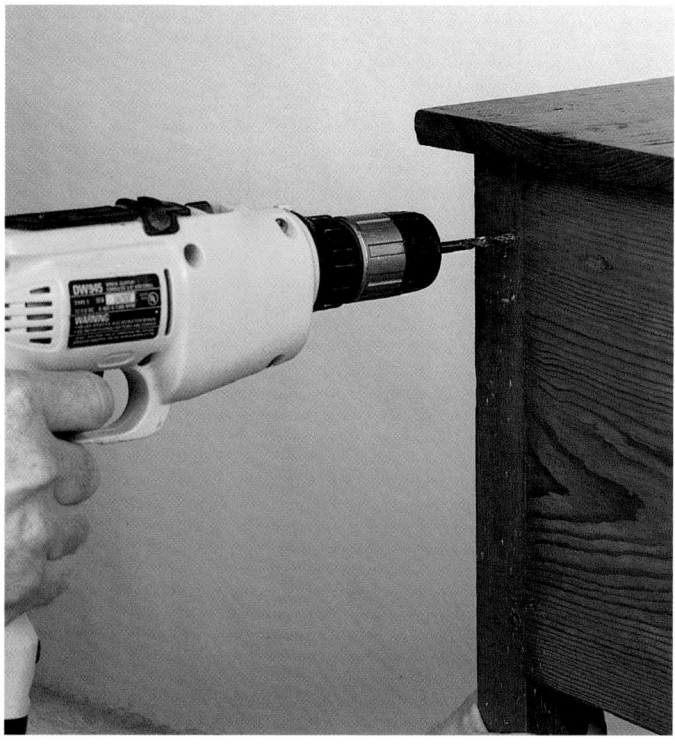

1 Drill out the wooden peg using a slightly smaller drill bit.

2 Loosen the peg shards using a narrow chisel. Grasp them with needle-nose pliers to remove them.

pinned joints

Pegs are usually easy to spot, but sometimes you have to look closely for nails because the nailhead may be countersunk and covered with wood putty. If you discover nails, try one of two removal processes:

- Pull the pin out with diagonal pliers, which may require digging around the head of the nail with a wood chisel.

- Drive the nail all the way through with a nail set, if possible, and pull it out the other side.

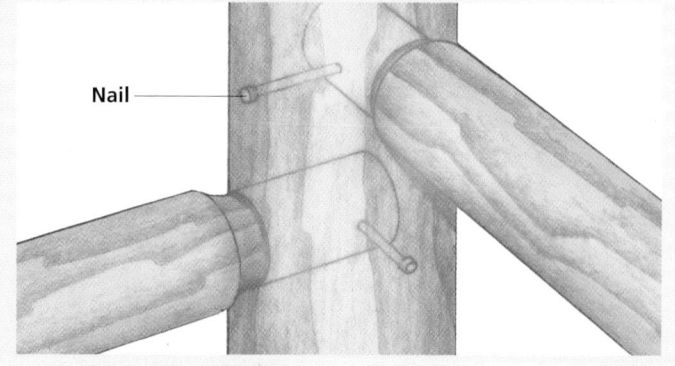

Nail

LOOSE JOINTS IN CHAIRS

Structurally speaking, chairs get the hardest use of any furniture. If you own—and use—chairs for 10 years or more, they will probably need at least some regluing, depending on their construction and frequency of use.

At first glance, chair repair seems simple and straight-forward. But don't be fooled by the chair's relatively small size. Chairs generally incorporate at least a dozen—and as many as 20 or more—joints in their basic construction. In addition, despite the fact that chairs are the one category of furniture that's virtually useless if not structurally sound, their design is often weak and fragile. To complicate matters further, chairs tend to break at their weakest point, which can be the most difficult place to restore to its original strength. These weak points are usually where two or more parts intersect to form joints. For example, a back post that has been mortised or drilled for adjoining seat rails can be weak and may break. Repairing this problem can be difficult because several joints converge in the damaged area, and a back post gets a considerable amount of stress from use.

Fortunately, many times the only problem with chairs is that the joints have loosened, which is easy to fix. (See pages 64–67.) Although chair styles and construction vary, the following procedures are basic and common to most chairs when they need regluing.

Loose Dowels, Rungs, and Tenons

After cleaning a joint and test-fitting it, you may find that it's too loose to form a strong joint. You'll need to take care of this obstacle before proceeding with regluing. Problems sometimes encountered when regluing joints include loose-fitting dowels, chair stretcher rails, or tenons.

Dowels. If dowels fit too loosely, the best solution is to remove each dowel and drill out the hole using a twist bit to accommodate the next-larger-size dowel. To keep the holes aligned you may need to use a doweling jig. (See "Using Dowels to Fix a Broken Joint," page 91, for how to use the jig.) Install the larger dowel pins, making sure you cut them to the correct length (slightly shorter than the depth of the hole to allow room for glue) before proceeding with your regluing schedule.

Chair Stretcher Rails. Chairs often have horizontal members called stretcher rails that run between the legs. A rounded stretcher rail is called a rung. If a stretcher fits too loosely in the joint, remove it from the chair and put it in a vise with the end facing up. Using a backsaw, cut a kerf in the center of the end of the rail

Loose Joints in Chairs. Although they're small, chairs are complicated structures with a large number of joints.

deep enough to accommodate a small wedge, and drill a small hole at the base of the kerf. Cut a wedge from a piece of hardwood the width of the stretcher diameter, and tap it into the kerf at the end of the rail until the rail end expands to the proper size. Cut off the end of the wedge, and then test-fit the stretcher rail into the hole before regluing it.

Tenons. If a tenon is too loose, remove it from the mortise and cut some shims (thin pieces of wood used to fill space) to the same size as the tenon. Veneer pieces will usually work for this purpose. Use as many shims as necessary to widen the thickness of the tenon, placing them wherever the tenon is loose fitting. Glue and clamp the shims to the tenon until the glue is dry. Next, test-fit the tenon into the mortise, sanding or trimming the shims if necessary for a precise fit before regluing.

Regluing Chair Joints without Disassembly

If a chair has an upholstered, caned, or rush-woven seat that's in good shape, you may not want to remove the seat or ruin it by cutting it out just to reglue a few loose joints. Other joints that are difficult or impossible to disassemble are the wedged joint and the shrink joint, usually used on older chairs to lock the legs and stretchers or rails together.

A wedged joint is formed when a wedge has been inserted into the end of a stretcher rail or rung, expanding the end of the member as the wedge is tapped into the hole. A shrink joint is created when a chair stretcher or leg is turned from dry wood with a knob-type end on it. This knob end is inserted into the hole of the other member while that wood is still green. As the green wood dries, it shrinks, tightening around the knob end of the dry wood member and locking the two pieces together.

If you encounter any of these situations, you may want to reglue the joints without taking them apart. This entails getting glue around the mating joint parts without actually being able to get at the parts themselves.

Difficulty Level:

TOOLS AND MATERIALS
- Drill and assorted bits   • Clamps
- Wood glue and injector   • Rag
- Appropriate size dowel

1 Drill a glue hole. Drill a small hole about ⅛ inch in diameter under the joint, on a slight angle directly into the mortise, or hollowed-out area, in the wood.

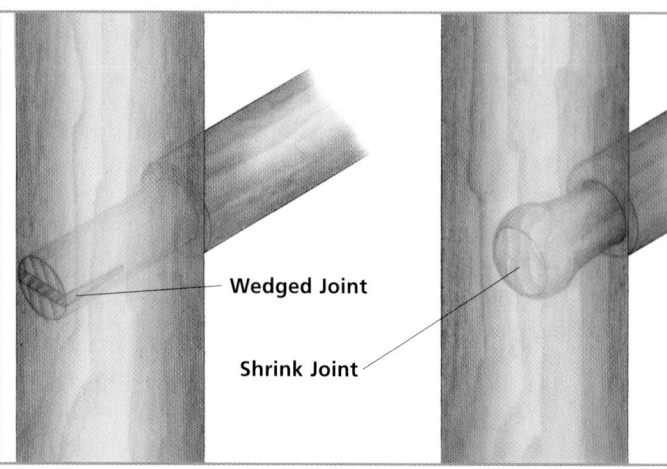

Regluing Joints without Disassembly. Wedged joints (left), where a wedge locks a chair stretcher or rung in place, and shrink joints (right), where the knoblike end of a chair member is held firmly in place when green wood in the mating member shrinks around it, are difficult to remove, even if they become loose.

2 Inject glue. Put about an ounce of polyvinyl or hide wood glue in a syringe-type glue injector (available from woodworkers' catalogs or hardware stores) or in a glue squeeze bottle with a narrow tip. Thin the glue by adding about 25 percent water, and mix it well. Insert the syringe or glue-bottle tip into the hole you just drilled, forcing the glue into the joint. Move the loose joint back and forth, being sure to work the glue throughout the joint.

3 Clamp the joint. Install a clamp on the joint, and then plug the glue hole with a small dowel pin of the appropriate diameter and clean up any glue that's been squeezed out of the joint. Allow the glued joint to dry for several hours.

1 Drill an inconspicuous, angled hole under the joint.

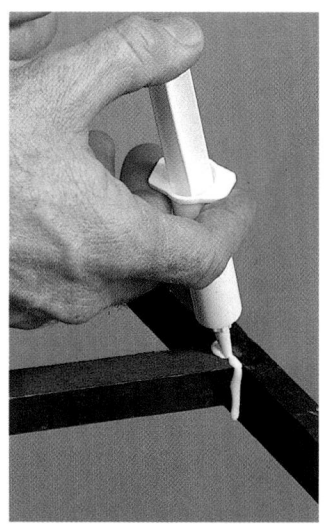

2 Insert the syringe tip into the hole, and inject glue into the joint.

3 Clamp the joint tightly, plug the access hole with a same-size wooden dowel pin, and clean up excess glue.

Regluing a Chair

In this case, you're able to take apart the entire chair, clean all the joints, and glue the chair back together.

Difficulty Level:

TOOLS AND MATERIALS

- Screwdrivers
- Masking tape and marker
- Rubber mallet
- Solvent or rasp, chisels, or ultility knife
- Clamps
- Rag
- Wood glue and glue brush or palette knife
- Mineral spirits, #0000 steel wool, and wax

1 Check the joints. If the seat is removable, take it off to check the joints. If the chair has a slip seat (a removable, upholstered seat that slips out of the chair frame), check under the seat for the screws that hold it in place. Remove the screws, and put them in a labeled plastic bag so you can find them when you're ready to reinstall the seat.

Some chairs don't have slip seats; the upholstery is attached directly to the chair seat rails. It may not be necessary to remove all the upholstery, only that which is around the loose joint. In this case, carefully remove only the upholstery necessary to work on the joint you want to fix. You can tack the upholstery back in place after you complete the job.

Check all the joints to find out which ones are loose by applying pressure to each joint. If there's any movement at all, you should probably reglue the joint, as it will continue to loosen with use. Also, if possible, determine what kind of joints (usually dowel or mortise-and-tenon) the chair has, and look closely to make sure pegs or nails are not driven through the tenons or dowels. If you find pegs or pins, you must drill them out or remove them before you try to separate the joint. (See "Removing Pegs from Joints" and "Pinned Joints, page 62")

2 Label and disassemble the chair parts. If the chair has corner blocks inside the seat frame, label them and the inside of the seat rails with masking tape and corresponding numbers. Remove the screws, and put them in a labeled bag. Using a mallet, tap the corner blocks loose.

NOTE: After removing corner blocks, check to see whether the screws fit tightly in the block screw holes. If so, enlarge the holes so the screws fit loosely in the block. When you reinstall the blocks to the chair frame, this will ensure that the screws act as a clamp, tightening into the chair frame and pulling the corner blocks up tight.

Label all chair parts with corresponding numbers using masking tape labels so you'll make no mistakes when reassembling the chair. Make sure the finish on the wood is sound before labeling if you're not refinishing the chair. Use blue painter's tape if you're unsure of the soundness of the finish, and be careful when peeling it off. Beginning with the loosest joint, tap it apart with a mallet. Continue tapping joints apart until you've removed all the loose parts. Be careful not to apply unnecessary force, which could split or break the chair.

Continued on next page.

1 Apply pressure to each joint to see which ones are loose and need to be repaired.

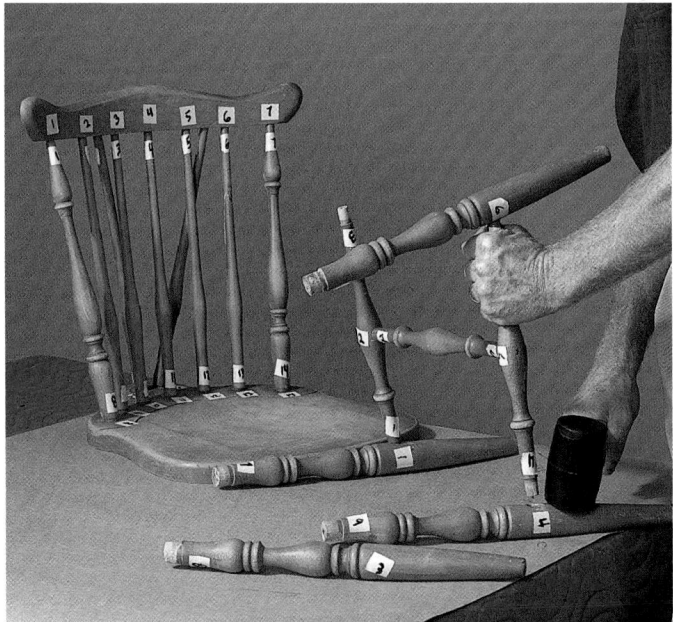

2 Label all the joints, and then knock them apart using a rubber mallet.

Continued from previous page.

3 Clean the joints. Clean old glue from the joints using adhesive solvent or by gently scraping with a rasp, a chisel, or the edge of a utility knife. To clean dowel holes, use an old drill bit of the proper size or a narrow wood chisel.

4 Test-fit the parts. After you've cleaned all the joints, assemble the entire chair without glue to make sure everything fits properly. You may be tempted to skip this step, but don't. It's frustrating to get glue on the joints only to find that something doesn't fit properly or you've accidentally mixed up the parts. If this happens, usually the glue will be set by the time you get the problem straightened out, and you'll have to clean the joints again.

5 Glue up the chair. Take the chair apart, and begin to apply hide or polyvinyl wood glue. Cover all the joint surfaces with a thin layer of glue, spreading it with a glue brush, a palette knife, or a small dowel. Assemble the joints as you apply the glue.

6 Clamp the joints. After you've assembled all the parts, apply clamps to pull all joints up snugly but not overly tight. Make sure you cushion steel clamp jaws with plastic caps or softwood blocks to keep from damaging the chair's finish. Wipe off all excess glue using a wet or damp rag, and check all the joints to make sure they're pulled up tight.

NOTE: If the wood surface is finished, you can allow the excess polyvinyl glue to set for about an hour or so, and then simply peel it off with the help of a razor blade or sharp wood chisel. Make sure you don't allow the glue to set completely, however, or you won't be able to remove it without damaging the finish.

7 Square up the chair. Set the chair on a level surface, and make sure everything is square. Check that the chair doesn't rock and that any slip seats will fit back into the seat framework. Let the chair dry overnight.

Remove all clamps and labels, and do your final cleanup using mineral spirits and #0000 steel wool. After cleaning, you may have to use polish or wax to brighten the finish.

3 Clean all old glue from the joints using solvent or by carefully scraping with a rasp, a chisel, or the edge of a utility knife.

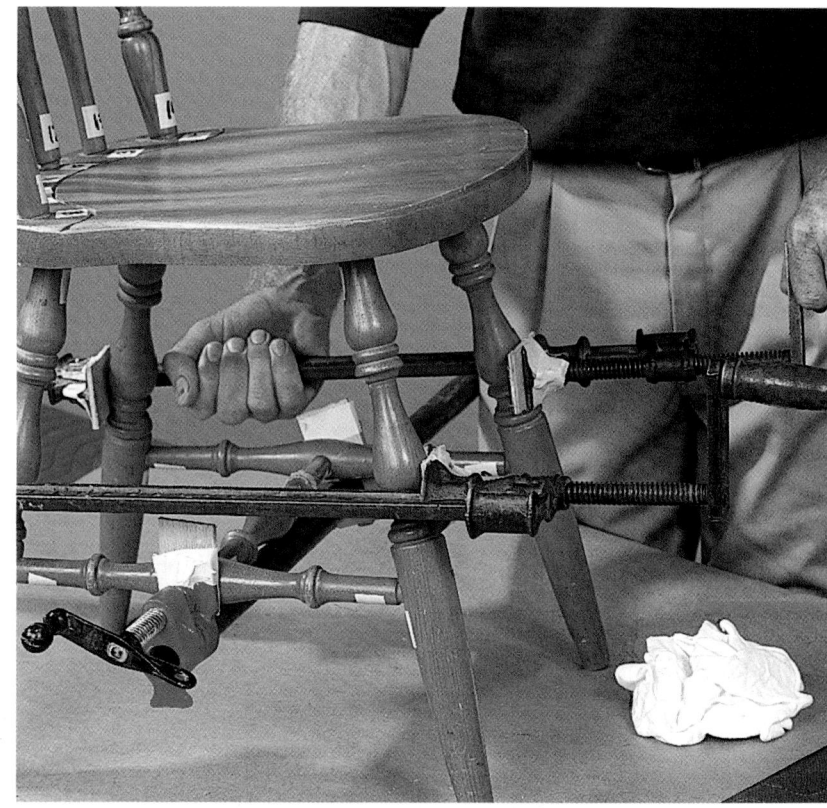

6 Once you've assembled all the joints, apply clamps where needed to snug up the joints.

4 Test-fit all the joints after cleaning to make sure everything goes together properly.

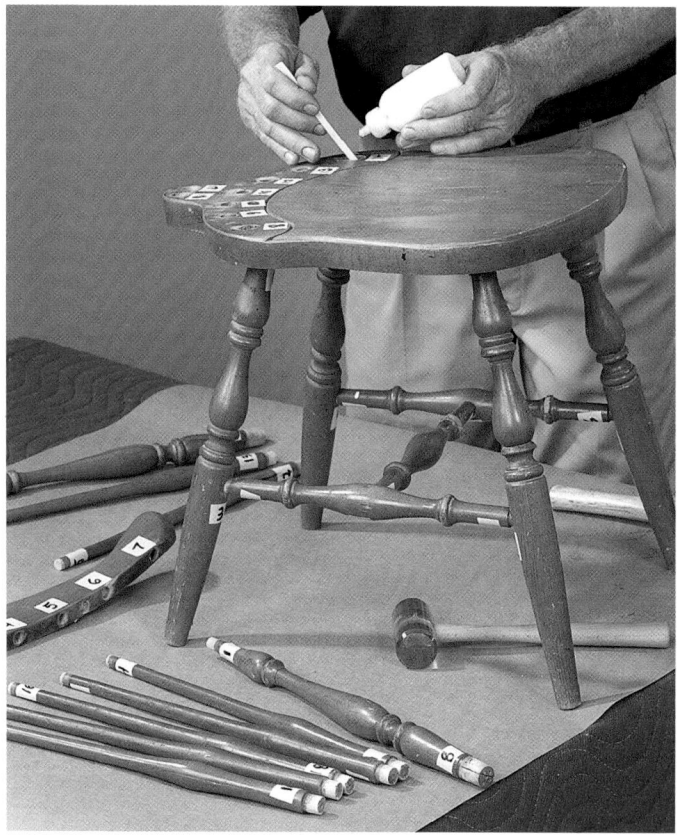

5 Apply hide or polyvinyl wood glue to all joint parts, assembling the joints as you go.

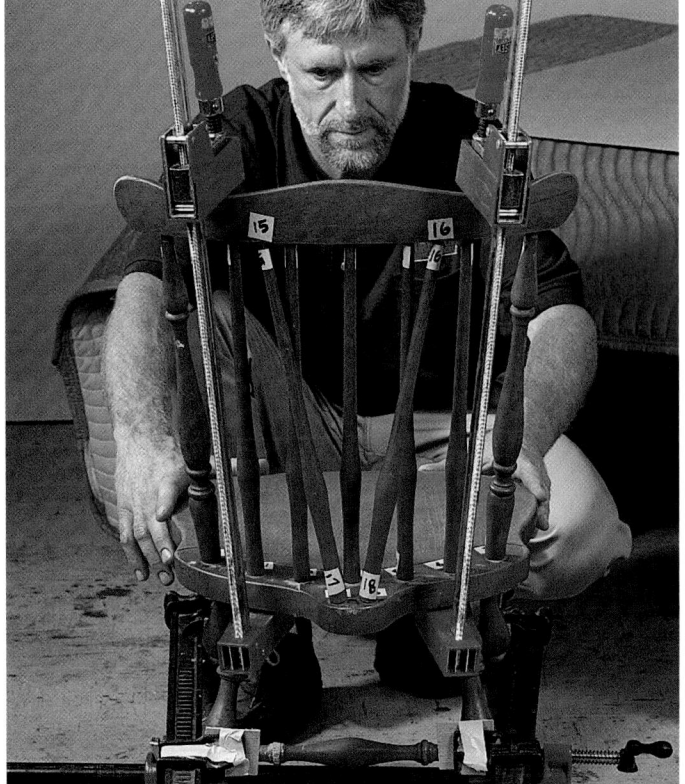

7 Check that the chair is square and doesn't rock by setting it on a level surface.

reinforcing joints

There are a few ways to tighten loose joints when regluing a chair. For rounded rungs, such as the type found on the chair shown here, install a small wedge on the end of the rung. Place the piece in a vise, and use a backsaw to cut a kerf in the end of the rung. Drill a hole at the base of the kerf. The hardwood wedge should be the width of the rung diameter. Cut off the edge of the wedge once the rung expands to its proper size. For a loose tenon, glue veneer shims to the tenon until the joint is tight.

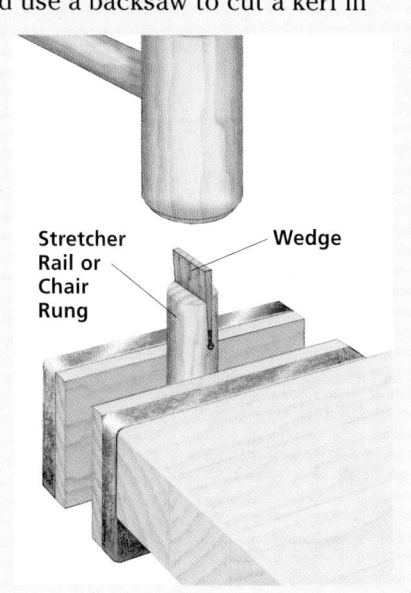

Stretcher Rail or Chair Rung

Wedge

LOOSE JOINTS IN TABLES

There are many kinds of tables: dining, coffee, end, bedside, sofa, console, card-and-game, and lamp tables. Although these tables have a variety of styles, they all consist of a flat top supported by legs or a base. Generally, the construction of the legs or base follows one of two basic designs: pedestal-type tables or frame-type ones.

The pedestal table is usually made up of a single column supported by three or four legs. A block is mounted to the top of the column, which in turn is mounted to the underside of the tabletop. Tilt-top tables are pedestal tables made so that their tops can tilt up to a vertical position, allowing them to be placed in the corner of a room.

The frame table consists of a frame with legs at each corner. The legs may be joined to the frame with bolts, dowel joints, or—in the best tables—mortise-and-tenon joints. The top is then attached to this leg-supported frame.

Whether you're dealing with a pedestal or frame table, your primary concern will be the legs or table base when you reglue loose joints.

Pedestal-Style Tables

Regluing pedestal-table legs can be challenging because of the odd angles you're likely to encounter when clamping some of the joints. With improvisation and special clamp blocks, however, you can overcome these difficulties. (See "Clamping Jigs for Pedestal Tables," opposite.)

Pedestal tables usually become loose in any of several areas: where the legs join the pedestal column, where the mounting block joins the top of the pedestal column, and where the top attaches to the mounting block. Legs are joined to pedestals in a variety of ways including dowels, mortise-and-tenons, sliding dovetails, and even lag screws on some hollow-pedestal Victorian-style tables. Some pedestals also have metal plates attached to their bottoms to lock the legs together at the column. If legs are loose and need to be reglued, remove the metal plate first and reinstall it after the job is complete.

If the legs seem loose, turn the table upside down and inspect the various joints to see which ones have movement in them. Then follow the appropriate instructions for regluing or tightening.

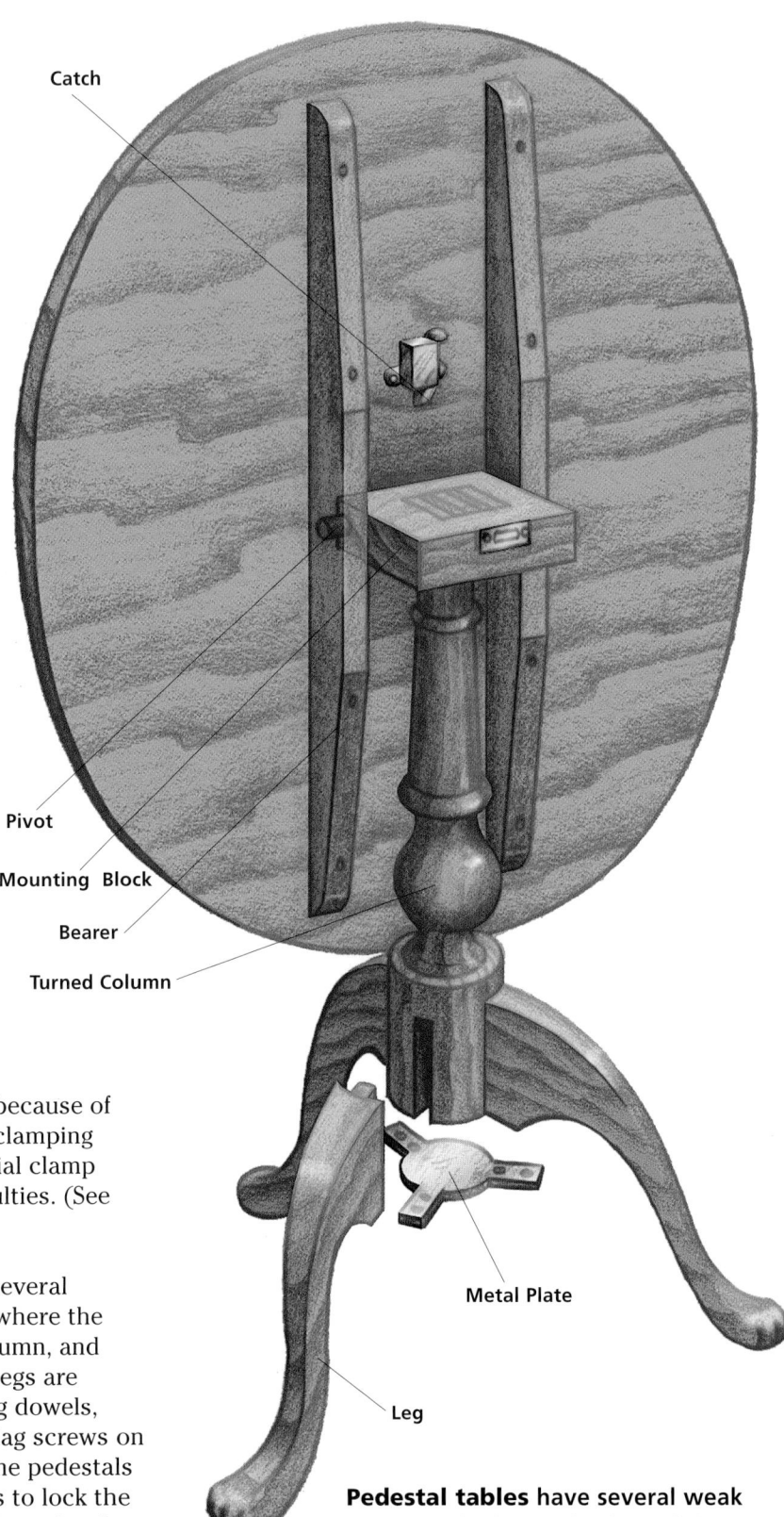

Catch

Pivot

Mounting Block

Bearer

Turned Column

Metal Plate

Leg

Pedestal tables have several weak spots: at the leg-and-column joint, at the mounting-block-and-column joint, and at the tabletop-and-mounting-block joint.

PRO TIP: clamping jigs for pedestal tables

As anyone who's worked in a furniture shop can tell you, clamping pedestal legs can be a challenging task. You may need to make a clamping jig to pull up the joints in certain pedestal-leg configurations. Here are two time-tested jigs, one using wood blocks and plywood and the other using ¾-inch plywood.

Make a block-and-plywood jig. Cut a solid piece of wood (about the same thickness as the leg) and a piece of ¼-inch plywood the same size. The length and width of these pieces will depend on the size of the pedestal legs to be glued. Make sure the block and plywood are large enough to fit the leg as illustrated. Trace the outline of the leg on the wood block as shown, and cut the block at the traced outlines.

Mount the two end pieces of the block onto the ¼-inch plywood as shown using glue and small nails. After the glue dries, the block is ready to use as illustrated. To protect the leg's finish you can glue felt to the inside edges of the block where it makes contact with the leg.

Make a plywood jig. Trace and cut out blocks of plywood to fit the legs so the plywood will hook over the toe as illustrated. Cut a notch at the top of the block as shown. You may want to line the block with felt or some other padding where it makes contact with the leg to prevent finish damage. You can also make the block thicker for large legs by gluing two pieces of plywood together. After fitting the legs to the pedestal column, pull them tight using a tourniquet clamp or a band clamp.

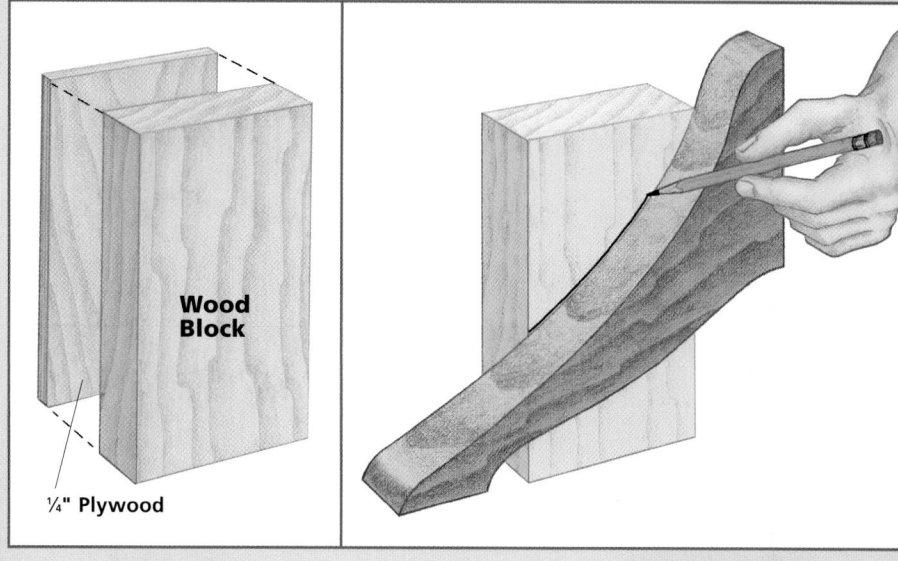

Wood Block

¼" Plywood

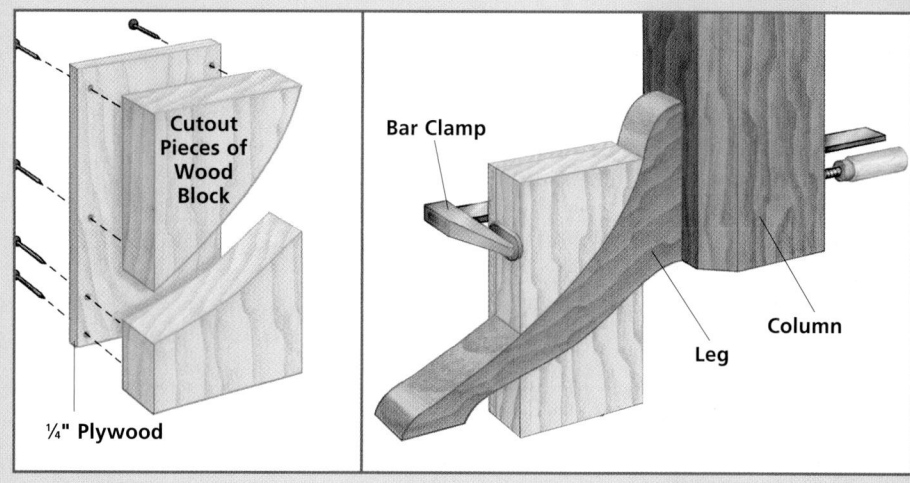

Cutout Pieces of Wood Block

¼" Plywood

Bar Clamp

Column

Leg

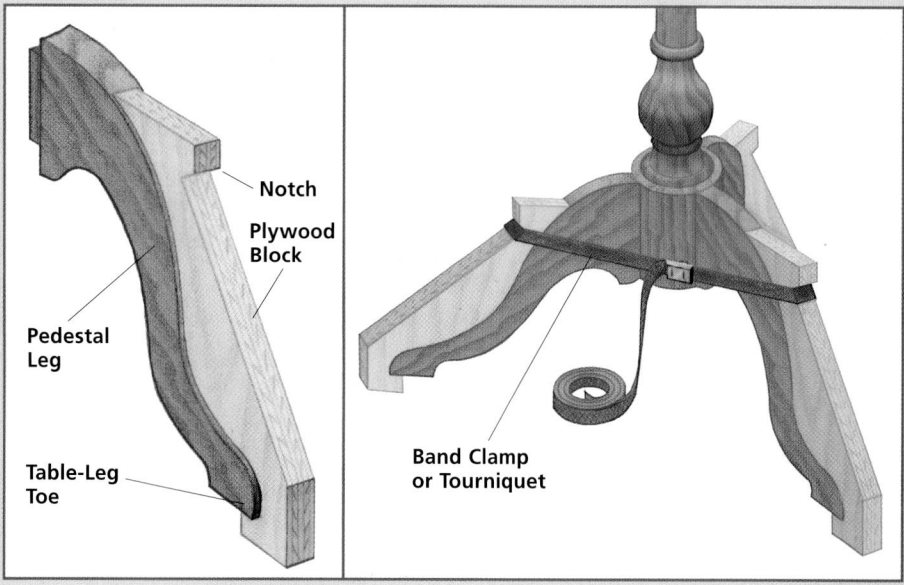

Notch

Plywood Block

Pedestal Leg

Table-Leg Toe

Band Clamp or Tourniquet

Repairing Dowel and Mortise-and-Tenon Leg Joints

If the pedestal column is solid and you can't see any evidence of the joint by looking at the bottom of the column, the legs are likely joined by either dowel or mortise-and-tenon joints. You'd reglue both kinds of joints in the same way.

Difficulty Level:

TOOLS AND MATERIALS
- Chisels
- Wedges (if necessary)
- Masking tape and marker
- Clamping jig (if necessary)
- Glue solvent or rasp, chisel, or utility knife
- Wood glue and glue brush or palette knife
- Mallet
- Clamps
- Rag

1 Remove the legs. Turn the pedestal upside down, and insert a wood chisel downward into the bottom of the leg joint. Tap the chisel with a mallet to loosen the joint. As the joint loosens at the bottom of the column, tap the leg on top of the foot to loosen the top of the leg joint. Alternately tap the bottom and top of the leg until it can be removed. If the joint is stubborn, make narrow hardwood wedges and drive them into the joint to help separate it.

2 Clean the joints. Make sure all the matching joint parts are labeled with numbers; then clean off old glue from all the joint surfaces using solvent or a chisel, knife, or wood rasp. Test-fit the legs to ensure that the joints fit properly, and install any clamps you'll use to be sure they'll pull the joints tight. If the clamps are too awkward or won't mount properly to tighten the joints, consider making a clamping jig before regluing the legs. (See "Clamping Jigs for Pedestal Tables," page 69.)

3 Glue the joints. Once you're sure the legs fit properly and you have the proper clamping method to tighten the joints, remove the legs from the pedestal again and apply glue to all joint surfaces, spreading it to a thin film. Assemble the joints as you go.

4 Reassemble the piece. Install the clamps and tighten them to pull the joints up snug; do not over-tighten. Clean excess glue from joints with a damp rag, and make sure they're tight. Be certain the legs are aligned properly with the pedestal and each other. After the piece dries, remove the clamps and clean up the finish with #0000 steel wool and mineral spirits.

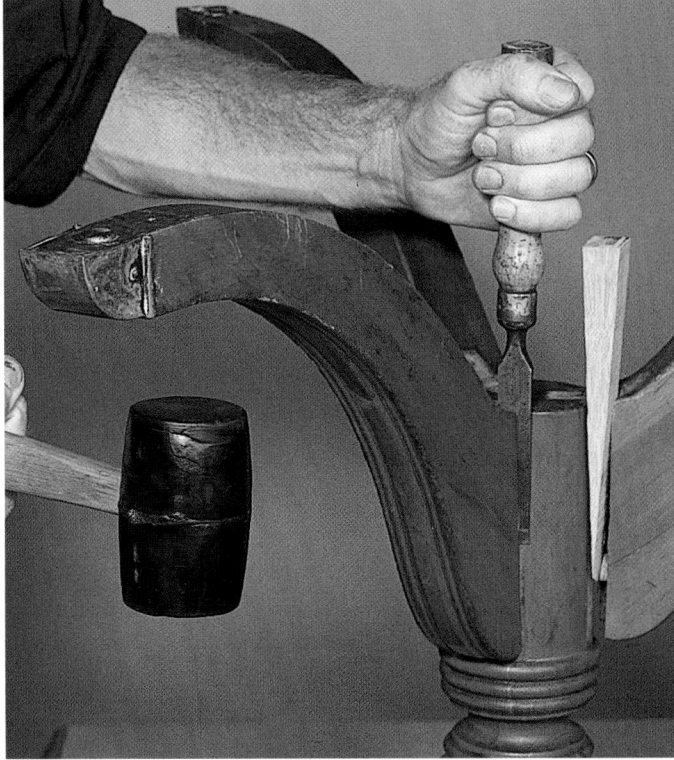

1 Use a chisel and mallet to loosen the leg joints. A wedge can help in loosening a stubborn leg.

3 Apply hide or polyvinyl wood glue to all joint surfaces, and assemble the joints as you glue them.

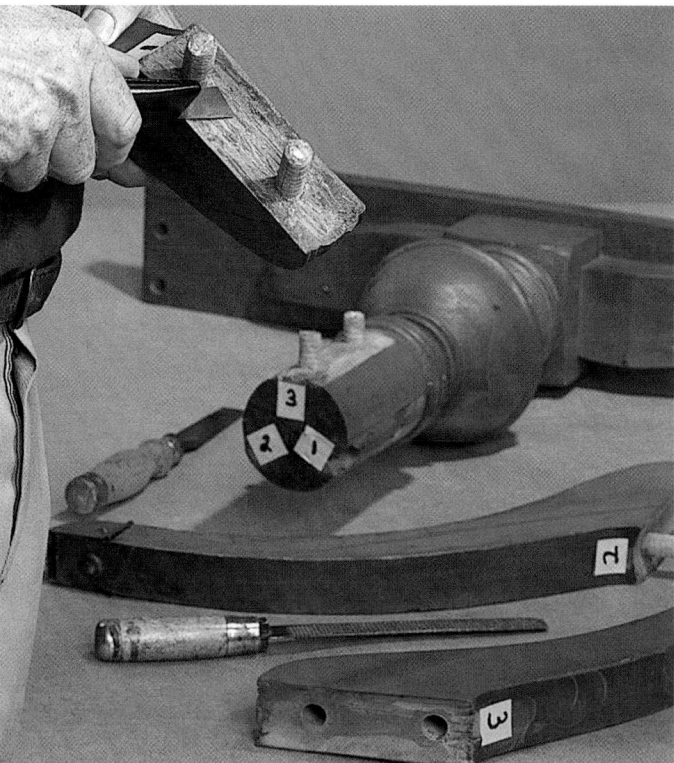

2 Label the joints; clean off old glue; and test-fit them using clamps to make sure the clamps fit.

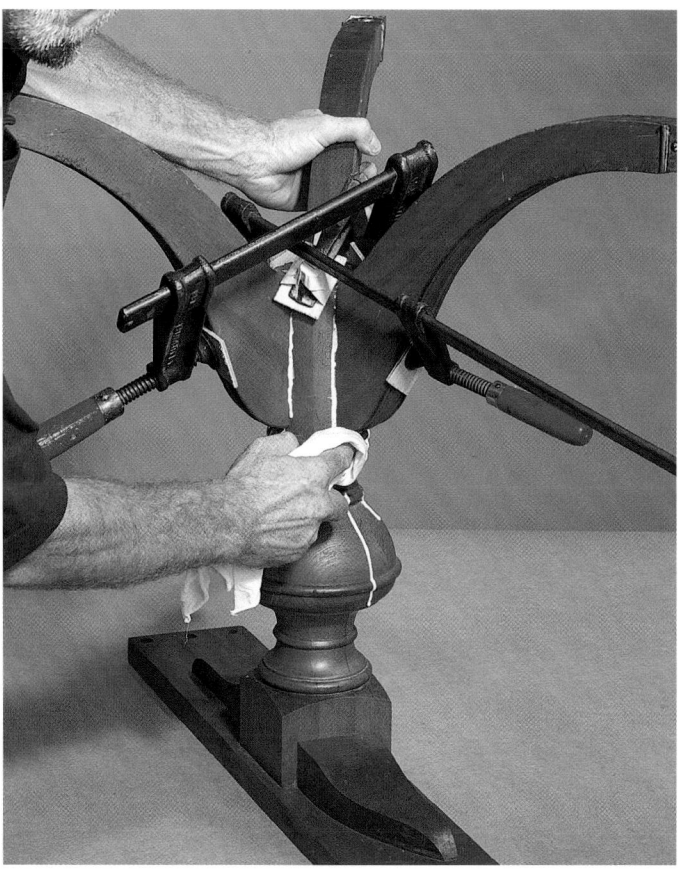

4 Apply clamps to tighten up the joints, and clean off glue squeeze-out using a damp rag.

sliding-dovetail joints

Sliding-dovetail joints are excellent for joining legs to a pedestal column. This joint virtually locks the leg into the column with a flared tenon, almost guaranteeing that the joint won't come apart. To determine whether the legs are mounted to the column with sliding dovetails, check the pedestal bottom and look for dovetail-shaped tenons extending into the column of the table.

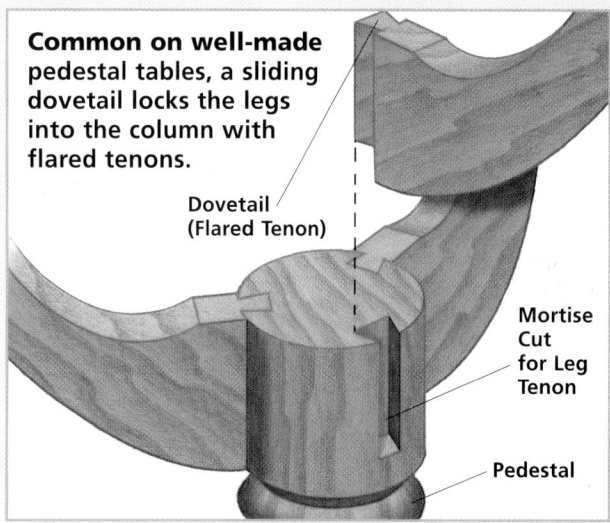

Common on well-made pedestal tables, a sliding dovetail locks the legs into the column with flared tenons.

Dovetail
(Flared Tenon)

Mortise Cut for Leg Tenon

Pedestal

Even though this kind of joint rarely if ever comes completely apart, it can loosen. Most often this is caused by the column itself splitting around the dovetail joints. If a split in the column is the problem, often you can work glue into the split and clamp it without having to remove the leg. If the dovetail itself is loose, you may need to remove the leg and repair the split in the column first.

To reglue sliding dovetails, hold the table base right side up and tilt it until the loose leg is off the floor or bench surface. Tap the top of the leg at the column with a rubber mallet to drive the dovetail down and out of the column. Clean old glue from joint surfaces using solvent or a chisel.

If there are splits in the column, repair them by working glue into them using a thin spatula, and clamping until the glue is dry. Reassemble the dry leg joint to ensure a proper fit. If the dovetails fit too loosely, glue a thin strip of veneer to one or both sides of the dovetail. After the glue dries, trim the shimmed dovetail to fit the mortise. Apply glue to all joint surfaces, and install the legs as you apply glue. You won't need clamps as long as you keep the pedestal upside down while it's drying.

Repairing a Loose Pedestal Tabletop

If the top of a pedestal table is wobbly or loose and the leg joints are tight, turn the table over and check where the mounting block joins the top of the pedestal or where the tabletop joins the mounting block. When you turn the table over, place it on a padded surface so you don't scratch the top.

The mounting block is usually attached to the pedestal with a mortise-and-tenon type joint. The top is usually attached to the mounting block with screws or bolts. Check these screws first to make sure they're tight. Sometimes a wobbly top can be stabilized simply by tightening the screws or bolts. If this doesn't help, the mounting block is probably loose where it joins the column, and you'll have to reglue it.

Difficulty Level:

TOOLS AND MATERIALS
- Screwdrivers
- Rubber mallet
- Clamps
- Rag
- Solvent or rasp, chisels, or utility knife
- Wood glue and glue brush or palette knife

1 Remove the top. With the table upside down on a padded surface, remove the screws that attach the tabletop to the mounting block, and remove the top.

2 Remove the mounting block. Check the top of the mounting block to see whether the tenon extends through the block. If so—and the joint is only slightly loose and hard to disassemble—drill a few small holes down the sides of the tenon and inject thinned glue (with 25 percent water) into the holes with a syringe or squeeze bottle, and work glue into any loose parts of the joint using a thin spatula. Clamp the joint, and let it dry. If the joint is loose enough to disassemble, tap on the bottom of the mounting block around the column to separate the two pieces. If the joint does not separate easily and the tenon is exposed on the top of the mounting block, turn the pedestal right side up and set the mounting block across an open vise or a pair of sawhorses. Use a wooden block and hammer to tap the tenon top, driving it out of the mounting block.

3 Clean the joint. Clean old glue from the joint using solvent or by gently scraping with a rasp, chisel, or knife. Test-fit the joint. If the tenon is wedged, you may want to remove the old wedge and make a new one from hardwood. Do not install the wedge until the final gluing sequence.

4 Glue and clamp the assembly. Disassemble the joint, and apply glue to the joint surfaces. Reassemble the mounting block to the column, tapping it into place. Apply clamps, and reinstall the tenon wedge if necessary. Clean excess glue from the joint, and check for tightness and alignment. Remount the top to the mounting block when the glue is dry.

lag-screw table-leg joints

When the pedestal column is hollow, special fasteners with a screw thread on one side and bolt thread on the other (sometimes called rail bolts or hanger bolts) are used to attach the legs. The fastener extends from the leg through the wall of the pedestal column and is held by a nut and washer.

If the legs become loose, tighten them by turning the pedestal upside down and reaching into the bottom of the hollow column to tighten the nut on the end of the bolt with an open-end wrench. As you tighten the nut, the leg should pull up tight. If the nut doesn't tighten, the screw side of the fastener is probably stripped out of the table leg. (See "Repairing a Tilting Tabletop," on page 74 for instructions on how to fix a stripped screw hole.)

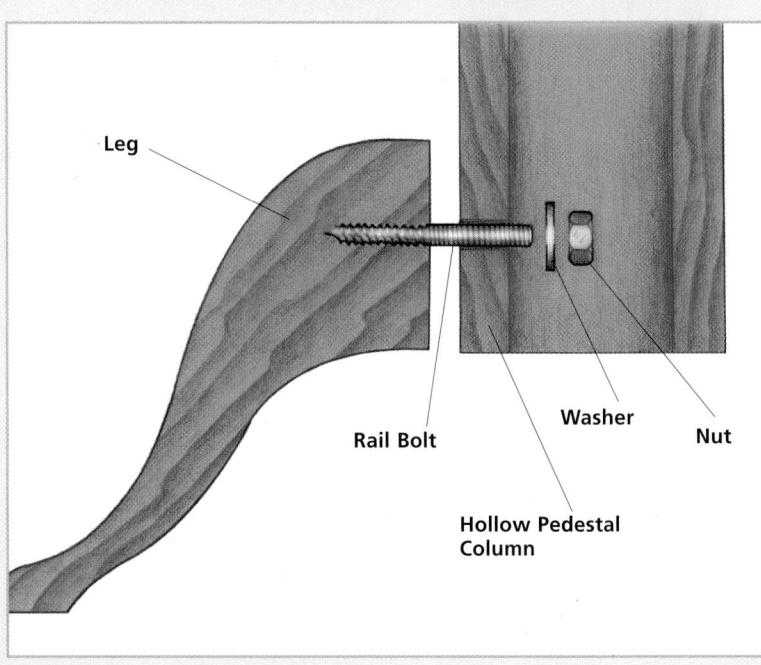

Leg
Rail Bolt
Washer
Nut
Hollow Pedestal Column

1 Back the screws out of the mounting block using a screwdriver, and remove the top.

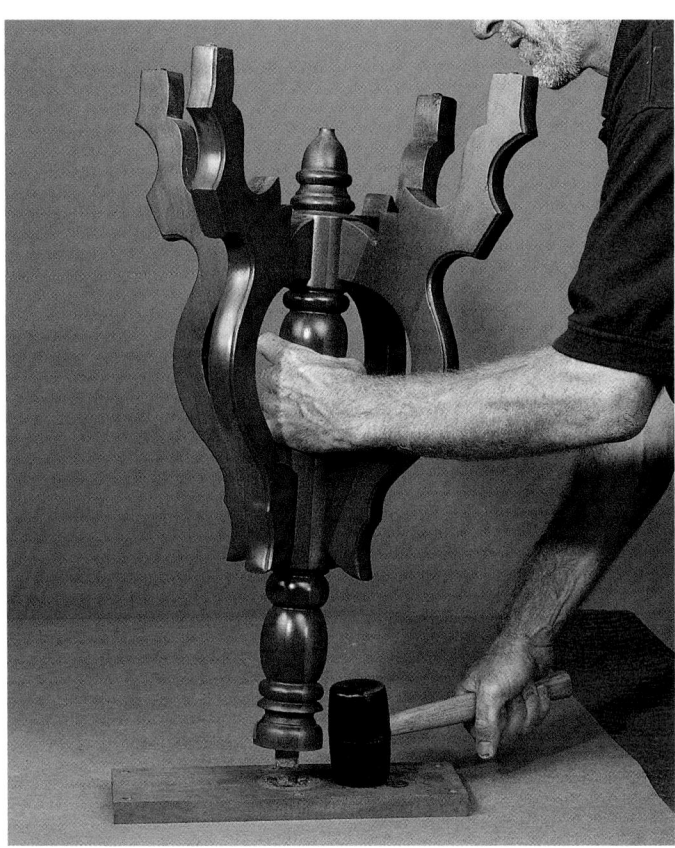

2 Tap on the mounting block using a rubber mallet to separate it from the pedestal column.

3 Clean the old glue off all joint surfaces. Use solvent or carefully scrape with a rasp, chisel, or knife, and test-fit the joint.

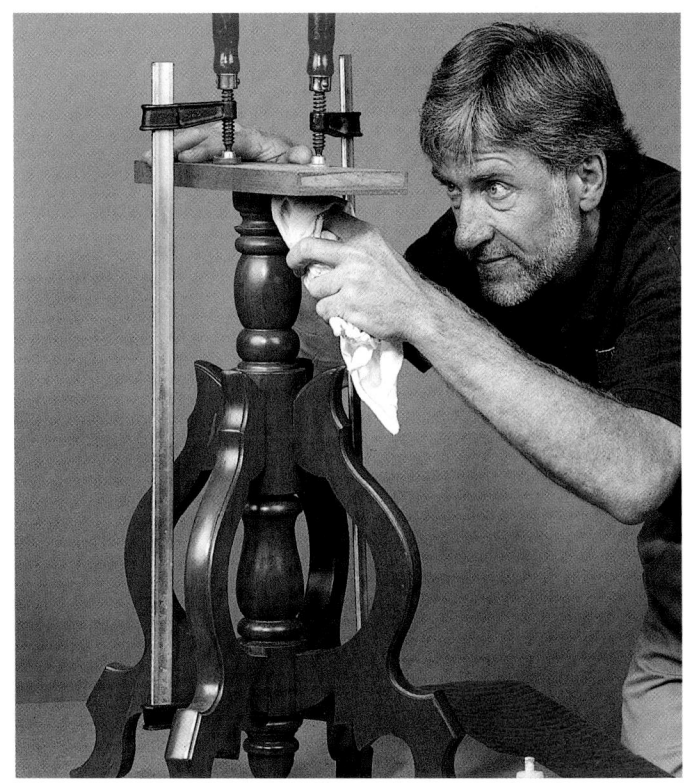

4 Apply glue to the joint parts, and clamp the joint. Clean off excess glue, and check the assembly for alignment.

Repairing a Tilting Tabletop

As mentioned previously, tilt-top tables have a pedestal base with a top that can swing up vertically. In most cases, two long pieces of wood called bearers are mounted with wood screws to the underside of the top. The mounting block is generally situated between these two bearers, with two dowel pivots on one end of the block extending into the bearers.

If the top of the table wobbles, it's probably because the screws holding the bearers are stripped. If one or more of the bearer mounting screws are stripped, install larger-gauge screws of the same length. If this doesn't work, remove the bearer and plug, and redrill the appropriate screw holes as follows.

Difficulty Level:

TOOLS AND MATERIALS
- Screwdrivers
- Drill and assorted bits
- Appropriate-size dowels
- Wood glue
- ¼-inch chisel
- Masking tape
- Fine-tooth backsaw
- Scratch awl

1 Remove the bearer. Turn the table upside down to remove the bearer from the tabletop. Be sure to use a padded surface so you don't mar the top. Remove any wooden buttons, or dig out the putty concealing the mounting screws using a ¼-inch chisel. Back the screws out using a screwdriver.

2 Drill new holes. Drill out the stripped screw holes in the tabletop. Use a ⅜-inch-diameter bit to install a same-diameter piece of dowel. Measure the depth of the tabletop, and mark a slightly shorter depth on the drill bit with tape so you don't drill the hole completely through the top.

Mark, cut, and install the dowels. After drilling the hole or holes, insert a section of dowel, and mark it for cutting. Cut the dowel to size with a fine-toothed saw, and install it with glue into the hole.

3 Drill new holes for bearer screws. When the glue is dry, set the bearer back in its original spot. Extend a scratch awl through the bearer's screw holes, and mark a center hole for drilling new pilot holes. Remove the bearer, and drill the holes for the bearer screws using the appropriate-size bit. Be sure to mark the depth on the drill bit to keep from drilling through the top.

4 Replace the bearer. Reinstall the bearer under the tabletop in its original position using the original screws. This time, however, they will tighten into the new holes you've made.

1 Dig out the putty or buttons hiding the screwheads, and back out the screws using a screwdriver.

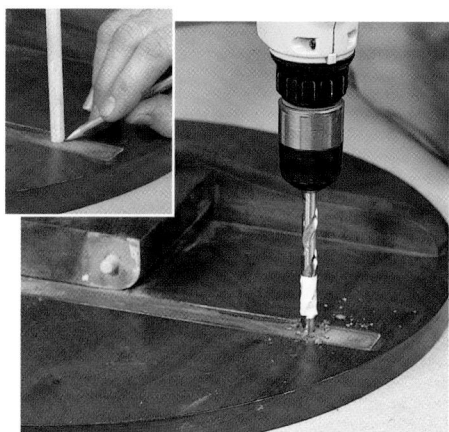

2 Drill out the stripped holes using a ⅜-in.-dia. bit. Mark the bit for depth using tape. Mark a ⅜-in.-dia. dowel (inset), cut it to length using a backsaw, and glue it in place.

3 Put the bearer back in place, and use a scratch awl to mark a center point for new holes.

4 After drilling the new screw holes, reinstall the bearer using the original screws if possible.

FRAME-STYLE TABLES

The legs of a frame table may be attached to the frame or apron through joinery or bolts. The majority of older frame-style tables have legs joined to apron rails with dowels or mortise-and-tenons.

Many modern tables, especially dining-room tables, use rail bolts (fasteners with a screw thread on one side and bolt thread on the other) to attach the legs to wooden corner blocks or metal corner braces on the table's underside. Though not a mark of high-quality construction, this kind of leg joint holds up fairly well and is easy to tighten unless the screw holes in the leg have been stripped.

To check for the kind of construction your table uses, turn the table over and look at each corner where the leg mounts. If you see a wooden corner block with no bolts or nuts visible, the legs are attached via joinery. If you see a corner block or metal brace with one or more bolts coming out of the leg and extending through the block or brace, the legs use rail bolts.

Regluing Table Legs

Because the joints in a frame table may take a large amount of stress over the years, especially if the table is moved often, as when adding and removing extension leaves, even mortise-and-tenon joints may come loose. You'll have to disassemble the joints and reglue the table.

 *Difficulty Level:*

TOOLS AND MATERIALS
- Screwdrivers
- Clamps
- ¼-inch chisel
- Chisels and mallet
- Rag
- Scratch awl
- Wood glue
- Masking tape and marker
- Solvent or rasp, chisel, or utility knife

1 Remove the tabletop. Turn the table upside down on a padded surface, and examine the underside to see how the top is attached to the base. Most tabletops are attached using screws through metal clips or wooden blocks or directly through the apron or frame of the base. Remove the screws, and place them in a sealable, labeled plastic bag. Look for additional glue blocks that may be used to attach the top. If you find any blocks, break them loose using a wood chisel and mallet. These can also be saved and reinstalled when reattaching the top.

Continued on next page.

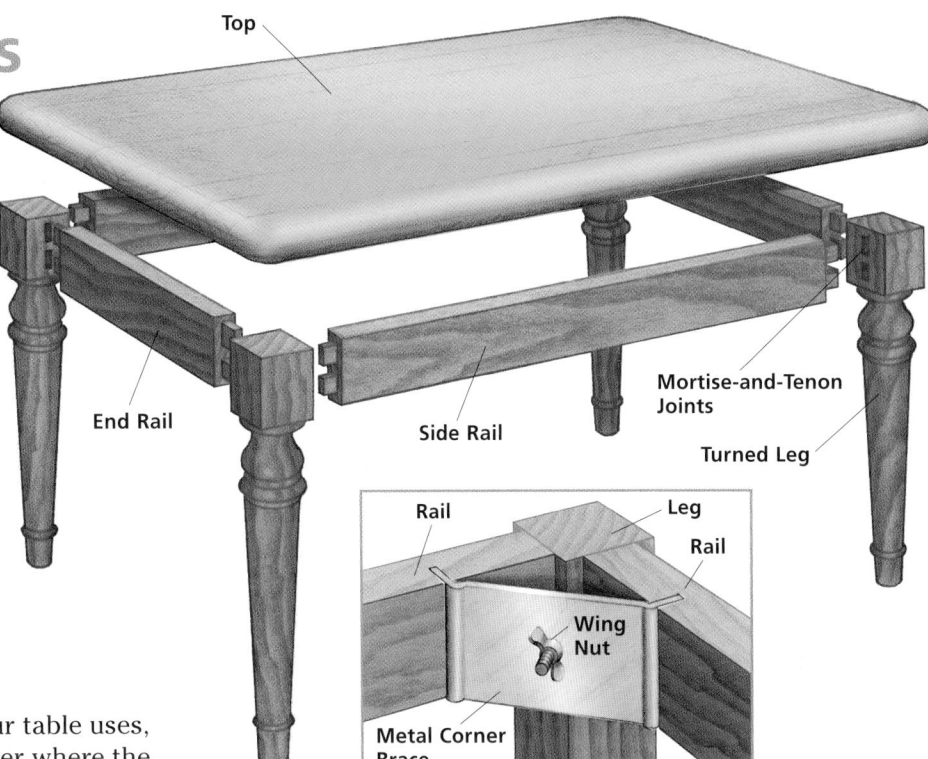

Frame-Style Tables. The connection between the legs and the rails of frame tables may be through joinery (main drawing) or through corner braces and bolts (inset).

1 Turn the table upside down, and remove the screws holding the tabletop to the rails.

Continued from previous page.

2 Label the joints. With the top removed, label all the leg joints using masking tape and a marking pen. Give each leg a number, and code the leg and adjoining joint part with the same number.

3 Separate the joints. Disassemble the labeled joints by striking the inside of each leg with a mallet and working the leg free by moving it back and forth gently but persuasively.

4 Clean the joint parts. Clean the mating parts of the joints using solvent or by gently scraping with a chisel, rasp, or knife edge. Make sure you remove all old glue, but be careful not to take off any wood in the scraping process, if you choose to go that route.

5 Reassemble the table. Apply glue to all the joints, and put the table frame back together again, using clamps. Make sure the tabletop fits properly and that the screw holes in the frame align with the holes in the top. It's a good idea to align these holes using a scratch awl and to reinsert the screws to hold the frame in the proper position before tightening down on the clamps, cleaning the glue and allowing the joints to dry.

2 Using masking tape and a marker, label all the joints you'll take apart so you don't get them mixed up.

3 Knock the joints loose using a mallet, and work the legs free from the rails.

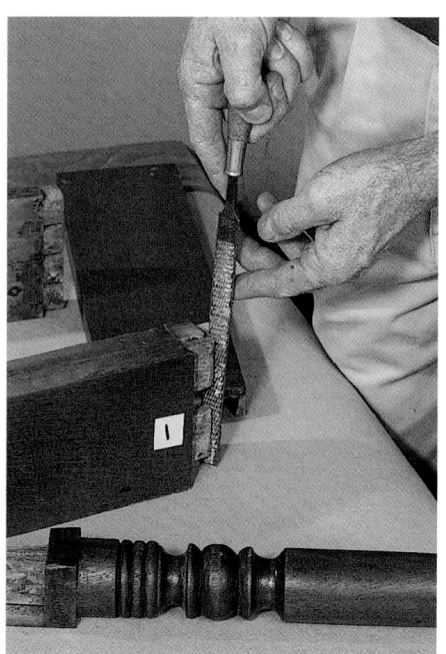

4 Use solvent or a rasp, chisel, or knife to remove all old glue from the joints.

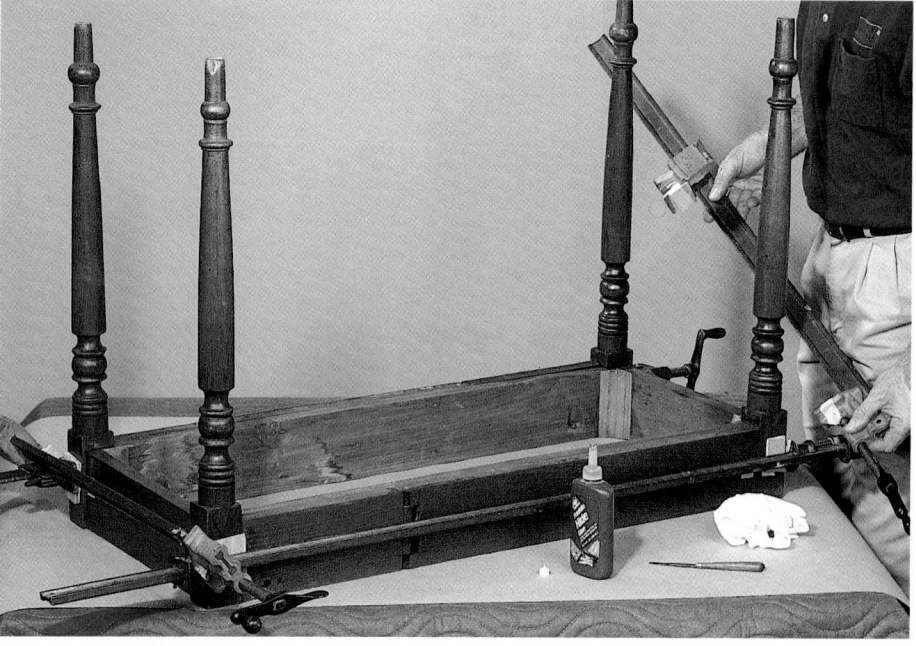

5 Glue and clamp the joints tight. Make sure that the legs and the table frame are square before allowing the glue to dry.

Repairing Bolted Legs

If your table has bolted legs and any of them are loose, try tightening the nut. If the nut continues to turn without pulling up the leg, the screw is stripped out in the leg. You'll need to plug the screw hole.

Difficulty Level:

TOOLS AND MATERIALS
- Adjustable or open-end wrench
- Appropriate-size dowel (if necessary)
- Pliers   • Drill and assorted bits
- Scratch awl   • Masking tape

1 Remove the leg. Turn the table upside down on a padded surface. Back the nut off the bolt using an adjustable or open-end wrench, and take the leg off the table.

2 Remove the bolt. Using a pair of pliers to grip it, try to tighten the screw part of the rail bolt farther into the leg. If the screw tightens into the leg, reinstall the leg on the table, inserting the bolt through the corner brace. If the screw doesn't tighten, remove the rail

bolt from the leg by unscrewing it or by pulling it out with the pliers. Drill and plug the screw hole in the leg with a slightly larger wood dowel. (See "Repairing a Tilting Tabletop," page 74, for how to plug a hole.)

Mark the new screw hole. Once you've plugged the leg, place it back into its original position on the table. Using a scratch awl extended through the hole in the corner block, mark the leg with a center hole where you'll install the rail bolt.

3 Install the bolt. Remove the leg, and drill a hole using the center mark you just made to begin drilling. When drilling, make sure you drill the hole at the same angle as that of the original hole. Usually you can do this simply by eyeballing it. Use the correct-size bit, which should be the same diameter as the threaded portion of the screw minus the threads. Drill to the correct depth by marking the drill bit with masking tape. Once you've drilled the hole, insert the rail bolt and tighten it down with pliers.

4 Reinstall the leg. Place the leg back in its original position on the table, insert the bolt through the corner brace, and tighten down on the nut to finish the job.

1 Turn the table upside down, and free the leg by removing the nut using an adjustable or open-end wrench.

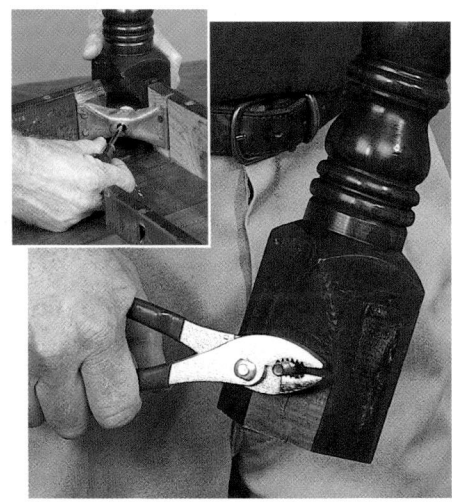

2 Remove a badly loosened bolt using pliers, and plug the stripped hole with a dowel. With the leg in proper position (inset), use a scratch awl to center-point a new bolt hole.

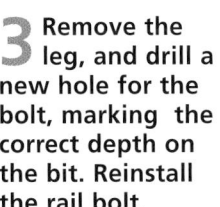

3 Remove the leg, and drill a new hole for the bolt, marking the correct depth on the bit. Reinstall the rail bolt.

4 Reattach the leg, with the bolt through the corner brace, and tighten down on the nut.

LOOSE JOINTS IN DRAWERS

Drawer corners usually use dovetail, dado, or rabbet joints to hold the main framework together. The drawer bottom then slides into the framework from the back, fitting into grooves in the sides and front. After sliding the bottom in, you then nail or screw it to the drawer back's bottom edge to hold it in place. Although corner joints of drawers are glued, drawer bottoms are not.

Loose Joints in Drawers. Most drawers have four glued dovetail, dado, and/or rabbet joints. The bottom panel sits in grooves and is not glued in place.

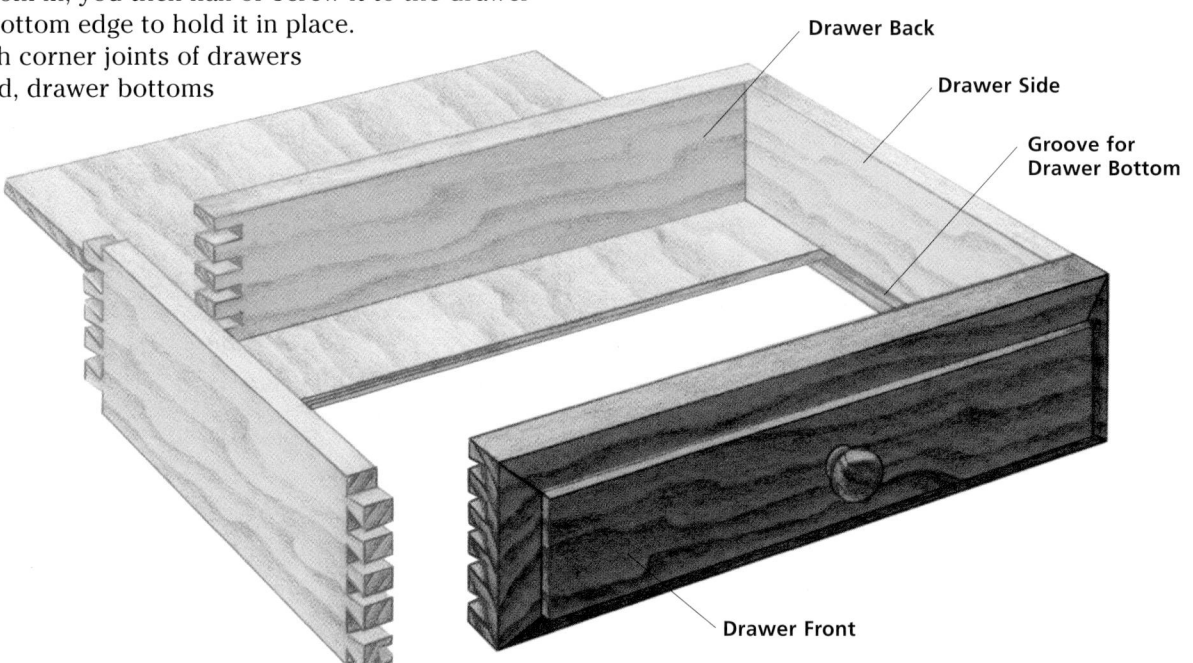

Drawer Back

Drawer Side

Groove for Drawer Bottom

Drawer Front

loose joints in casegood bases and feet

Casegood carcases often have turned or bracket feet, or enclosed frame- or box-type bases.

Turned Feet. Turned feet are usually attached to the chest with a dowel pin. If this type of foot is loose, clean the joint, reglue it, and clamp it.

Bracket Feet. Bracket feet are created from two wood brackets mitered together to form a right angle. If they are loose, check for screws attaching them to the case. If the feet are only screw-mounted, you may be able to tighten the screws. Replace damaged glue blocks.

Bases. Frame- or box-type bases may consist of boards set on edge on which the carcase sits. To free the frame from the carcase, first remove any screws; then knock glue blocks loose. If the frame has loose joints, knock them apart and then clean and reglue them. Replace any missing glue blocks, and remount the base to the cabinet. Clamp until dry, and check for squareness. Also make sure the frame will line up with the casegood upon reinstallation.

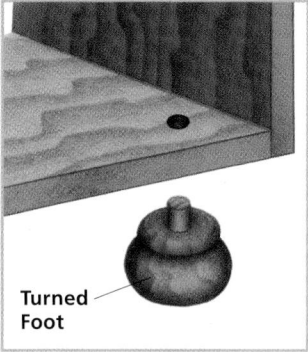

Turned Foot

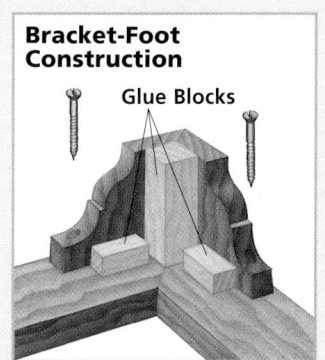

Bracket-Foot Construction

Glue Blocks

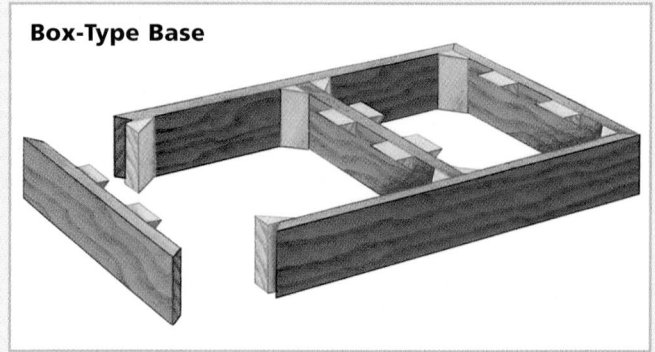

Box-Type Base

Regluing a Drawer

Difficulty Level:

TOOLS AND MATERIALS
- Clamps
- Wood glue
- Masking tape and marker
- Square or measuring tape
- Glue solvent or rasp, chisel, or utility knife
- Rag
- Screwdrivers and hammer

1 Remove the bottom. Turn the drawer upside down on your workbench, and remove the nails or screws holding the drawer bottom to the drawer back. If the drawer has a center guide mounted on the bottom to keep the drawer running straight in the chest, you may need to remove it first. Pull the bottom panel toward the back, removing it from the drawer frame.

2 Knock out the sides. Label the side joint parts, and knock the sides outward using a hammer and softwood block held against the inside corners. On most drawers, the sides should be knocked outward from the drawer front and back to keep from breaking the wood in the joint. Examine drawer joints carefully before knocking them loose.

3 Remove old glue from the joints. Clean the drawer joints of old glue using solvent or a chisel, wood rasp, or knife edge. Assemble the drawer joints without glue to be sure they fit properly; make any necessary adjustments; and then take them all apart again.

4 Glue and reassemble the drawer. Apply glue to all joint surfaces, assembling the joints as you go. Install clamps to pull the joints up snugly, but don't overtighten them. You might want to use large wood blocks to ensure that the full width of the drawer sides will pull up tight without using additional clamps. Clean off excess glue with a damp rag, and check the drawer for squareness. Reinsert the drawer bottom, and drive nails or screws into the bottom edge of the drawer to hold the panel in place.

1 Remove the nails or screws holding the drawer bottom, and then slide it out the back.

2 Knock the drawer sides outward from the drawer front and back after labeling the joints.

3 Clean all old glue from the joints, and test-fit the drawer parts.

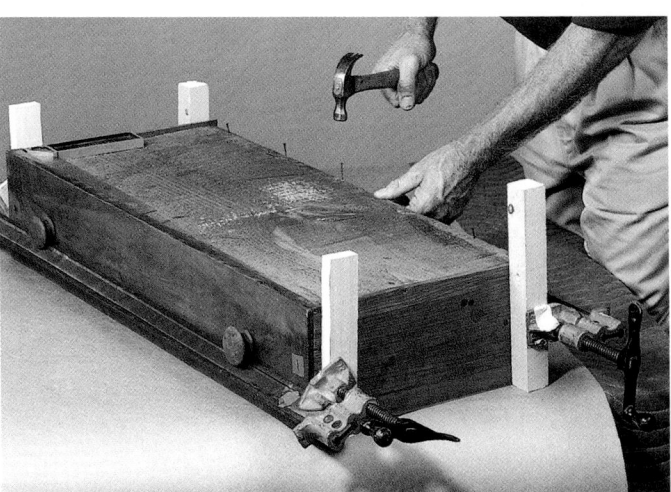

4 Glue and clamp the drawer, and reinstall the drawer bottom, nailing it back in place.

LOOSE MIRROR AND PICTURE-FRAME JOINTS

Mitered corner joints used in mirror and picture frames usually use some kind of reinforcement. Some frames have a back attached to them; others may be reinforced with nails, dowel pins, or splines. If the miter joints are loose, examine them to see what type of reinforcement was used—if any—before you take them apart and reglue them. Often, when you reglue a miter joint, you'll want to reinforce it with pins or splines.

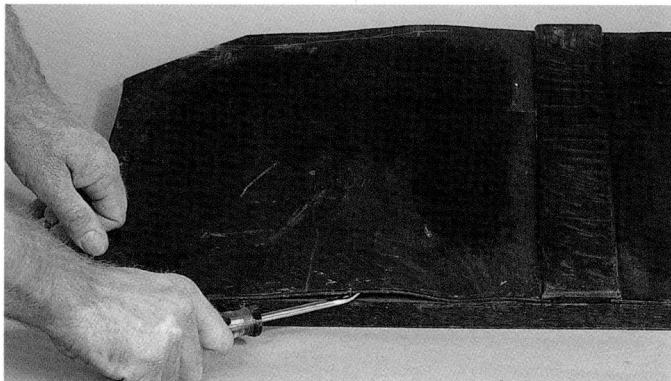

1 Remove the back from the frame, and then remove any picture, mirror, or glass and put it aside.

2 Using a mallet, gently knock the joints apart, and remove any splines or other reinforcement.

Regluing a Mitered Mirror Frame

Difficulty Level:

TOOLS AND MATERIALS
- Hammer
- Plywood
- Measuring tape
- Wood glue and glue brush or palette knife
- Diagonal pliers, screwdriver and nail puller
- Chisels and glue solvent, wood rasp, or utility knife
- Rubber mallet
- Clamps

1 **Remove the backing.** Most pictures and mirrors have a backing that's attached to the frame with small nails. Remove the back, along with any picture, glass, or mirror by prying and removing the nails with a small nail puller, diagonal pliers, or a screwdriver and hammer.

2 **Disassemble the joints.** Tap the joints apart with a mallet, removing any nails or other reinforcement.

3 **Clean off old glue.** Clean the joints with glue solvent or by scraping off the old glue with a wood rasp, chisel, or knife edge. Be careful not to chip the wood.

3 Remove all old glue from the joints using solvent or by gently scraping them clean with a rasp, chisel, or knife.

PRO TIP: reinforcing a miter joint

After you glue up a miter joint, you might want to reinforce it with finishing nails. To install the nails, you'll need to drill pilot holes so that you don't split the wood. The pilot hole must be large enough so that the nail can pierce the wood without splitting it but is still tight in the hole. Fill the holes with putty or colored wax sticks to conceal them. Another way to reinforce the miter is by installing a spline in the joint.

Clamp the frame in a vise, and cut a kerf across the miter joint using a doevetail saw or backsaw.

Cut a spline to match the size of the kerf; glue the spline and the slot; push the spline into place.

Once the glue is dry, cut the spline flush with the frame; trim it; and touch it up to match using stain.

4 Clamp the frame. After cleaning the joints, assemble the frame parts and clamp them without glue. Picture framing or miter clamps work well for frames.

If you don't have one of those clamps, use a strap clamp. Be sure the frame is laid flat, and clamp it to a flat bench or board so it doesn't get warped or twisted when you pull the joints tight. (See photo.) Remove the clamps, and apply glue to the joint surfaces. Assemble the frame pieces again, and reinstall the clamps, making sure the joints are aligned and tight. Also, make sure the frame is square by measuring diagonally from corner to corner. When the two diagonal measurements are the same, the frame is square. Clean off excess glue.

4 After test-fitting, clamp the frame, laying it flat on plywood, and make sure it's square.

6
Structural Repairs II: Broken Joints

When you discover broken joints while repairing furniture, a simple regluing may appear to answer the problem. That quick fix is usually not enough, however. Because joints are designed to withstand stress, you must repair them back to their original strength if at all possible. In most cases, you'll have to reinforce the joint. Sometimes you'll find you need to rebuild the joint completely, depending upon the kind of joint it is.

BROKEN CHAIR JOINTS

Joints frequently break in chair foot rails and stretchers (rungs) or in chair-back spindles and posts. These joints get a lot of stress, and when one breaks, it puts undue strain on the others, causing them to also crack or break. If a foot rail or spindle breaks at or near the joint, you should be able to repair rather than replace it.

Repairing a Broken Chair-Rung Joint

Difficulty Level:

TOOLS AND MATERIALS
- Drill and assorted bits
- Backsaw
- Chisels or wood rasp
- Dowels
- Clamps
- Rag
- Wood glue and glue brush or palette knife

1 **Examine the break.** Remove the rung or foot rail from the chair, and examine the broken piece left in the hole. If the piece is solid and glued tight, as in the first photo, top right, don't plug the hole. If the piece is loose, drill it out using a slightly smaller-size bit, and then clean the hole using a narrow wood chisel. Next, plug the hole using the correct size wood dowel, gluing it in and cutting it flush with the surface.

2 **Drill a pilot hole.** Using a small-diameter bit ($\frac{1}{16}$ to $\frac{1}{8}$ inch), drill a pilot hole into the center of the plugged hole, making sure to follow the same angle as that of the original chair rung.

3 **Drill the chair rung.** Clamp the chair rung in a vise with the broken end up, and drill a pilot hole in the center of its end using a $\frac{1}{8}$- to $\frac{1}{4}$-inch bit. To ensure a straight hole, use another person to sight across the drill bit and chair rung as you drill. Following

4 Glue up a new runner. Measure the cut, and fit a new piece of wood for the runner. If you make the patch slightly larger, you can plane or sand it after attaching it. Plane the joint edge of the patch, making it dead straight for a good fit with the drawer-side edge. Glue and clamp the new runner in position. Remove any excess glue with a damp rag, and then let the glue dry for two hours.

5 Plane the patch. If you removed the drawer side (Step 2), reinstall it. Smooth the runner with a block plane, and trim it at the back if necessary. Fit the drawer to the casegood carcase by planing and sanding the new runner until it runs smoothly. Stain, finish, and touch up the patch where necessary. As a last step, apply wax to the runner.

1 To repair a damaged drawer runner, first scribe a straight line above the damaged area.

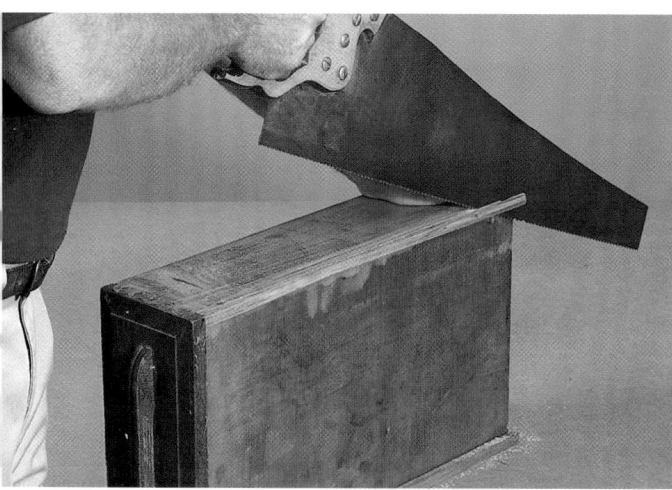

2 Using a handsaw, cut away the damaged area. Remove the drawer side if necessary.

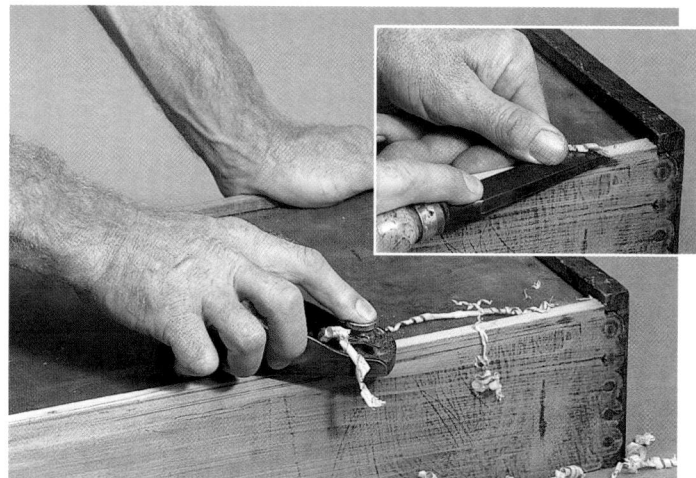

3 Plane the bottom of the runner cut to smooth it. Use a chisel to smooth hard-to-get-at areas (inset).

4 Cut a new strip of wood for the runner. Glue and clamp the new runner in position on the drawer.

5 Plane the runner edge until the drawer fits and works smoothly in the cabinet.

Switching Interior Drawer Runners

If the runners inside the cabinet are worn or damaged, you can sometimes remove them, switch them to the other side of the cabinet, and turn them upside down. This gives the drawer a new surface to run on while still using the original runners.

If this won't work because of the runners' design—or if a runner is missing—you may need to make new ones to match. Remove the old runner to get the exact measurements you need for the new one. Try to duplicate the original type of wood if you're working with old collectible or antique cabinets, as this will help to preserve their character. On newer cabinets this is not as important, and any hardwood will work fine. If runners are mounted using screws or nails, drill pilot holes for these fasteners to keep them from splitting the wood.

Freeing Stuck Drawers

If you can't open or close a drawer or if it gets stuck in one position, the wood in the drawer sides may have swollen, making the drawer too large for its opening. To be sure, check the following items:

■ If the drawer is lockable, check to make sure it's not locked; if it is and the key is lost, try other drawer keys to see whether they'll work. If that doesn't work, remove the drawer's back panel or reach through an upper drawer opening and try to remove the lock. As a last resort, try to pry the drawer rail up to clear the lock bolt. If you're afraid this will damage the piece, call a locksmith.

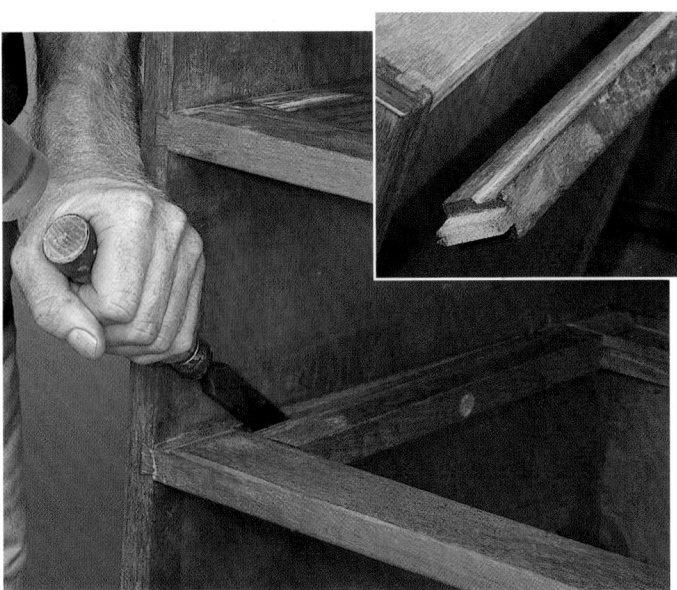

Sometimes you can remove worn runners (inset) inside a casegood and switch them to the other side of the carcase by turning them upside down. Use a mallet and chisel for removal.

■ Drawers are sometimes made to fit only their particular opening; if they get exchanged with another drawer, they won't work well. Move the drawers around to different openings to see whether this solves the problem.

■ Remove the drawer above the stuck one, and investigate to make sure nothing inside is preventing the drawer from opening. You can remove the back of the piece of furniture to look inside if necessary. You may find that a dust panel above the drawer has warped or fallen down in front of the back of the drawer or below it, preventing it from opening.

■ If you've checked all these things and still not found your problem, the drawer is most likely swollen. Remove the drawer; if it's badly stuck and you can't free it, try removing the cabinet back and tapping along the back edge of the drawer with a hammer to free it. After removing the drawer, try to determine where the drawer is sticking by looking for shiny areas on the wood. Use a belt sander or a sharp block plane to sand or plane these areas down enough for the drawer to move freely. This procedure is often a matter of trial and error; just continue to plane or sand until the drawer works well. Lastly, wax the runners to keep them working smoothly.

Repairing Warped Drawer Bottoms

Often drawer bottoms made from solid wood can warp or split. To correct a warp, you can usually remove the bottom, flip it over, and reinstall it. Repair splits and cracks by gluing and clamping them. If a drawer bottom is warped or damaged beyond repair, you'll have to replace it. The easiest way to do this job is by using a piece of ¼-inch-thick plywood. Luaun plywood, available at home centers or lumberyards, works well for this. Remove the old bottom, cut the new panel to size, slide the new panel in place, and attach it.

Missing Drawer Stops

When you close a drawer, in most cases it should stop flush with the front edge of the furniture. If the drawer seems to go too far into the opening when you close it, you're probably missing the drawer stops.

Most wooden casegoods use small blocks of wood mounted at the back or front to stop the drawer in the proper position. The stops can break loose and get lost or damaged. Remove the drawer, and look inside the cabinet to see where the old stop blocks were mounted. You'll find that most stops are mounted on the rearmost rail at the back of the carcase. Sometimes you'll find stops installed on the front rail, just behind the face of the drawer front. Clean old glue from these areas to prepare for the new blocks.

Replacing Back Drawer Stops

Difficulty Level:

TOOLS AND MATERIALS
- Block plane
- Measuring tape
- Saw to cut blocks
- Wood glue and glue brush or palette knife
- Scrap plywood or one-by blocks and shims as necessary

1 Measure for the stops. Push the drawer all the way into the cabinet until it hits the back. While the drawer is pushed all the way back, measure from the front edge of the cabinet to the front edge of the drawer. Use this measurement to determine the size blocks you'll need to act as drawer stops.

2 Install the stops. Cut the appropriate-size blocks from scrap ¾-inch plywood or one-by lumber. Remove the drawer, and place the blocks at the back of the cabinet. Gently reinstall the drawer until it makes contact with the new drawer stops. Check to see whether the drawer front is flush with the carcase front. For fine-tuning, trim the block with a block plane to bring the drawer farther into the carcase, or glue veneer shims to the front of the block to move the drawer out. Attach the block.

1 To determine the width of the drawer stops, push the drawer in and measure from the front.

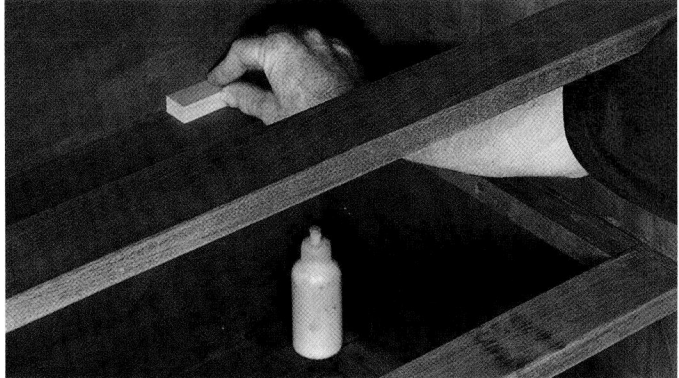

2 Cut the block; test-fit it; apply glue to the block; and install it in the back of the carcase.

Replacing Front Drawer Stops

Difficulty Level:

TOOLS AND MATERIALS
- Measuring tape
- Combination square
- Scratch awl
- Saw to cut blocks
- Brads
- Hammer
- Nail set
- Wood glue and palette knife
- Scrap ¼-inch plywood or solid wood

1 Measure the drawer front. Measure the thickness of the drawer front at the bottom edge. You'll use this measurement to determine how far back from the cabinet front to mount drawer stops on the drawer rail.

2 Scribe a reference line. Set a combination square to the measurement you obtained in Step 1, and scribe a reference line on the drawer rail where you want to install a stop as shown in the photo.

Install the stops by cutting them from ¼-inch solid wood or plywood, and align them on the reference line you marked on the drawer rail. Mount the blocks using glue and small brads. Countersink the brads using a nail set. Install the drawer to double-check the drawer stop position.

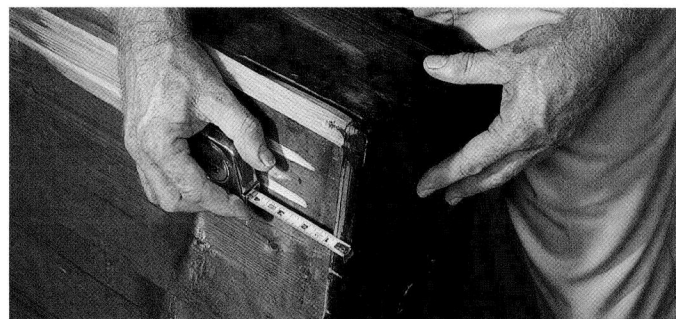

1 When installing front drawer stops, measure the thickness of the drawer front.

2 Scribe a line on the drawer rail (left). Glue and nail stops, aligning them with the reference line (right).

VENEER REPAIR

Whether antique or contemporary, much furniture available today uses veneer, mostly for large flat areas. Veneer can be used to produce beautifully figured furniture surfaces that hold up well, provided the furniture is well cared for and the environmental conditions are favorable. But veneer can easily develop problems such as loose edges, bubbles, and chips. Because even minor veneer problems can develop into major problems if they're neglected, it's important to take care of them. Sometimes veneer difficulties aren't evident unless you look closely.

Repairing a Loose Veneer Edge

The most common veneer problem—and the easiest by far to repair—is the loose or popped up edge. Loose veneer edges can often be repaired without having to cut the veneered surface. In this case you'd work from the open edge.

Difficulty Level:

TOOLS AND MATERIALS
- Utility or razor knife
- Wood glue and palette knife
- Wax paper or plastic wrap
- Rag
- Clamps
- Clamping blocks

1 Clean out old glue. Use a thin blade, such as that in a utility or razor knife, to clean the area under the loose veneer. Thoroughly scrape out all old glue with the knife blade.

2 Reglue the edge. Spread wood glue under the loose veneer, using a palette knife to work the glue well into the loose areas. Using a veneer roller, roll the glued area lightly at first, and then increase pressure, forcing excess glue out to the edge.

3 Clamp the veneer. Clean up the excess glue with a damp rag. Lay wax paper or plastic wrap and a flat block that spans the repair area on the finish surface. Either ½- or ¾-inch plywood makes a good block. Place a similar block beneath the repair area, and apply three or more clamps, one at each end and one or more across the middle. Leave the clamps in place until the repair is dry, at least 2 hours.

1 Before repairing loose veneer, clean out as much old glue as possible using a thin blade.

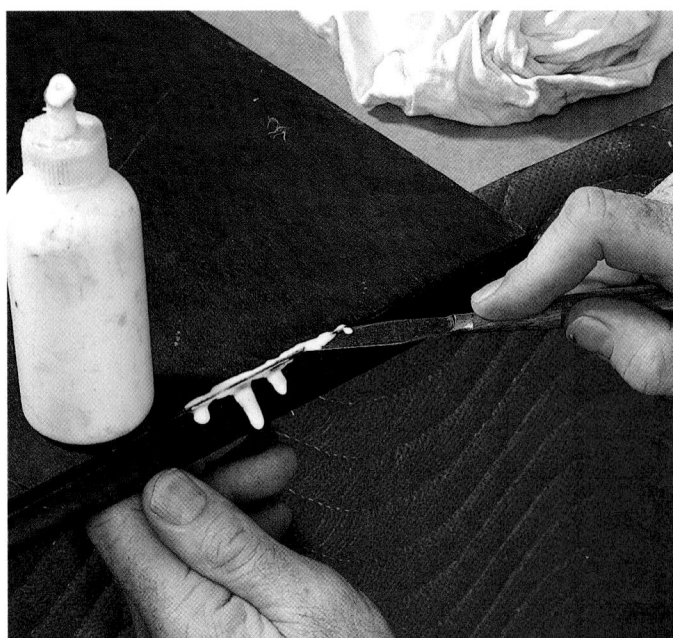

2 Work wood glue under the loose veneer using a palette knife or other thin-blade tool.

3 Clean up excess glue, and then clamp the veneer tight using a firm flat block over wax paper.

Regluing a Veneer Bubble

Difficulty Level:

TOOLS AND MATERIALS
- Damp cloth
- Wood glue and palette knife
- Veneer roller
- Rag
- Wax paper/plastic wrap
- Clamps
- Clamping blocks

1 Soften the veneer. Apply a damp cloth to the bubbled area to soften the veneer. Keep the cloth in place for about 30 seconds, or until you can see that the veneer is flexible.

2 Apply glue to the bubble. Cut a slit in the bubble, following the grain's direction, if it's not already split. Work wood glue into all parts of the bubble through the slit or split with a palette knife. Make sure the glue reaches all loose areas.

3 Roll the area. Use a veneer roller to roll the repair area flat, forcing extra glue out the bubble. Apply light pressure at first, and then increase the pressure, rolling toward the slit or split to allow excess glue to escape. Clean the glue seepage with a damp rag.

4 Clamp the bubble. Lay a sheet of wax paper or plastic wrap over the blister, and clamp the area with flat blocks under the jaws of the clamp. Make the blocks just slightly bigger than the repair area. If you can't reach the area with a clamp, use a heavy weight, such as large books, a concrete block, a bucket of water, or anything that can provide the necessary pressure to press the veneer flat. Allow the glue to dry for about 4 hours.

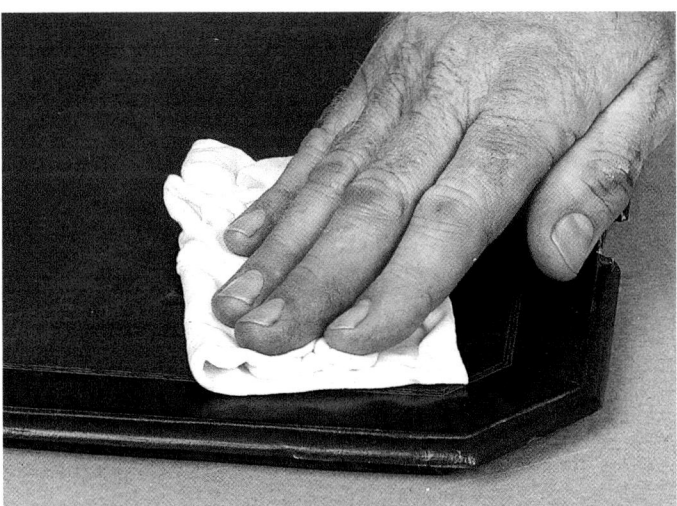

1 To reglue a veneer bubble, apply a damp rag to the bubble to make the veneer more pliable.

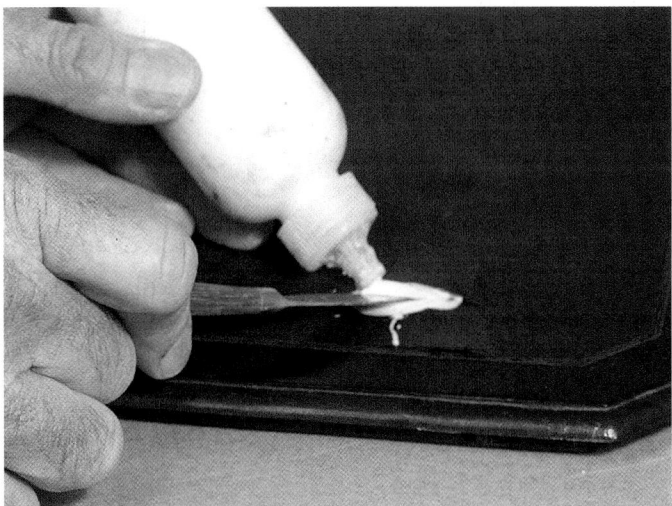

2 If the veneer is not split, cut it with the grain. Then work wood glue under the bubble.

3 Use a veneer roller to roll the bubble flat and force any excess glue out from under the veneer.

4 Clamp the bubble flat using a sturdy flat block over wax paper until the glue dries.

Fixing a Veneer Bubble Using Heat

Sometimes, especially on older pieces on which hide glue was probably used, you can fix a bubble by pressing it back into place and reactivating the old glue with heat. If the bubble doesn't adhere, you'll have to reglue it. (See "Regluing a Veneer Bubble," page 99.)

Difficulty Level:

TOOLS AND MATERIALS
- Cotton cloth
- Household iron

1 **Cover the bubble.** Place a clean cotton cloth over the bubble. You can dampen the cloth, but be sure to wring it mostly dry so you won't damage the furniture's finish if you leave it in place for too long.

2 **Lay an iron on the cloth.** Gradually press the veneer back into place using an electric household iron set on medium heat. Leave the iron in place for no more than 2 or 3 seconds at a time to avoid damaging the finish.

After the bubble is flat, remove the cloth and briefly apply the iron to the wood surface to press the bubbled area. Don't leave the iron down for more than 1 or 2 seconds.

1 To reactivate the glue under a veneer bubble, begin by laying a damp cloth over the bubble.

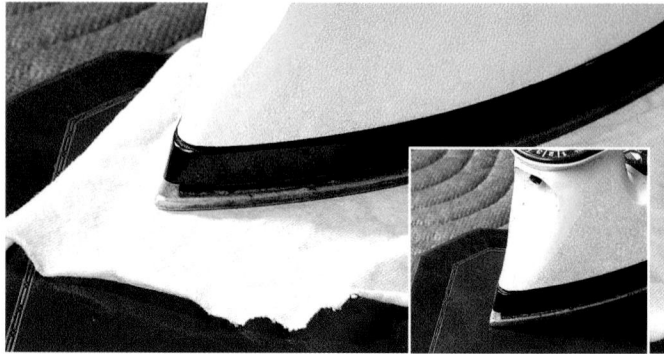

2 Apply a hot iron to the cloth for a few seconds to press the veneer flat. Then apply the iron directly to the spot for a few more seconds (inset).

Repairing Veneer Edges

When veneer becomes loose and isn't repaired, often it breaks or chips, and pieces get lost. This happens frequently on edges that get hit or scraped. If veneer is missing on an edge, you can patch it.

Difficulty Level:

TOOLS AND MATERIALS
- Piece of veneer to match the existing furniture
- Utility knife
- Masking tape
- Straightedge
- Chisel
- Wood glue and palette knife
- Rag
- Wax paper
- Clamping blocks
- Clamps
- Sandpaper/block
- Stain and finish

1 **Tape veneer over the damaged area.** Decide on the type of veneer and the size of the patch you'll need to cover the damaged area. (See "Wood Identification," page 13, for tips on matching wood.) Cut a piece of veneer to match as closely as possible, making it a little bigger than the damaged area. Line up the grain in the patch with the wood to be patched, and tape the cut piece of veneer firmly over the damaged area.

2 **Cut the patch.** Using a utility knife and a straightedge, make a V-shaped cut in the patch, fanning out to the outer edge of the patch. Cut through the patch and into the old veneer underneath.

3 **Cut out the damaged area.** Remove the patch, and cut the old veneer following the V-shaped knife cut that should be visible. Use a sharp wood chisel to clean out the damaged area. Scrape the surface with the edge of a chisel or razor blade, cleaning old glue from the surface.

4 **Glue and clamp the patch.** Apply wood glue to the cut-out area, and tape the veneer patch in place, making sure it fits tight. Cover the patch with wax paper or plastic wrap, and clamp it in place using flat blocks under the clamp's jaws. Make the blocks slightly larger than the patched area. Let the glue dry for about 2 hours.

5 **Sand the patch.** When the glue is thoroughly dry, block-sand the patch flush with the surrounding wood. Use 120-grit sandpaper.

6 **Trim the patch.** After you've sanded the patch well, trim the edge to match that of the rest of the top, using a utility knife. Touch up the sanded and trimmed patch using stain and finish to match the surrounding wood.

1 Cut a similar piece of veneer, and tape it over the damaged area, lining up the grain.

2 Make a V-shape cut over the damaged area. Make several passes to scribe the surface below.

3 Remove the new veneer, and then cut out and remove the V-shaped area in the old veneer surface.

4 Glue the new patch in place, and then clamp it using a strong flat block over wax paper.

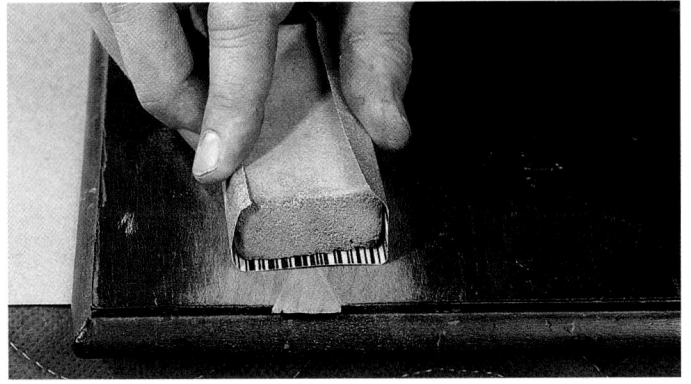

5 When the glue is dry, remove the clamp, and sand the patched area flush with the surrounding surface.

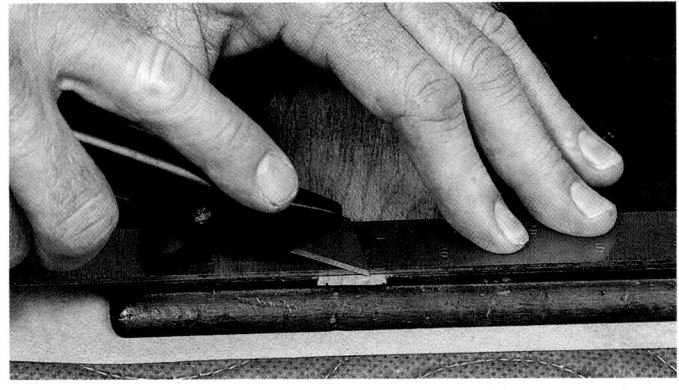

6 Trim the patched area using a utility knife, and then touch it up to match the surrounding wood.

PRO TIP: center-patching veneer

Sometimes veneer gets damaged in the center part of a veneered surface. You'll make the repair in the same way as for a veneer edge, with the following alterations:

• **Don't make a V-shape cut** in the veneer patch. Instead, cut the patch shape to align with the wood grain as much as possible, and be careful never to cut straight across the grain. A diamond-shaped patch is often recommended in order to make the patch as invisible as possible.

• **If you find that a clamp** won't reach the patch, cover the patch with wax paper and a wood block, and then put a heavy object on top of the block and allow the glue to dry.

Removing Veneer

If a veneered surface has extensive damage or most of the surface is loose or bubbled, you'll have to remove the old veneer and prepare the substrate for new veneer.

Difficulty Level:

TOOLS AND MATERIALS
- Wet towel
- Household iron
- Scraper, knife blade
- Rag
- 120-grit sandpaper
- Power sander or sanding block

1 Soak the veneer with a wet towel. Strip all finish from the veneer surface. (See "Using a Chemical Remover," page 132.) Place a wet towel over the surface, and allow it to soak, checking it every few hours to see whether the old veneer has loosened. Allow the veneer to soak overnight if necessary.

2 Soften the glue with heat. Once the veneer is well soaked, use a hot household iron on the same damp towel to soften the glue and further loosen the veneer. At the same time, work a wide spatula or putty knife under the veneer, lifting it. You can also use a heat gun to apply heat under the veneer surface as you peel the veneer up.

3 Clean off the old glue. After removing the old veneer, prepare the subsurface by cleaning off the old glue. Use a damp rag or glue solvent to continue to soften the glue, and scrape the surface clean with the edge of a sharp chisel or a utility-knife blade.

4 Repair and sand the subsurface. When the surface is clean, check it for defects such as small chips and cracks, and repair them using wood putty. Repairing defects in the surface to be veneered is important because they can show up through the veneer, particularly after you apply the finish. Sand the surface well using a power sander or a sanding block with 120-grit sandpaper until the surface is even and smooth.

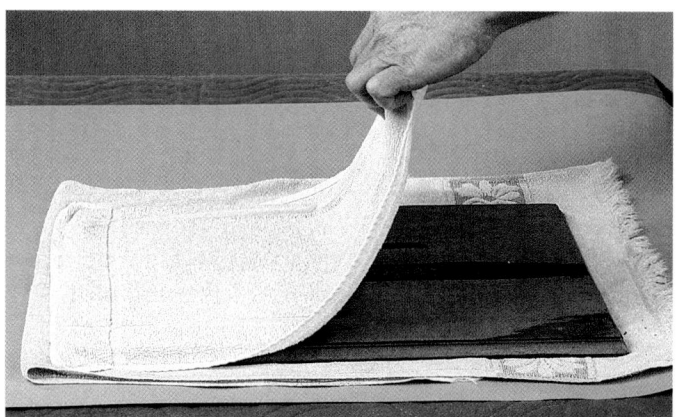

1 Strip the finish from the veneer surface, and then thoroughly soak the veneer using a wet towel.

2 When the veneer begins to loosen, use a hot iron and wide spatula or scraper to remove it.

3 Use a utility knife blade or chisel edge to scrape any remaining old glue from the surface.

4 Sand the surface well using 120-grit sandpaper and a power sander to prepare it for new veneer.

Applying Veneer and Adhesive Sheets

One of the easiest ways to apply veneer is to use thin pressure-sensitive veneer. This is a flexible product with a factory-applied adhesive on one side. To use, cut it to size; leaving a slight overhang that can be trimmed after application. Peel off the backing; position it on the work; and then press and smooth it onto the surface. You need to be precise in positioning because once it sticks, you can't reposition it. Pressure-sensitive veneer needs an extremely smooth subsurface. Some suppliers recommend coating the subsurface with a couple of coats of shellac or lacquer before applying the veneer.

Iron-on adhesive sheets are another helpful product developed for veneer application. These adhesive sheets are heat-sensitive, with a paper backing for easy application. They are best used with thin, flexible veneer.

Difficulty Level:

TOOLS AND MATERIALS
- Adhesive sheet
- Household iron
- Veneer
- 120-, 180-, 220-grit sandpaper
- Veneer roller
- Utility knife or veneer saw
- Sanding block

1 Position the adhesive sheet. Veneer adhesive sheets come with paper on one side. After you've prepared the substrate surface, position the sheet on it, paper side up. Use an iron set on the "cotton" setting to press the adhesive sheet onto the surface. After the sheet adheres, use a veneer roller to go over it, applying pressure as it cools. After the sheet cools, remove the paper.

2 Iron the veneer in place. Cut the veneer to fit the surface, with a fraction left over on all sides. Position on top of the cooled adhesive sheet, and place the sheet's paper backing on top of the veneer. Iron over the surface of the veneer until it seems firmly attached. When you've finished ironing the veneer, firmly press it in place and smooth it with a veneer roller.

3 Cut from underneath. Turn the veneered panel upside down on a flat surface. Be sure the surface is smooth so you don't damage the veneer. While firmly holding the panel, use a veneer saw or sharp utility knife to trim away any overhang at the edges. Turn the panel right side up, and use a sanding block and sandpaper to smooth the edges. To prepare the veneer for finishing, block-sand it with 120-grit sandpaper followed by 180- and 220-grit paper. If you use a machine sander, such as a random-orbit sander, be careful not to round off or cut through the edges of the panel. Finish the surface as you would any solid-wood surface.

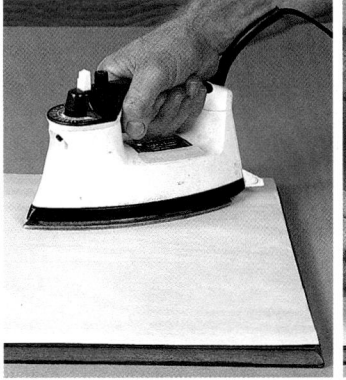 

1 Position the adhesive sheet, paper side up; press it with an iron (left); and remove the paper (right).

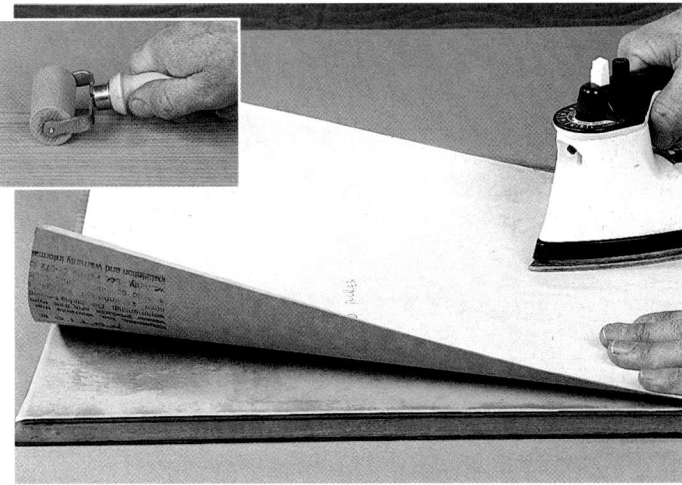

2 Cut the veneer to fit; place the adhesive-sheet paper on top; and press the veneer with a hot iron. After ironing, remove the paper and firmly roll over the veneer using a veneer roller (inset).

3 Turn the panel veneer-side down on a flat surface, and trim the overhang using a utility knife (left). Turn the panel upright, and sand the edges and top using 120-grit, and then 180- to 220-grit, sandpaper (right).

CASTERS AND GLIDES

Casters are small wheels, rollers, or balls mounted under the feet or base of furniture so it can roll. Casters are mounted to furniture by a plate attached to the wood with screws, or through a shaft that gets inserted into a metal sleeve in the wood. Plate-mounted casters are the most sturdy but require a large flat area on the bottom of the furniture. Casters with a shaft, called stem casters, are used primarily on narrow wood, such as chair legs, and they can often develop problems. Glides are flat metal or plastic buttons attached to the feet that enable the furniture to slide easily.

Replacing Glides

Glides usually have pointed tabs or a pointed shaft, such as a nail, that you drive into the wood to attach them. You can pry off worn or missing glides and replace them with new ones. To get the right replacement glide, consider the floor the piece rests on: carpet may not require glides, but plastic glides work well on floors that are tile or wood. Metal glides with a fabric tab attached are also available to keep them from scratching floor surfaces.

Difficulty Level:

TOOLS AND MATERIALS
- Flat-bladed screwdriver
- Hammer
- Needle-nose pliers
- Replacement glide

1 Remove the glide. Turn the furniture upside down, and use a thin flat-blade screwdriver to work under the button and pry it up. Then use needle-nose pliers to grasp the shaft, tapping it out with a small hammer.

2 Install the new glide. Hold the glide's shaft in position with a pair of needle-nose pliers, and tap the glide into the wood using a hammer.

1 You can usually remove a glide by prying it off with a thin, flat-bladed screwdriver.

2 Hold the new glide in place with needle-nose pliers, and then tap it into place using a hammer.

PRO TIP: solving simple step-caster problems

Caster problems may result when caster wheels break or become worn flat on one side. If this is the case, replace the caster. You can sometimes find replacement casters to match your original, but more likely you'll have to replace all of them. Another option for some pieces is to remove casters altogether and replace them with furniture glides. If doing so won't change the height of the piece enough to matter and the function isn't affected, the piece may be fine without casters. If the piece is old, save the original casters in case you decided to reinstall them at a later date.

Caster wheels such as this one that have been worn flat will have to be replaced. To get a match, it's sometimes necessary to replace the set.

Casters and glides make furniture easier to move, and they protect the floor. Casters may be the stem type or plate type; glides may simply fit over the feet of furniture or be attached by nailing or screwing them into the furniture leg.

Tightening a Stem Caster

A common problem with stem casters is that they continually fall out because they don't stay inserted in their metal sleeves. When this happens, you need to tighten the assembly.

Difficulty Level:

TOOLS AND MATERIALS
- Scratch awl or flat-bladed screwdriver
- Small wood block   • Mallet
- Adjustable pliers

1 Pry out the caster sleeve. Pull the caster and stem from the metal sleeve, and remove the sleeve using a scratch awl or flat-bladed screwdriver. Fit the tool under the teeth of the serrated flange, and pry up the sleeve, using a small wood block as a fulcrum. You may need to use pliers and a mallet to tap the sleeve out of the hole.

Using adjustable pliers, squeeze the bottom end of the metal sleeve together so the tabs snap over the stem end of the caster when it's inserted.

2 Replace the sleeve and caster. Put the metal sleeve back into the hole, and tap it down using a mallet until it's tight. Reinstall the stem caster, tapping it down into position until it snaps in place in the metal sleeve.

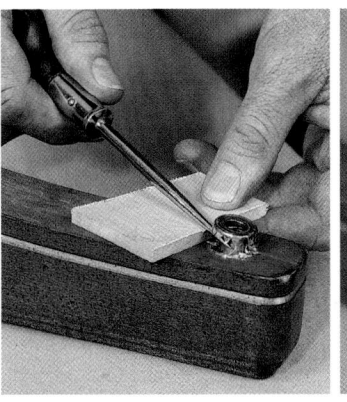 

1 Pry up the caster sleeve using a scratch awl or thin screwdriver and a wood block (left). To tighten the sleeve so that the caster stem will stay in place, squeeze the bottom end using pliers (right).

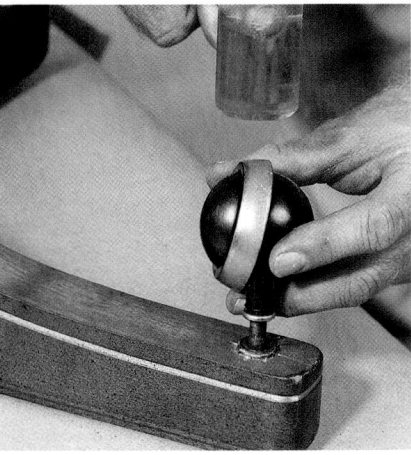

2 Reinstall the metal sleeve, and insert the caster, tapping it down until it snaps into place.

Shimming a Stem Caster

Stem casters can also get loose and fall out because the metal sleeve in which they're inserted becomes loose when the wood around it wears or splits. If the wood isn't split, but the hole is just worn, you can shim the caster.

Difficulty Level:

TOOLS AND MATERIALS
- Slender shims
- Wood glue and palette knife
- Needle-nose pliers
- Hammer

1 Insert the shim. Remove the loose metal sleeve and stem caster from the worn hole. Cut one or two slender hardwood shims, and apply wood glue to one side and inside the hole. Hold the shim or shims with needle-nose pliers, and insert them, gluing them to the side of the hole.

2 Reinstall the sleeve and caster. Insert the metal sleeve in the hole to see whether it's tight. If so, drive the sleeve into the hole using a hammer, and then reinstall the stem caster.

1 Remove the loose caster sleeve, and insert glued shims so they stick in the hole.

PRO TIP: tighten a plate caster

Plate casters rarely develop problems, but if they do, it's usually because the screws holding the caster plate are stripped from the wood. If this is the problem, you may be able to move or turn the plate slightly to provide new wood into which you can drive the screws. (left) If you can't turn the plate, you'll have to plug the screw holes. (right)

 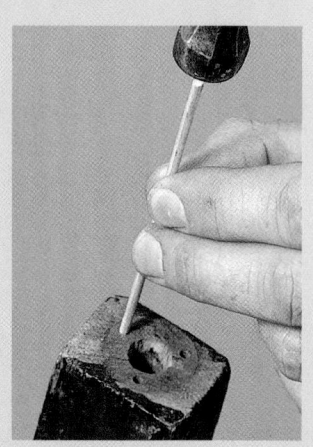

2 Tap the caster sleeve back into the hole using a hammer, and then replace the caster stem.

Repairing Splits around a Stem Caster

Difficulty Level:

TOOLS AND MATERIALS
- Rag
- Mallet
- Backsaw
- Drill and assorted bits
- Wood glue
- Clamps
- Dowels
- Masking tape
- Palette knife

1 Glue up the split. When the wood around the hole is split, remove the metal sleeve, and then glue and clamp the split tight. Clean up any glue seepage. If the split or splits are minor, you can tap the metal sleeve back into the hole while the wood is still clamped, and let the glue dry thoroughly overnight before removing the clamps. If the splits are major, go on to the next step.

2 Plug the old caster hole. After gluing and clamping the splits, plug the caster hole with the correct-size dowel. Prepare the dowel by chamfering the ends and cutting a groove in it; then apply glue to the dowel and caster hole. Drive the dowel into the hole using a mallet. Allow the glue to dry overnight, and then cut the dowel flush using a backsaw.

3 Drill a bigger hole. With the caster hole plugged, drill a hole about ⅛ to ¼ inch larger in diameter and ⅛ to ¼ inch longer than the original caster hole. Be sure to center this new hole on the plugged hole.

4 Plug the bigger hole. Choose a dowel the same diameter as, and a little longer than, the hole you drilled in Step 3. Prepare the dowel (with a chamfer and groove), and then glue and install it. Allow the glue to dry overnight; then cut the dowel flush using a backsaw.

5 Drill for the caster sleeve. With the larger hole plugged, center and drill the proper size hole for the metal caster sleeve. The sleeve should fit snugly. Measure the caster stem for correct depth; mark the drill bit with masking tape; and drill the hole straight.

6 Install the caster. Reinstall the metal caster sleeve, seating it in the new hole with a few gentle but firm taps from a hammer; then drive the caster back in place using a mallet.

1 Put the split pieces back together, and then glue and clamp them without the caster in place.

2 Prepare the correct-size dowel, and plug the old caster hole. Allow the glue to dry.

3 After cutting the dowel flush, drill for a larger-diameter dowel centered on the original hole.

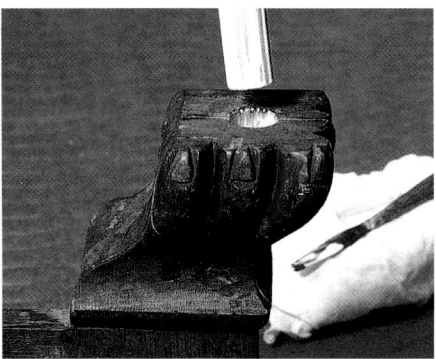

4 Prepare the larger-diameter dowel, and plug the new hole. Allow the glue to dry overnight.

5 After cutting the new, larger dowel flush, drill a hole sized for the original caster sleeve.

6 Drive the caster sleeve into the new hole using a hammer, and then install the caster.

8

Cleaning and Reviving Old Finishes

For many things, new is better. But that's not necessarily true for furniture finishes. If an old piece of furniture has been maintained well enough that it still has its original finish, most professional restorers would say that the finish should be saved. An original finish is considered an intrinsic part of the furniture, and removing it may devalue the piece and detract from its beauty. Of course, there are times when stripping and refinishing is not detrimental, and may even be necessary. A piece of furniture that has been poorly refinished or severely damaged by water, heat, or smoke may be a good candidate for refinishing. This chapter describes how to inspect the finish on your piece and decide on the best approach with these criteria in mind. If there's some question about which approach to take—reviving or refinishing — try cleaning the old finish first. You can always strip and refinish it later.

IS THE FINISH ORIGINAL?

Years of use and the natural aging of a finish can result in a pleasing effect called *patina,* which is the combination of a naturally distressed finish and deep wood color. To attempt to duplicate patina with a new finish is extremely difficult at best, and usually results in an artificial look. That's a good reason for reviving an original finish. In addition, saving the old finish usually means less work, mess, time, and money. Stripping an old finish requires the use of strong chemicals with hazardous fumes—you'll need protective clothing and good ventilation. But how do you know whether you have a finish worth saving? To determine whether your piece's finish is original, you must become a detective and search for clues.

A refinished piece often looks new, without normal wear signs such as stains, scratches, or dents; if there are scratches or dents, they have been finished over and are in the wood rather than the finish. Sanding marks can also show up on a refinished piece. Coarse sandpaper may have left scratches, or a power sander may have scarred the surface with small vibrator marks or orbital sander markings. Traces of old finish can also be left in corners, crevices, and carvings, usually appearing darker than the new finish.

Look for runs in the finish, usually indicating it's not original. Inspect backs, undersides, and inside furniture for telltale signs of refinishing; many refinishers don't clean up these areas well, and you'll be able to find traces of old finish or

Although this finish has a few new scratches and dents, the piece also shows scratches and dents in the wood itself that have been finished over, indicating that the finish is not original.

Traces of old paint on the underside of the piece at the top show that it has been refinished. The finish runs on the edge of the middle piece indicate that a finish has been applied since the piece was made. Light-colored run marks on the inside back edge of the bottom piece show that it has been stripped before.

residue left by the stripping process and light-colored streaks where solvent ran across the area, removing color. Also look under hardware for signs of an older, darker finish.

There are good indications of a fine old finish that you can look for, as well. If the finish looks rich and mellow, with normal age and wear signs, it could be old. Some old finishes are also cracked, crazed, or "alligatored," a term used to describe a finish surface resembling alligator hide. Old finishes may be sun bleached in one or more areas from exposure to sunlight through a window. If an older finish has been waxed or oiled regularly, it can appear dark, soiled, and dingy because of dirt and dust accumulation. You can usually remedy this with a good cleaning, which will return the piece to its original color.

Some old finishes like this one have become "alligatored," a term used to describe a cracked or crazed finish that resembles an alligator hide.

identifying the type of finish

If you decide to preserve the original finish after doing a cleaning and touch up, you may need to apply a top coat of finish over the old one to protect and renew it. If you do, it's always good to use the same type of finish as the original, which means you must first identify the original one.

Most furniture finishes are either shellac, lacquer, or varnish. Occasionally you'll find oil, wax, or painted finishes. Early furniture—dating from or before the eighteenth century—was usually finished with linseed oil and beeswax. This continued into the 1800s when shellac finishing became popular, beginning with the French polish technique (1810 to 1820). In the early 1900s, lacquer began to be used; by the 1950s, most manufactured furniture had a lacquer finish. Varnishes have also been used for many years, particularly among custom cabinetmakers.

Penetrating Finishes. You can usually identify oil finishes by their appearance. Because they are a penetrating, rather than a film-building, finish, oil finishes give wood a natural look with very little if any film on the wood surface. Look across the wood, allowing the light to reflect off the surface; if the wood grain appears open, reflecting the light, and the sheen is dull rather than glossy, it may very well be an oil finish.

Film Finishes. To check for shellac, lacquer, or varnish, use the solvent test. Using mineral spirits on a rag, clean a spot in an inconspicuous area. Then apply denatured alcohol on a white cotton rag to the same spot; let the alcohol soak in for a few minutes; and rub the spot with the rag. If the finish begins to dissolve and the rag picks up brown stains, you probably have a shellac finish. If not, go to the next solvent, lacquer thinner, and repeat the process to see whether the finish dissolves; if so, the finish is lacquer. If the finish still doesn't dissolve, or if it crinkles and lifts, you can assume it's some type of varnish. Most varnishes are vulnerable to methylene chloride-type paint and varnish removers.

Some recently-developed varnishes, however, are next to impossible to dissolve or remove, and they can't be recoated. If you encounter this type of finish, you'll soon know it. The best approach is to leave it alone. After all, it was designed to last indefinitely.

CLEANING AN ORIGINAL FINISH

Once you've handled any major repairs and decided to preserve the existing finish, the next step is cleaning the finish. You can do any necessary finish repairs after cleaning. (See Chapter 9, "Repairing Minor Surface Damage," starting on page 116.)

Cleaning the finish involves removing anything on top of it, such as dirt, grime, fingerprints, oils, polishes, and waxes. Ideally, after you've completed this step, only the clean, intact finish will remain.

One method of cleaning a finish is to use warm, not hot, water and mild dishwashing detergent (the kind

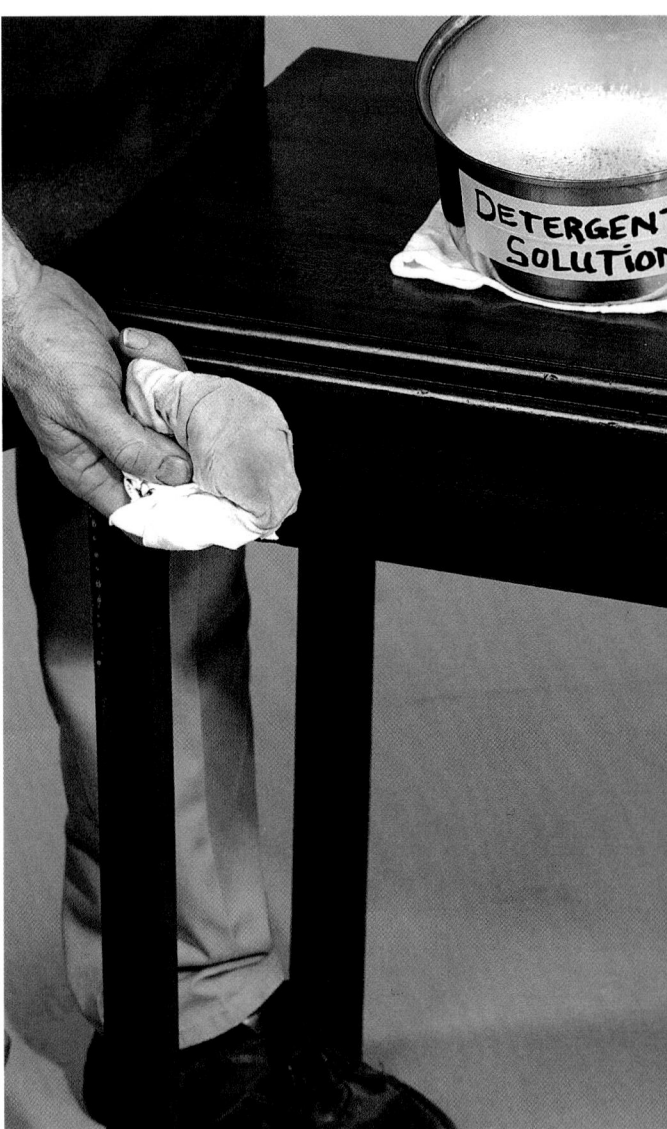

A solution of warm water and dishwashing detergent may be used to gently clean an old finish. Note the dirt on the rag.

used for hand dishwashing, not dishwashers). Another method uses mineral spirits, or paint thinner. Whichever method you choose, always try the cleaner in an inconspicuous area before you apply it to the entire piece. That way you won't damage the finish or the wood.

Using Detergent

A water-and-detergent solution works best on painted finishes but can be used on clear finishes, too. Mix detergent in water as you would to wash dishes, using a rag to wash down the furniture starting at the top and working down. An old washcloth or a piece of cheesecloth works well for this. Don't saturate the surface, or the water may damage the wood. Wring the cloth out till it's almost dry, and work one section at a time, rinsing the cloth often to remove dirt. Be careful not to snag any loose wood or veneer with the rag. Next, rinse the furniture surfaces using a clean cloth dipped in clear water. Finish using a clean, dry rag to rub down all wet surfaces.

Using Mineral Spirits

Use the same type of rag as you would for detergent, and wash the piece, starting at the top and working down. Rinse the rag often in the mineral spirits, wringing it out each time. Clean one area at a time, and wipe

it dry with a clean rag. If the clean rag still picks up dirt, wash the piece down again using more mineral spirits and a clean rag. Dry the finish as much as possible using a dry rag, allowing it to air-dry for an hour or two before doing any additional work on it.

With both the detergent and the mineral spirits methods, you can substitute #0000 steel wool for the cleaning rag when you have excessive dirt or wax buildup. Make sure you rub in the direction of the wood grain when using steel wool, as it will leave subtle rub marks on the finish surface.

A thorough cleaning job should take no more than about 30 minutes for all but the largest pieces of furniture. Also, you don't have to start and finish in one day. You can begin a cleaning job, and then stop and pick it up the next day.

Is Cleaning Enough?

Examine the finish closely after cleaning to determine its condition. If the finish seems to be in good shape with the exception of being a little dull, a good waxing or polishing will probably bring it back to life. You may find that it needs more than a good coat of polish or wax to revive it, however. If the finish itself appears sound but has dents, nicks, scratches, or water stains, you can fix these problems fairly easily before waxing. (See "Water Rings, Stains & Candle Wax" and "Nicks, Dents & Scratches," pages 116 and 120.) If you find that the finish is alligatored, crazed, or cracked, these problems are more severe and you'll have to address them before you can wax or polish the finish. (See "Reviving an Alligatored, Cracked, or Crazed Finish," on page 113.)

A finish can also appear hazy or foggy and may need special attention to revive it. (See "Reviving Furniture Finishes," page 114.) Some pieces of furniture have a finish that is fine in one area yet breaking down and dissolving in another; an example of this is an armchair with soiled or worn finish on the arms. The finish may be so weak in these areas that a good cleaning removes it completely, exposing the wood underneath. In this case you'll have to strip and refinish the whole piece rather than just revive the finish.

Mineral spirits (paint thinner) also works well to remove any oil, polish, wax, or dirt from an old finish surface.

WAXING AND POLISHING

Waxes and polishes are meant to protect and beautify finishes. Although neither wax nor polish offers a high degree of protection, wax is the better of the two; it's a little harder to apply but offers more protection and needs to be applied about once a year. Polish offers a quick, easy way to liven up a dull finish. Don't use polishes that contain silicones, as they're incompatible with most finishes and will eventually harm them; instead, choose a good cream polish.

Applying Cream Polishes

To apply cream polish, dip a clean, soft rag into the polish or pour some onto the rag. Apply to the finish using overlapping tight circles, and continue to apply polish until you cover the entire surface with a thin coat. Let the polish harden for 30 to 45 minutes, and then use a clean, soft cloth or a lamb's-wool electric drill attachment to buff the surface vigorously until it shines.

Applying Paste Wax

A good furniture paste wax provides a thin, hard, protective coating that can't be beat for the final touch to a good finish. For waxing a dark finish, dark or amber paste wax works best; for waxing a light or bleached wood finish, use clear paste wax.

Difficulty Level: 🔨🔨🔨

TOOLS AND MATERIALS
- Furniture paste wax
- Electric drill with lamb's-wool pad
- #0000 steel wool
- Soft rag

1 Apply the wax. Wipe a soft rag or #0000 steel-wool pad in the wax, and apply a light, even coat to the finish surface. If you're using steel wool, rub the wax onto the surface in the direction of the wood grain. An exception to this rule is when you're waxing turnings, or small shaped or carved parts of furniture. You can use steel wool in any direction when applying the wax to these areas. Apply the wax on one section of the furniture at a time, and be sure to cover the surface with a thin, even coat.

Rub down the waxed area using a clean, soft rag in a circular motion. Allow the waxed surface to sit undisturbed for about 15 minutes.

2 Buff the wax. Using a clean, soft rag, buff the surface with the grain until it produces a shine. If you want to polish to a higher luster, let the wax harden longer, and then buff the surface again using a lamb's-wool buffing attachment in an electric drill.

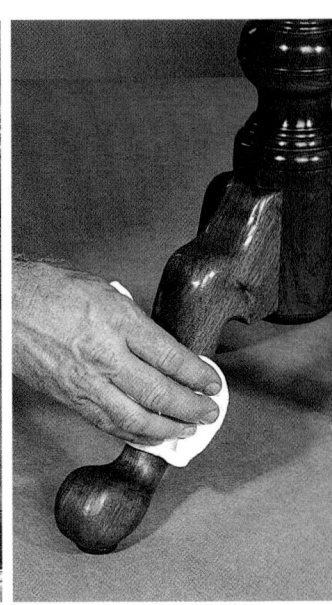

1 Using a #0000 steel-wool pad, apply a light, even coat of paste wax to the finish surface (left). Rub the waxed surface down using a clean, soft rag (right), and buff in a circular pattern.

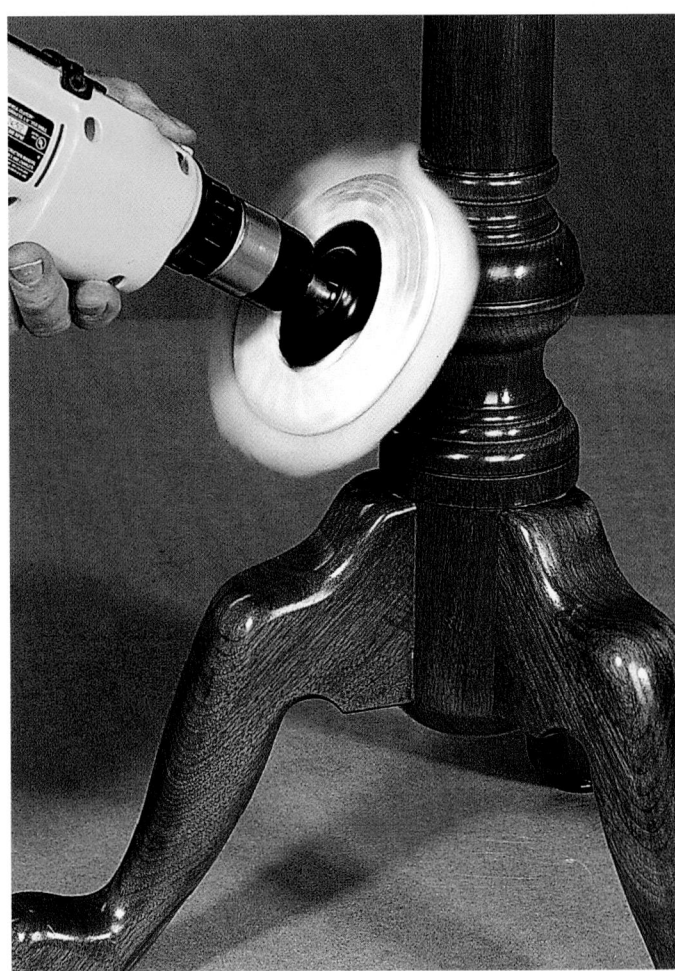

2 After the wax dries, use a lamb's-wool buffing attachment in an electric drill to polish the surface to a high luster.

REVIVING THE OLD FINISH

When a finish is alligatored, cracked, or crazed, it generally appears lifeless and tends to hide the natural beauty of the wood underneath.

An alligatored finish has intersecting cracks or ridges that give it a rough, textured look. Cracked or crazed finishes have small, irregular cracks that randomly crisscross the finish surface. These cracks are usually caused by overexposure to heat or sunlight, which causes the finish to dry out and shrink.

Other finishes can appear hazy or foggy. A painted or oil finish may simply need brightening up. There are ways to deal with all these problems, and in most cases the finish can be improved without stripping and refinishing.

Reviving an Alligatored, Cracked, or Crazed Finish

To restore an alligatored, cracked, or crazed finish to its original beauty, you must eliminate the tiny cracks or ridges in the finish. Even though these cracks are small, they can be deep, often going all the way down to the wood surface. Sanding them would remove so much of the finish that you would essentially be refinishing it. A better approach is to reamalgamate the finish, or dissolve and redistribute it, allowing it to flow together, thus eliminating cracks or ridges. This process will work on shellac and most lacquer finishes as long as the finish is free of wax and dirt. Varnish will not reamalgamate and must be treated differently. (See "Reviving Varnish," page 114.)

Difficulty Level:

TOOLS AND MATERIALS
- Denatured alcohol or lacquer thinner
- 2- or 2½-inch China bristle brush
- #0000 steel wool
- Tack cloth
- 3-lb. shellac or aerosol lacquer
- Furniture paste wax
- Soft rag
- Open-mouthed jar

1 Apply solvent. Using denatured alcohol for shellac and lacquer thinner for a lacquer finish, pour the correct solvent into an open-mouthed jar large enough to accept a 2- or 2½-inch paint brush. Set the surface to be renewed facing upward on a horizontal plane so that the solvent doesn't run when you apply it. Apply the solvent to the finish with a pure bristle brush, using light strokes in the direction of the grain. Don't be in a hurry; do one horizontal section at a time, allowing the solvent a few minutes to work. You may have to apply several coats of solvent before the finish softens enough to begin to flow out, so watch it closely. After the sol-

vent begins to work and the small cracks and ridges in the finish begin to disappear, move on to the next section until you finish the entire piece.

Allow the finish to dry completely (about 4 hours), and then inspect it. You can repeat the amalgamation process if necessary. If the surface seems smooth, you can do one of two things: rub the piece down in the same direction as the grain using #0000 steel wool dipped in paste wax, followed by buffing to complete the job, or rub the surface down well with dry #000 or #0000 steel wool.

2 Apply a top coat of new finish. If you did not wax the piece, recoat it with shellac or lacquer. Be sure to rub the surface well with a tack cloth to remove all steel-wool residue before applying the finish. If you use shellac, apply a 3-pound cut of commercially prepared shellac with a pure bristle brush. If you want to apply lacquer, use an aerosol can of finishing lacquer to apply a light coat. Be sure to have adequate ventilation when spraying. After the finish is dry (either shellac or lacquer), rub the surface down with #0000 steel wool and paste wax, and follow with a vigorous buffing.

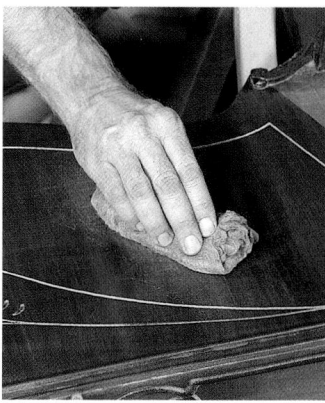

1 Apply the appropriate solvent to the surface using a pure bristle brush with light strokes in the direction of the wood grain (left). After the finish surface has completely dried, rub the piece down in the direction of the grain using #0000 steel wool (right).

2 After tacking the surface to remove any steel-wool residue, recoat the piece using the appropriate finish.

Renewing an Oil Finish

An oil finish is probably the easiest finish of all to renew because it's a penetrating finish rather than a film finish. Oil continues to penetrate the wood over time, and more finish can always be added.

Because oil finishes are interchangeable, there should be no compatibility problem between the finish already on the piece and the oil finish you use to recoat it. Either a tung oil or a penetrating resin oil such as Danish oil should work fine.

Difficulty Level:

TOOLS AND MATERIALS
- Mineral spirits, paint thinner, or turpentine
- Soft rags
- Oil finish
- #0000 steel wool

1 Clean the surface. Use mineral spirits, or paint thinner, and a rag to clean the surface of the furniture.

2 Apply thinned finish. Thin new oil finish by adding 25 to 50 percent turpentine or mineral spirits, and then freely apply it to the surface with a soft, absorbent rag. Allow the oil to penetrate for 15 minutes.

3 Wipe the excess. Wipe off the oil that hasn't penetrated with a rag. Allow the surface to dry for 3 hours.

4 Apply straight oil. Using new, unthinned oil finish, liberally apply the oil using the same kind of rag as in Step 2. Let the oil penetrate for about 15 minutes, and then wipe off the excess. Let the piece dry over-night, and dispose of the rag. (See "Dispose of Used Rags Properly," page 21.)

5 Rub with steel wool. The next day, rub down the oiled finish using #0000 steel wool to give it a hand-rubbed look. Buff the surface lightly using a soft cloth.

reviving furniture finishes

Reviving a Hazy or Foggy Finish

Some finishes have a hazy or foggy appearance that remains after cleaning. The fact that the haze doesn't go away with cleaning indicates that the problem is in the finish, and it usually requires more than just a coat of wax to correct.

To determine the best solution, wet the hazy surface with mineral spirits to see whether the haze disappears. If it does, you can probably eliminate it entirely by applying a coat of finish.

Rub the surface down well with #000 or #0000 steel wool; then use a tack rag to remove any dust and steel-wool residue. Be sure to use the appropriate finish for the piece, applying shellac with a pure bristle brush and applying lacquer from an aerosol can. Follow either application with a #0000 steel wool rub-down using paste wax and a final buffing using a clean, soft rag.

Reviving Varnish

Varnish is a tough, enduring finish, but when problems develop they are difficult to fix without refinishing. Alligatored or crazed finishes will not dissolve and flow back together as reamalgamated lacquer and shellac will, but you may still be able to improve the look of the overall finish by applying a coat of Danish oil. Danish oil works much like a scratch-cover polish except that it will dry rather than stay tacky

and dull looking. Because it will penetrate any cracks or scratches in the damaged finish or wood, you can use a colored Danish oil finish to restore color to these areas.

Use a soft, absorbent rag to apply, being sure to wipe it into any scratches, cracks, or crevices. Allow the oil to penetrate these areas for about 15 minutes, and then wipe off excess oil with a clean, soft rag. Allow the finish to dry overnight; then apply a coat of paste wax. Buff the surface to finish the process.

Reviving a Painted Finish

Painted finishes are not necessarily all the same. Opaque coatings for furniture can be pigmented shellac, pigmented lacquer, pigmented oil varnish (oil-based paint), or pigmented water-based finish (latex paint). Some old pieces were painted with milk paint, developed during colonial times, using milk or buttermilk as a base.

If you have a painted antique piece with its original finish, it's better to consider imperfections as a part of the furniture's charm, and just clean and wax it carefully. Other painted pieces can sometimes be rejuvenated with a clear coat of finish. First rub the surface using #000 or #0000 steel wool or scuff-sand using 280 to 320-grit sandpaper; then apply the finish. Once dry, follow with a clear paste wax applied with #0000 steel wool, and buff the surface.

1 To renew an old oil finish, first use paint thinner to clean the surface.

2 Apply a thinned coat of new oil finish to the surface, and allow it to penetrate.

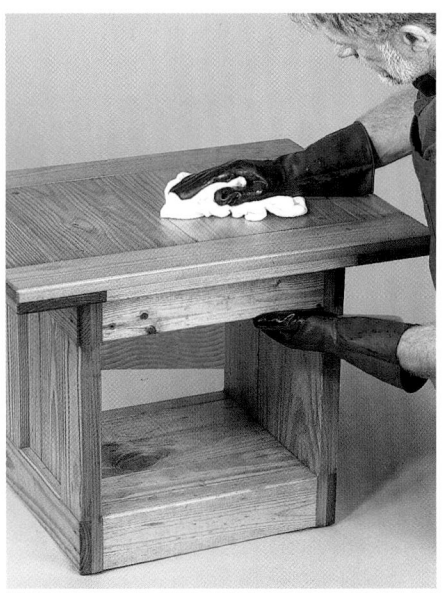

3 Wipe off the excess oil, and allow the surface to dry for about 3 hours.

4 Apply a coat of the unthinned oil finish, and allow it to penetrate before wiping off the excess.

5 After the finish is dry (overnight), rub it down using #0000 steel wool in the direction of the wood grain; then buff it.

9 Repairing Minor Surface Damage

An important aspect of preserving and renewing a finish is repairing and touching up minor—and sometimes not so minor—damage to the finish surface. All the repairs in this chapter can be done without having to refinish the entire piece of furniture.

Of course, you'll want to remove water rings and stains from the finish. Many times an otherwise beautiful finish is ruined by scratches or a deep gouge. Cigarette burns and candle-wax drippings are other common surface problems. Even crushed corners and wood that has been chewed by pets can be repaired without refinishing.

WATER RINGS, STAINS, AND CANDLE WAX

Water and other liquids can cause rings or stains in finish and wood. Shellac finishes are more susceptible to this problem than other types. Stains that are in the finish are usually white, while stains that have seeped through the finish and into the wood will appear dark or black.

Dark moisture stains can't be removed without refinishing, and even then they are difficult to get out. You may be able to remove the finish, bleach the stain, and refinish the surface.

White stains, or those still in the finish, can often be removed without stripping. The longer the stain is in the finish, the deeper it will penetrate into the surface of the wood. The deeper moisture penetrates, the harder the stain is to remove, so it's important to remove stains as soon as possible.

Finish discoloration that's caused by moisture is a result of moisture being trapped in or under the finish. To get rid of the discoloration, you must get rid of the trapped moisture. This can be done in one of two ways: use a chemical called an amalgamator to soften the finish long enough for moisture to evaporate, or use an abrasive to cut into the finish to the depth of the moisture, allowing moisture to escape and causing the stain to disappear.

Removing a Moisture Stain Using Amalgamator

Amalgamator is an alcohol-based mixture sold by finish and touch-up supply stores to soften an area of the finish and cause the moisture stain to dissipate. The technique for applying the amalgamator to the finish surface is similar to that used for French polishing. (See "French Polishing," page 150.) If you can't get amalgamator, try using denatured alcohol instead, but be careful not to cut too deeply into the finish.

Difficulty Level:

TOOLS AND MATERIALS
- Soft cotton rag
- #0000 steel wool
- Amalgamator
- Furniture paste wax

1 Apply amalgamator to a pad. Use a soft cotton rag to make an applicator pad. Ball or roll up the rag in a comfortable size to hold in one hand (about the size of a large egg). Smooth out the part of the rag that will make contact with the finish surface. There should be no wrinkles or creases. Apply amalgamator to the pad, allowing it to soak into the rag.

2 Disperse the amalgamator. Tap the padding rag into the palm of your other hand, causing the amalgamator to spread into the rag until the surface of the rag is damp, but not wet.

3 Pad the stain. Pad over the surface of the finish on top of the stain with a pendulum-like stroke in the direction of the wood grain. Briefly touch the pad to the stain surface, and then lift it off, keeping the pad in motion when it's in contact with the finish surface. The water stain may not immediately disappear, so continue to pad the area, adding more amalgamator to the rag if necessary. The trick is to keep your padding rag damp enough to soften the finish but not wet enough to cut through the finish to the wood surface.

4 Blend-in the repair area. When the stain is gone, allow the area to dry. Next, rub the finish down with #0000 steel wool to blend the sheen. Paste-wax the finish if necessary.

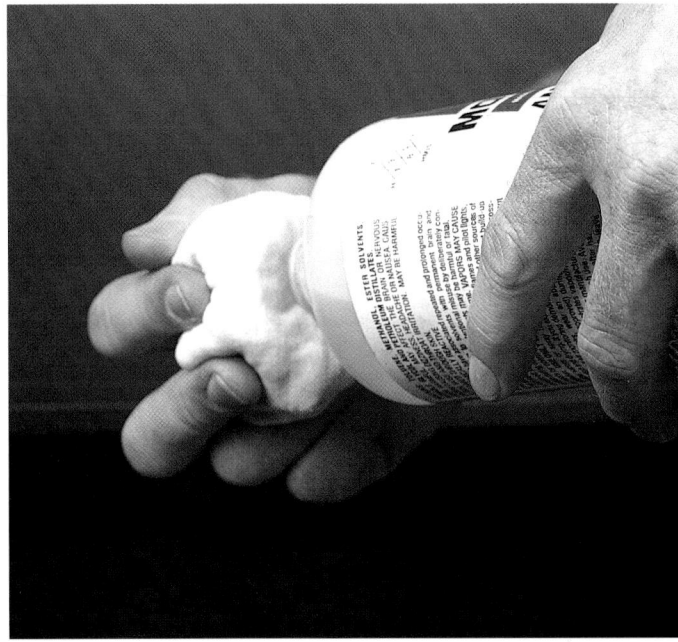

1 Make an applicator pad for the amalgamator by balling up a soft cotton rag.

2 After applying the amalgamator solvent to the applicator, tap the rag into the palm of your hand.

3 Pad the stained finish with the rag using pendulum-like strokes in the direction of the wood grain.

4 After rubbing the surface down with #0000 steel wool, apply paste wax and buff the area.

Removing a Moisture Stain Using Abrasives

You can use any number of fine abrasives to remove a water stain from the finish, including #0000 steel wool, rottenstone, pumice, and 600-grit wet-or-dry sandpaper. Adventuresome refinishers have even used toothpaste or cigar ashes as abrasives. The depth of the stain will

1 Use #0000 steel wool to rub over the stained area. Apply firm pressure in the direction of the grain.

2 Sand with 600-, 500-, or 400-grit wet-or-dry sandpaper. Use mineral spirits or soapy water as a lubricant.

determine which one will work for you. Start with a mild abrasive. If that doesn't work, go to sandpaper. The less cutting into the finish you have to do to get rid of the stain, however, the better.

Difficulty Level:

TOOLS AND MATERIALS
- #0000 steel wool
- Furniture paste wax
- 600-grit sandpaper (plus 500- or 400-grit if necessary)

1 **Rub the stain area using steel wool.** Rub #0000 steel wool over the stained area of the finish, rubbing with the grain and using firm pressure. If the stain is shallow, this may remove it. If not, go to Step 2.

2 **Rub the area using sandpaper.** Use 600-grit wet-or-dry sandpaper and a felt block to sand the stained area if steel wool doesn't get the stain out. A little soapy water or mineral spirits will work as a lubricant for the sandpaper. Use firm pressure, and sand the area well, rubbing in the direction of the grain. If the stain doesn't disappear, go to a coarser wet-or-dry paper (500- or 400-grit), but remember that coarser papers may dull the sheen in the repair area and can even cut through the finish to the wood, so be careful. If you use a coarser paper, follow it by sanding with 600-grit paper to try to bring back the sheen.

3 **Rub the area, again using steel wool.** Rub out the finish using #0000 steel wool and paste wax, if necessary, to blend the repair area with the rest of the finish.

3 Rub in the grain direction using #0000 steel wool with paste wax. Follow by buffing with a soft rag.

Removing Candle Wax from a Finish

A common problem on tabletop finishes is candle-wax drippings. When the hot wax drips onto the finish and hardens, it can be difficult to remove without damaging the finish—but not if you follow this procedure.

Difficulty Level:

TOOLS AND MATERIALS
- Ice cube
- Soft cotton rag
- Credit card or plastic scraper
- Cream polish and #0000 steel wool

1 Freeze the wax. Use an ice cube to harden the wax drippings, making them brittle.

2 Scrape the area. Use a plastic paint scraper or the edge of a credit card to scrape all the wax from the finish surface as gently as possible.

3 Rub out the affected area. Apply a cream polish to the surface using #0000 steel wool. Rub with the grain of the wood; this will remove any remaining wax residue.

4 Polish the area. Buff the repair area to a luster similar to that of the surrounding finish using a soft cotton cloth.

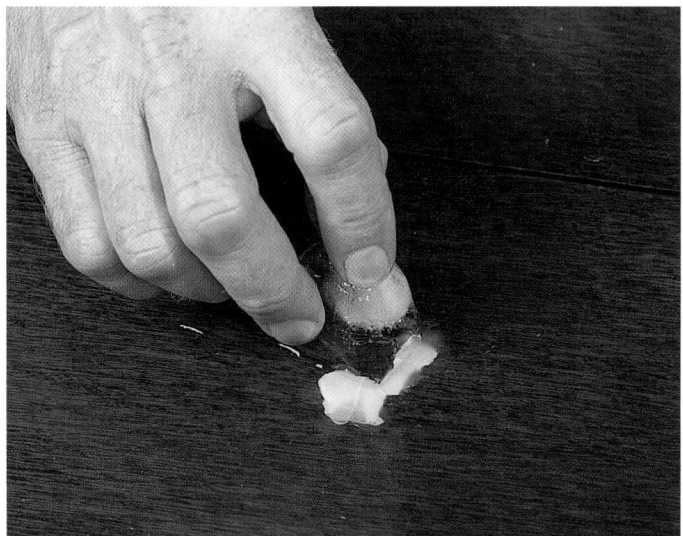

1 To remove candle wax from a finish, use an ice cube to freeze—or at least stiffen—the wax.

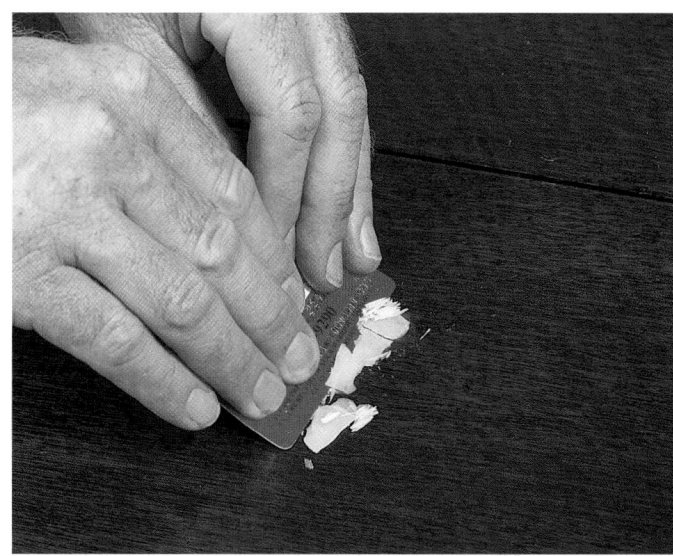

2 Use the edge of a plastic card or a nonmarring plastic scraper to scrape the wax free.

3 Apply cream polish to the area with #0000 steel wool, rubbing in the direction of the wood grain.

4 Rub the area with a clean soft cloth to restore the sheen.

NICKS, DENTS, AND SCRATCHES

An easy way to touch up nicks and scratches is to use a furniture touch-up marker of the appropriate color.

You can touch up nicks, dents, and scratches in a number of ways. If the piece you're restoring is old and has a lot of imperfections, use pigmented oil stain to touch them up. Use this technique when you don't want to render scratched areas invisible, but instead are willing to allow the furniture to have an old, distressed look. If the finish is free from wax, dirt, and polish, use a pigmented oil stain of the appropriate color. Apply the stain to damaged areas with an artist's touch-up brush. Wipe off any excess using a dry rag, and then apply a spray finish over the damaged areas. (For larger damaged areas, see "Covering Scratches over a Large Area," below.)

Another quick, easy method to touch up nicks, dents, or scratches is to use a furniture touch-up marker in the appropriate color. These are usually available at paint and hardware stores or home centers. If you can't find them there, try woodworkers' or furniture-supply catalogs. Touch-up markers look—and work— basically the same as permanent marking pens, except they contain a stain/polish mixture that colors defects to match or blend in with the surrounding finish. Matching the finish exactly is usually not crucial. A marker close to the same color will work fine. Wax sticks, such as touch-up markers, are available in a variety of wood and finish colors for filling in surface defects. Although a wax stick will not always make a scratch, dent, or nick invisible, it's a quick way to help disguise these marks, making them much less objectionable. There are two ways to fill a defect with a wax stick, and either of them will work fine, so use the one you find easier. (See "Fixing Defects Using a Wax Stick," opposite page.)

Covering Scratches over a Large Area

Difficulty Level:

TOOLS AND MATERIALS
- Pigmented oil stain
- Soft cotton rag
- Aerosol lacquer, polyurethane, or shellac finish

1 Apply stain to the top. Clean the surface you want to renew using either mineral spirits or detergent and water. (See "Cleaning an Original Finish," page 110.) Using a rag, wipe matching pigmented oil stain over large damaged areas, such as a table top, then go immediately to the next step.

2 Wipe off excess. Using a clean soft cotton rag, wipe any excess stain off the finish surface. Allow the stain to dry for the time prescribed on the label.

3 Apply new finish. Apply a coat of finish over the affected areas or over the entire piece if needed. For lacquer finishes, an aerosol lacquer works well. Spray one section at a time using long, overlapping strokes in the same direction as the grain. Apply a second coat if needed.

Other types of finishes, such as polyurethane and shellac, also come in aerosol cans but the finish works a bit differently than lacquer. Polyurethane is slower-drying and tends to run if you're not careful; shellac dries quickly, sometimes blushing (turning white) as a result of moisture getting trapped under the finish. If you use an aerosol finish, it can be quick and easy, but experiment first to familiarize yourself with how the finish goes on the surface. Be sure the can is warm so the finish sprays smoothly. If the can is too cold, set it in a pan of warm water for about a minute before spraying.

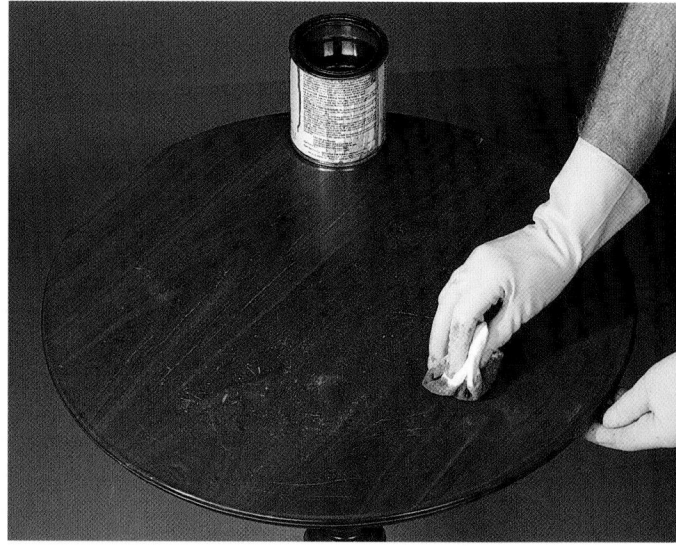

1 After cleaning the finish surface, apply matching pigmented oil stain over the damaged area.

Fixing Defects Using a Wax Stick

Difficulty Level:

TOOLS AND MATERIALS
- Colored wax stick
- Soft cotton rag
- Burn-in knife (optional)
- Sanding block

1 Fill the defect. Rub the wax stick across the surface defect, forcing the wax into the recessed area until it's filled. You can also use a hot burn-in knife to melt the tip of the wax stick, dripping wax into the defect. (See "Electric Appliances," page 31, for information about burn-in knives.)

2 Level the repair. When the defect is filled with the colored wax, wrap a soft rag tightly around a sanding block, rubbing back and forth over the wax filler until it's level with the surrounding surface. Keep changing the rag to a clean area, and continue rubbing until you've removed all the excess wax on the surrounding surface.

1 Rub the wax stick across the defect, forcing the wax into it (top), or use a hot burn-in knife to melt the wax, dripping it into the defect (bottom).

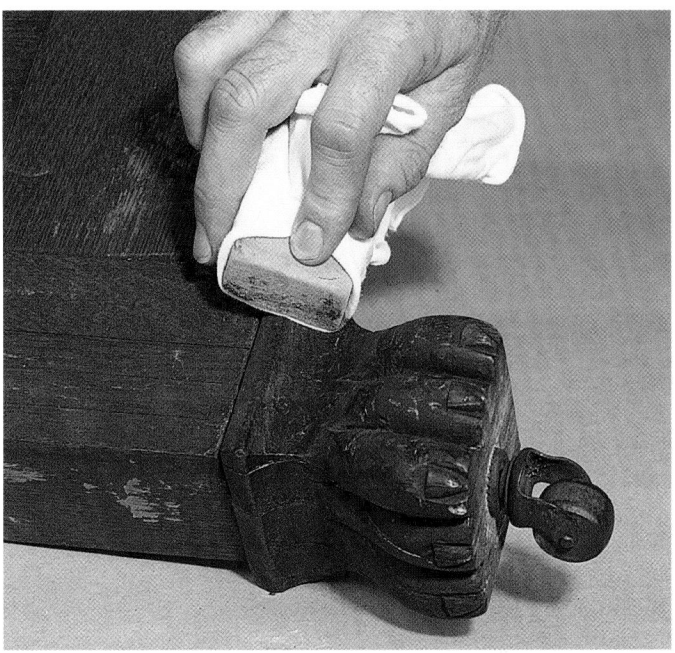

2 Use a soft rag wrapped around a sanding block to rub over the filled defect, leveling the wax with the surrounding surface.

2 Use a clean soft rag to wipe off as much excess oil stain as you can.

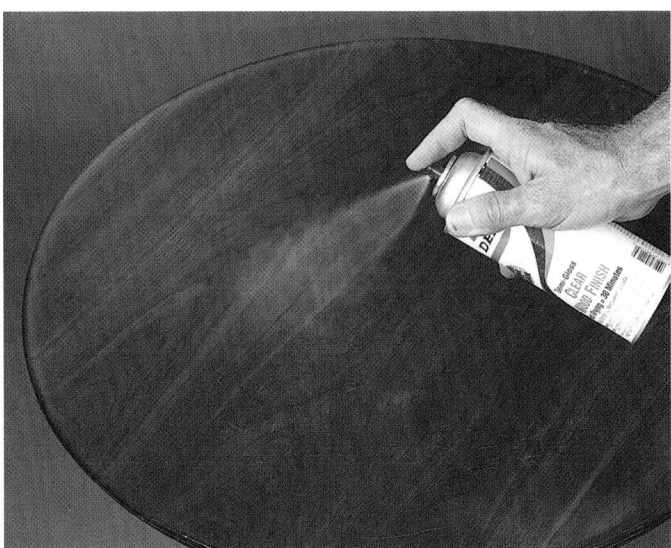

3 After the stain dries, spray a coat of finish over the stained area.

CIGARETTE BURNS AND GOUGES

On some pieces of furniture, a cigarette burn or gouge could be considered part of the piece's natural character. An example of this kind of furniture is a piece with a lot of wear and distress, to the point that one more spot doesn't detract from the overall look. On most furniture pieces, however, it appears as simply unwanted damage. If the gouge is objectionable, you can do a simple repair using a touch-up pen or artist's brush and oil stain. You can also repair the gouged area by filling it with a wax stick as described on page 121.

If the gouge is in a conspicuous area, such as a tabletop, however, or if you're dealing with a cigarette burn, the best method of repair may be to burn-in the defect, using hot-melt finish resin sticks (burn-in sticks) and a burn-in knife. (See "Electric Appliances," page 31, for information about burn-in knives and resin sticks.) Nicks, dents, and scratches can also be repaired using this burn-in method.

The basic steps for burning-in a defect are almost the same whether the defect is a dent, scratch, cigarette burn, or gouge. The only differences are in the first step of preparing the affected surface for the melted stick.

Burn-in sticks have a limited shelf life: if you've had one longer than six months, check it before applying the stick to the finish. If it gets rubbery or gummy when melted with the proper heat, the stick is too old; if it liquefies when melted, it's good.

Because the burn-in process may take some skill to perfect, work on a few practice pieces before jumping to the real thing.

Repairing Damage with a Burn-in Knife

Difficulty Level:

TOOLS AND MATERIALS
- Utility-knife blade
- Touch-up stain and finish
- Soft cotton rag
- Various grades of wet-or-dry sandpaper
- Burn-in knife and resin stick
- Artist's brush
- #0000 steel wool

1 **Dig out the defect.** For cigarette burns, use a utility-knife blade edge to scratch out all charred surfaces, removing only what's necessary to reach a solid clean surface (finish or wood). For gouges, use a utility-knife blade to remove any ragged or loose finish or wood fibers in the gouge and around the edge. For scratches, nicks, or dents, begin with Step 2.

2 **Melt the resin.** Heat up the burn-in knife, and choose a resin stick that matches the surrounding finish color as closely as possible. For defects that have not lost their finish color, use a transparent amber stick or a transparent clear stick for a natural finish over light wood. If the finish color is lost and you need to use a colored stick, usually it's best to match the background color with the idea of adding grain lines over the burn-in after it's sanded. When the knife gets hot, touch the tip to the burn-in stick and see if it begins to melt. If not, heat the knife again until it melts or liquefies the stick when touched. If the liquid resin bubbles or blisters, the knife is too hot and needs to cool. Maintain knife temperature as much as possible so the burn-in resin melts on its tip.

3 **Apply the resin.** Transfer a small amount of the stick onto the knife tip, immediately pressing it into the defect, melting it in place. Make sure that the resin is still in liquid form when you press it into the defect so it fuses well to the surface. Continue to transfer enough of the stick to the defect until it's just a fraction

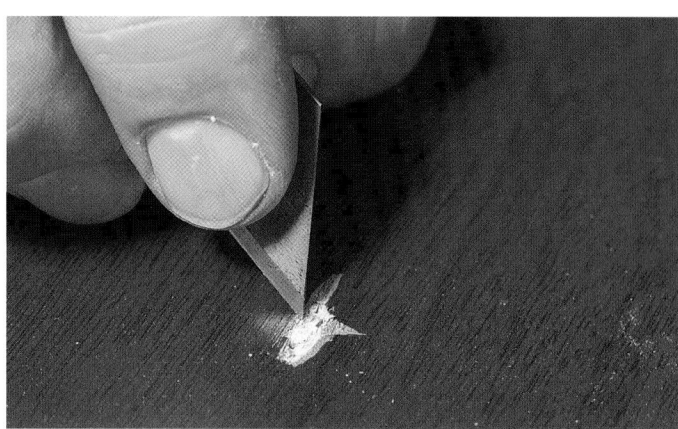

1 Before burning-in a damaged area, you may need to remove any loose finish or wood fibers using a utility knife.

4 Use fine-grit wet-or-dry sandpaper with mineral spirits or soapy water to block-sand the burn-in.

higher than the surrounding surface. Holding the burn-in knife as you would a pencil, use the bottom convex surface of the knife tip to pass over the burned-in defect surface, smoothing and flattening it as much as possible. Keep your knife tip at the right temperature during this step.

4 **Sand the resin.** Sand the burn-in surface using a felt block and 600-grit wet-or-dry sandpaper. Use soapy water or mineral spirits as a lubricant. The idea here is to level the burn-in surface smooth with the surrounding area without cutting through the existing finish. You might be able to use 500-grit or even 400-grit wet-or-dry paper during this step, but be careful or you'll cut through the finish surface and possibly lose the finish color in this area. It's better to use finer-grit paper unless the finish film is exceptionally thick.

5 **Touch up the repair.** After you have leveled the burn-in, wipe over the area using a rag dampened with water or paint thinner to clean away sanding residue and to look at the repair color. If necessary, use

a fine sable touch-up brush to paint in grain lines over the burned-in area, matching them to the surrounding wood. Use a pigmented oil stain for this, and work off a palette surface such as a paper plate or the back of a piece of wet-or-dry sandpaper. Graining pens and pencils are also available from touch-up supply houses. Use your creativity on this step; use whatever color or grain figure you think you need to blend the repair to the surrounding wood. Often you can continue existing grain lines and figure through the repaired area to fool the eye.

6 **Spray and rub out the repair area.** Allow the touch-up stain to dry. When used for touching up in this manner, most oil stains will dry in about 5 to 10 minutes. Spray the dried spot with an aerosol can of the appropriate finish.

Rub out the repair with steel wool, and let the finish dry. (Read the label of the finish you're using to determine how long to allow it to dry.) Rub the area down with the grain, using #0000 steel wool to blend the sheen with the surrounding finish.

2 When the burn-in knife gets hot enough to melt the lacquer stick, transfer a small amount of the stick to the knife tip.

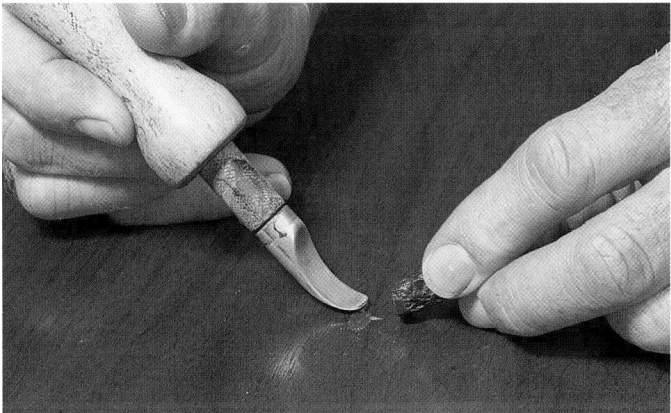

3 Press the melted lacquer into the defect until it is fused with the surface. Build up the damaged area until it's slightly higher than the surrounding surface.

5 After sanding, use a fine sable brush and pigment from a pigmented oil stain to paint grain lines across the repair area.

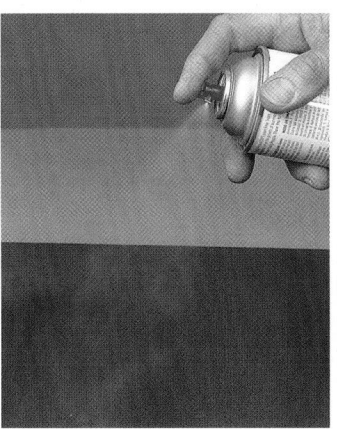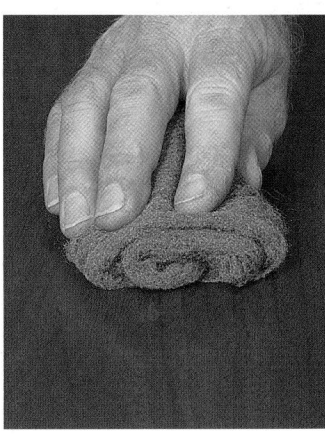

6 After the stain dries, spray finish over the area (left). Going with the wood grain, rub the area down using #0000 steel wool to blend (right).

CRUSHED CORNERS AND CHEWED WOOD

Crushed corners and chewed wood are common problems. A piece of furniture can appear to be ruined when a corner is crushed during a moving accident, or a leg or pedestal is used as a chew toy by the family puppy. This type of damage may look bad and seem tough to fix, but repair is entirely possible, and there are tricks to make it easier.

Using auto-body filler is the easiest way to fix both problems. In most cases, you can shape and finish this product to look like the surrounding wood. (See "Repairing Chewed Wood with Filler," page 126.) The filler has the hardness of wood and will last indefinitely. In some cases, however, you might not want to use filler material. If you have a high-quality, old piece of furniture, for example, you'll need to patch the area with matching wood and finish to match.

Repairing a Crushed Corner with Wood

To repair a crushed corner with wood, you must prepare the damaged area before applying the wood patch. You then apply the patch, shape it to form, and finish it to match.

Difficulty Level:

TOOLS AND MATERIALS
- Dovetail saw or backsaw
- Matching wood scrap
- Touch-up stain and finish
- Wood glue and palette knife
- Sandpaper and sanding block
- Tack cloth and wood filler if necessary
- Clamps (hammer, nail, and drill if necessary)
- Artist's brush
- Soft cotton rag
- #0000 steel wool
- Block plane

1 Cut out the damaged area. Using a dovetail saw or backsaw, cut away only the rough, damaged area with a straight cut, going with the grain.

2 Plane the corner. Plane the corner's cut surface flat and smooth using a sharp block plane. Don't take off too much wood, and make sure the cut is as plumb as possible.

3 Cut and plane the patch. Cut a piece of similar wood large enough to patch the area. Make the patch a little larger than necessary; you can shape and sand it after you apply it. Plane the joining surface of the patch completely flat and plumb to match the planed surface of the corner.

4 Clamp the patch in place. Test-fit and clamp the patch to the corner. If necessary, tap a small nail or brad through the patch into the corner to keep the patch from sliding on the diagonal surface when you clamp it. Predrill the nailhole to avoid splitting the

1 Make a cut as clean and straight as possible in the direction of the wood grain to remove the damaged wood.

4 Test-fit and clamp the patch to the corner without glue. Once you're sure you have a good fit, apply glue to both joint surfaces, and re-clamp the patch.

5 When the glue is dry, remove the clamps, and shape the patch to conform to the surrounding surface.

wood. Drive the nail only as far as necessary to hold the patch and leave the nailhead extending. (You'll remove it later.) Remove the patch with the nail in it for gluing. Apply glue to the joining surfaces, spreading it with a palette knife. Put the patch in place, lining up the nail (if you're using one) with the matching nailhole; tap the nail to seat it; clamp the patch as before; and allow the assembly to dry for at least 4 hours.

5 Shape the edge. Remove the clamps and any nails or brads used to hold the patch in place. Using a sharp block plane or belt sander, carefully shape the patch to match the existing surface. Fine-tune the shaping with a sharp chisel, especially for rounded surfaces.

6 Sand the patch. Block-sand the surface using 120-grit sandpaper, again fine-tuning the shape of the patch to the surrounding wood. Finally, block-sand the surface with 180-grit sandpaper, making sure you remove all surface defects, including coarse sanding marks or plane- and chisel-blade marks.

7 Touch up the patch. Remove all fine sanding residue and surface dust using a tack cloth, and fill the wood with paste wood filler if it needs one. (See "Filling Open-Grain Wood," page 144.) Stain the patch and any sanded wood to match the surrounding finish color. After the stain is dry (according to label instructions), apply a coat of finish. Let the finish dry, again according to the label instructions.

Light-sand the area using 320-grit sandpaper. If the patch needs additional touching up, use a pigmented wiping stain to do finer color matching. Use artist's brushes and a soft rag to blend the color on the wood's surface. You can also use aerosol shading stains, available from finishing supply and touch-up supply houses. Apply another coat of finish, and let it dry. Use 280- to 320-grit sandpaper or #0000 steel wool to smooth the surface. Apply as many coats as necessary to build up the new finish to the existing one. Rub the final finish coat down with #0000 steel wool, blending the sheen to the surrounding finish.

2 Use a sharp block plane to smooth the wood surface where you made the saw cut.

3 After cutting a piece of wood for the patch, use the block plane to smooth the surface of the patch that will be joined to the corner until you have a good fit.

6 Block-sand the patch smooth with the adjoining surfaces.

7 Touch up the patch using oil stain to match the surrounding wood color. When the stain is dry, apply finish.

Repairing Chewed Wood Using Filler

Difficulty Level: 🪶🪶🪶

TOOLS AND MATERIALS
- Wood chisel
- Grain filler (if necessary)
- #0000 steel wool; rag
- Sandpaper (80- to 120-grit, 180-grit, and 320-grit)
- Auto-body filler and dry stain
- Touch-up stain and finish
- Artist's brush

1 Clean the damaged area. Use a wood chisel to cut out all loose or damaged wood from the area. Do not smooth the damaged area because a rough surface provides better adhesion for the filler material. If the damaged wood is too smooth, use the chisel to make some cuts in the wood into which the filler can bite.

2 Apply the filler. Put auto-body filler on a mixing board surface (a piece of cardboard will work fine.) You can add dry pigmented stains to the body filler to match the wood color more closely, although this isn't necessary because you can touch up the filler during finishing. Add cream hardener according to the label directions, and mix it into the filler thoroughly. Apply the putty to the damaged area using a palette knife to force it into the rough surface. Fill the entire damaged area. The area may require additional applications of the filler so that it can be shaped to the original surface form.

3 Rough-shape the repair. When the auto-body filler is dry (usually after 5–10 minutes), use a wood chisel to sculpt the patch close to the desired shape.

4 Sand the repair. Next, use 80- to 120-grit sandpaper (with a block if you're sanding flat surfaces) to fine-tune the putty's shape, sanding the edges smooth and flush with surrounding wood. Once you're satisfied with the repair, sand the surface with 180-grit paper to remove course sanding marks.

5 Stain the patch and sanded area. If any of the surrounding wood was sanded and it's open-grain wood, fill the sanded wood and patch area with paste wood filler. Stain the patch and sanded area to match surrounding wood.

6 Apply the finish. Once stain dries, apply a coat of finish. When the finish dries, light-sand the surface with 320-grit paper, and touch up with artist's brushes using pigmented oil stains. You can also use aerosol shading stains to shade the repaired area, blending it into the surrounding finish. Apply as many coats of finish as necessary, using 320-grit paper or #0000 steel wool between coats. Be careful not to cut through the stain color. Rub down the final coat with #0000 steel wool to blend the sheen with the surrounding finish.

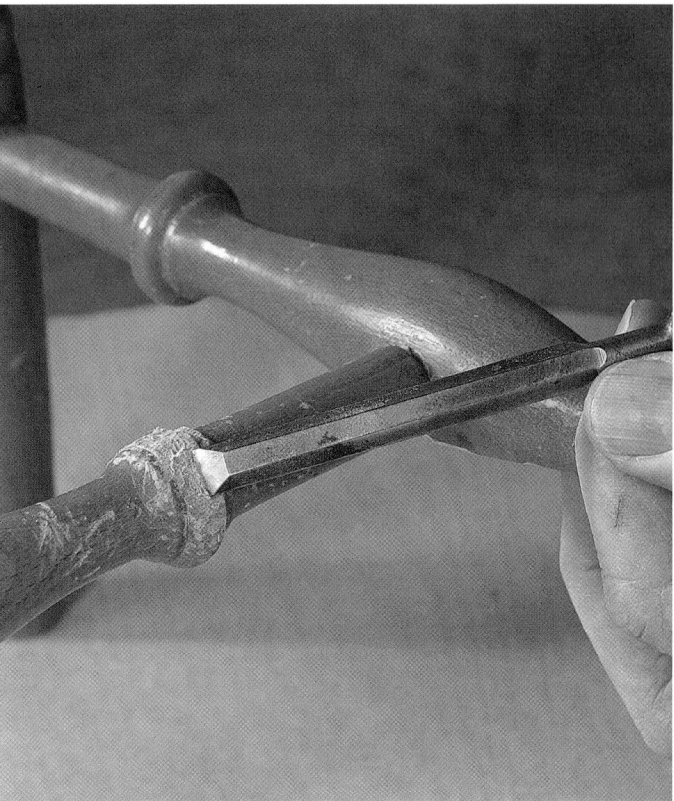

1 Use a wood chisel to cut out any loose wood fibers from the damaged area.

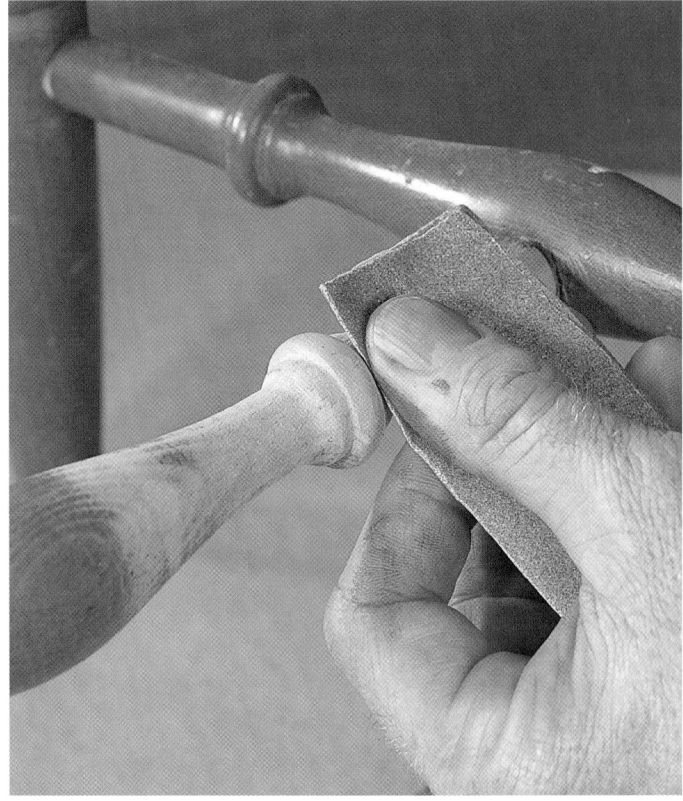

4 Sand the repair smooth with the surrounding wood surface.

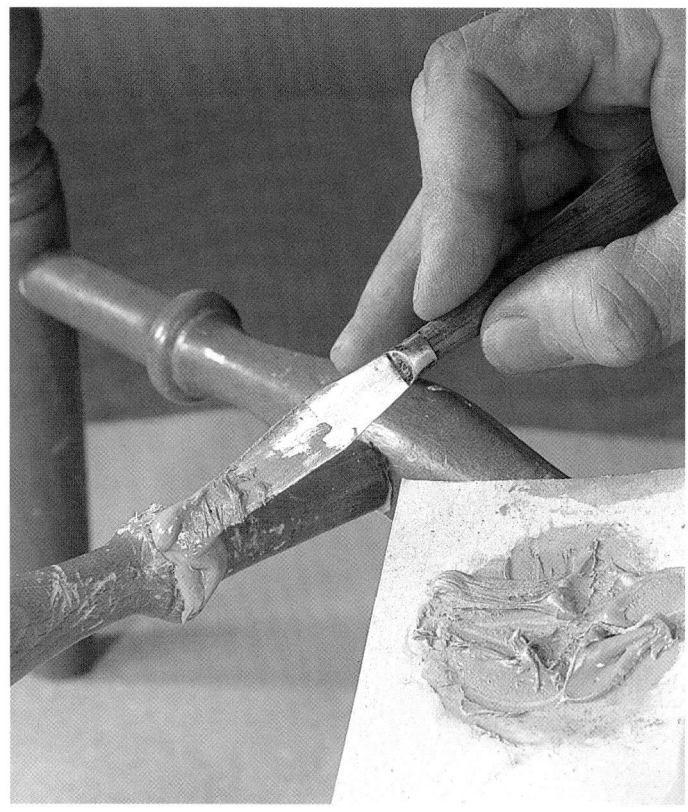

2 Mix the body filler, and apply it to the damaged area, forcing it into the damaged wood surface so that it will adhere well.

3 When the filler is dry, use a wood chisel to shape the filled area to the desired shape.

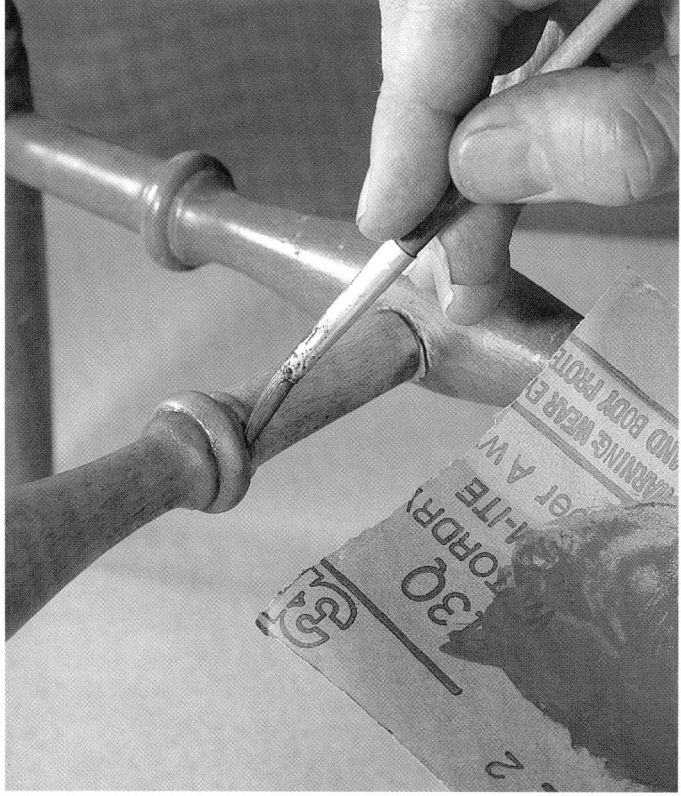

5 Stain the repaired area to match the surrounding wood as closely as possible.

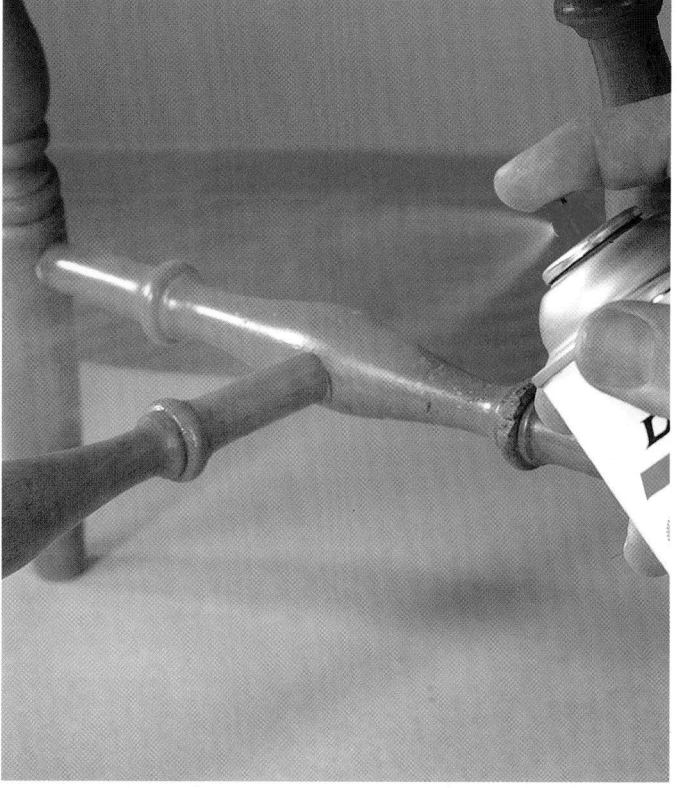

6 Apply as many coats of finish as necessary to blend with the surrounding finish.

10
Stripping and Bleaching Furniture

Stripping, or removing the old finish, is usually the messiest part of furniture restoration. If you don't want any mess at all, you might want to consider having the finish removed by a professional furniture stripper. But because some stripping processes can actually harm furniture, read through this chapter to learn more before making a decision. For certain types of projects, you can save money by doing your own stripping, providing that you have the right materials and supplies.

Remember, stripping and refinishing an antique or collectible can greatly reduce its value. Removing the old finish from a piece of furniture is a drastic step in the restoration process. Before deciding to strip a piece, make sure you can't preserve and renew the original finish.

WHEN TO STRIP THE FINISH

If you've scrutinized the finish and learned it's not original or if the refinishing job is a poor one, you may want to strip and refinish the piece. (See "Is the Finish Original?" page 108.) Another prime candidate for stripping and refinishing is a piece that originally had a wood finish but has since been painted over. Usually you'll find that the paint was applied directly over the original finish. This makes the piece easier to strip because the paint pigments have not penetrated the wood grain. Stripping and refinishing this kind of piece often exposes beautiful wood hidden under an opaque finish.

Keep in mind, however, that some pieces were made to be painted; stripping them usually uncovers inferior or unmatching wood pieces that will not finish well. If the paint has been applied to raw wood, it's usually an indication that the piece was meant to have a painted finish. In such cases you may still need to strip the paint to repaint the piece, or you may be able to simply repaint over the old color. To find out whether the paint was directly applied to the wood surface or atop another finish, scrape the paint or apply solvent to a small, inconspicuous area. If the paint pigment remains in the wood grain, it was probably painted originally; if not, the paint is over a natural wood finish and refinishing may be in order.

Another case for stripping is if the finish is so far gone or damaged that it simply cannot be renewed. Old finishes can become brittle or flaky as a result of age and mistreatment. Finishes can also be damaged by water or fire and often can't be restored without stripping and refinishing. Water can make some finishes lift and discolor permanently, while heat and smoke can blister or blacken finishes. You might also choose to strip and refinish a piece if you don't like the finish color or shade. For example, if you're putting a piece in a par-

Some finishes, like this one, have been damaged to such an extent that they will need to be replaced.

These chairs originally had a clear finish over wood but were painted sometime in the past. Note the chipping, which is common on furniture that wasn't meant to be painted. Stripping these chairs will likely reveal attractive wood.

ticular room or with another piece of furniture, you may want to blend the piece with the rest of the room's decor. But before you do anything, consider the piece itself: if it's valuable and blessed with an original finish, you'd be better off saving the finish and buying another piece of furniture to fill your needs.

STRIPPING METHODS

Once you've decided to strip and finish, what's the best method? Generally speaking, there are three ways to strip wood: with heat, by sanding, or with chemicals. Although each method will work, it is not necessarily the most appropriate choice for stripping some kinds of furniture.

Heat-Stripping the Finish

Stripping with heat means using either a propane torch or a heat gun. In this method, you hold the torch or gun to the finish to bubble and lift it; then remove the finish or paint using a scraper. The idea is to heat the surface just enough to loosen or lift the finish but not enough to burn or scratch the wood underneath.

Although this type of stripping may work fine in some limited applications, such as stripping household exterior woodwork that will be repainted, it is much too dangerous for furniture. If you choose to strip any wood using a heat gun or torch, keep a fire extinguisher close by, and wear an organic vapor mask, goggles, and heat-resistant gloves.

Stripping the Finish by Sanding

Sanding off a finish may seem like a logical approach to stripping, but it turns the job into a laborious, time-consuming task when it doesn't have to be.

Usually a belt sander or some other type of power sander is used to sand a finish off, and much of the wood is also removed in the process. Belt-sanding can leave an uneven wood surface, and it completely destroys the wood's patina, ruining—or nearly ruining—a good piece of furniture. Removing a finish by sanding also produces hazardous dust particles, requiring the use of a mask and goggles.

Chemical Stripping

Various methods are used for chemical stripping, some of which are practical for the do-it-yourselfer. Other methods, such as dipping, are commercial-only applications.

Dipping Methods. One method used by commercial shops is to dip the furniture into a tank of hot caustic solution until the finish is dissolved, then washing it with a neutralizing agent. This process can be damaging to delicate parts and to veneer. It can also loosen joints in the furniture, raise the grain of the wood, and harm the wood's patina. For this reason, I would not recommend hot-tank stripping for most furniture.

Another dipping method uses a cold chemical solution. Sometimes the stripping solution is hosed over the piece of furniture, keeping it wet until the finish is dissolved. Although this method is not as harsh as the hot-tank dipping method and will not loosen joints, it may still raise the wood grain and leave the wood gray or otherwise discolored. It's often difficult to restore the wood's beauty during the finishing process.

Hand Method. Stripping furniture by hand is perhaps the most recognizable method of chemical stripping, and it is the simplest and best method for the do-it-yourselfer. You apply a chemical solvent to the finish, dissolving and/or lifting it, and then either scrub or scrape off the finish by hand. This method requires more work and can be a little slower than commercial dipping, but it has many advantages. The most important advantage is that stripping furniture by hand won't damage furniture as easily as dipping. It doesn't destroy the beauty of the wood and doesn't loosen joints or damage veneer. Also, most finish removers designed for use by hand will not raise the wood grain. All these features mean less work in the finishing process.

The supplies you need for hand stripping are readily available. You can choose from a variety of brands and types of finish removers at home centers, hardware, or paint stores. Read labels carefully to identify which stripper is best for your project.

Methylene Chloride. Chemical removers contain solvents such as toluene, methanol, acetone, and methylene chloride. Other chemicals, such as di-basic esters and N-methyl pyrrolidone are also used and are considered safer because of their slow evaporation rate, among other things. Because methylene chloride is one of the strongest finish-remover chemicals, the more of it in the formula, the more effective the stripper will be; strippers with little or no methylene chloride usually work slower and are classified as solvent wood refinishers rather than finish removers. Methylene chloride is also

Chemical stripping by hand is the simplest and best method for the do-it-yourselfer. The chemical dissolves or lifts the finish, allowing you to scrape or scrub the wood surface clean.

nonflammable, which means the more of it contained in a stripper, the less flammable the stripper. If a remover contains methylene chloride and is labeled nonflammable, you can be sure it contains enough of the chemical to be fast and effective in removing most finishes.

Paint and varnish removers are available in liquid, semipaste, or paste form, so the consistency can be anything from a runny liquid to a gel. The liquid remover works best for horizontal surfaces. Paste or semipaste works well for vertical surfaces due to its clinging ability.

If you need to remove synthetic finishes, such as polyurethanes or epoxies, synthetic finish removers are also available.

Post-Stripping Wash-Down. Some removers contain waxes, which slow down their evaporation time, allowing them to work on the finish surface. These removers require the furniture to be washed down with a solvent such as mineral spirits or lacquer thinner after the finish is removed to clean off any wax residue left on the wood. Other removers contain detergents and require washing the surface with water after the finish is dissolved. But because water can raise wood grain and loosen joints and veneer, you may want to consider using a nonwater-wash remover. Finally, there are also removers, called no-wash removers, that claim to require no after-wash.

Wood Refinishers. Wood refinishers are solvents used to partially remove the finish, leaving a thin film of the original finish on the wood. Doing this preserves the original color and patina of the wood and eliminates many of the steps involved in refinishing. However, they will work only on shellac and lacquer.

Wood is composed of innumerable channel-like fibers packed together. With open-grain wood, the upper fibers form crevices that must be filled for a smooth surface.

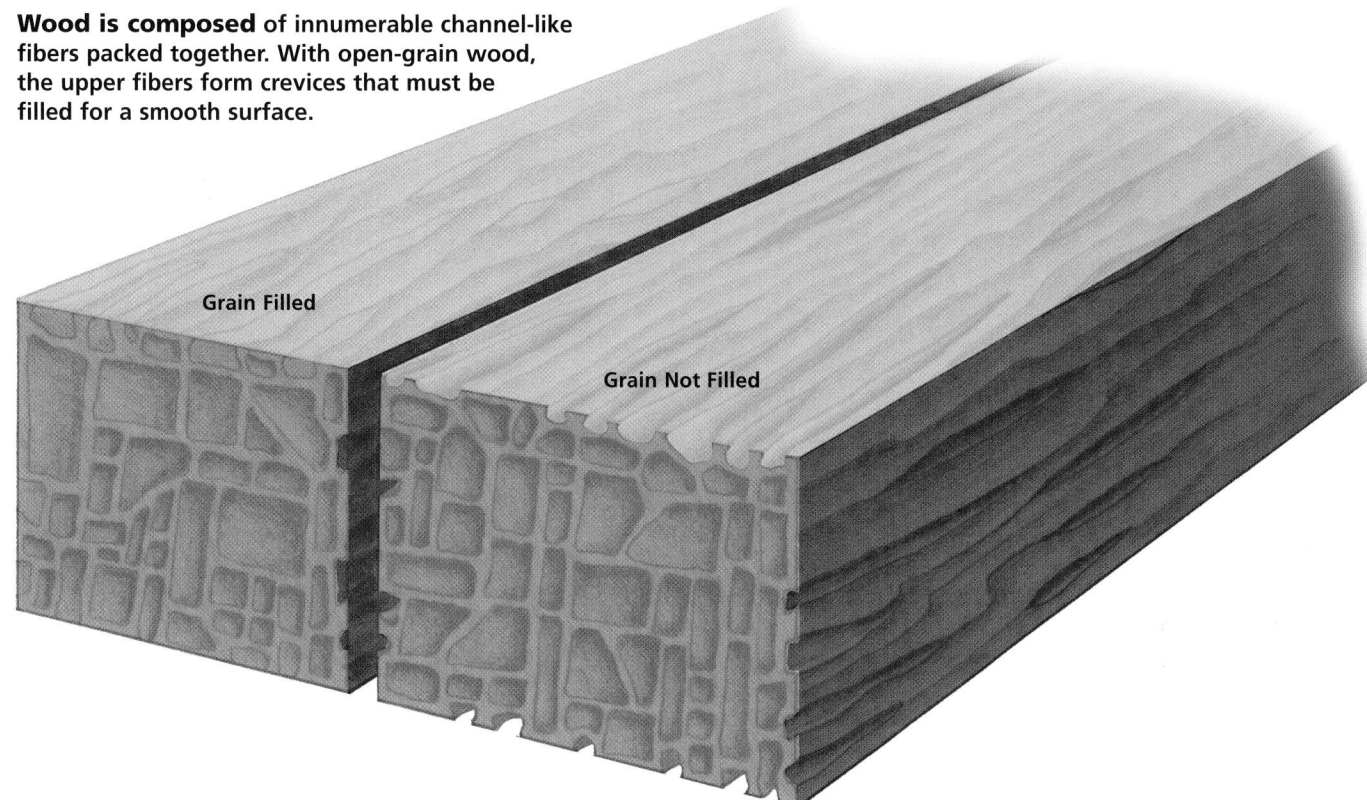

Grain Filled

Grain Not Filled

Another small but potentially important difference is that oil-based filler may not be compatible with water-based finishes, while water-based filler, once dry, is compatible with both water and solvent-based finishes. Whichever filler you decide to use, be sure to read and follow label directions closely.

Filler Color. Wood filler is available in a variety of colors, including natural. While wood filler is not meant to add a lot of color to wood, it will have some effect, primarily in the open grain of the wood because this is where most of the filler stays. If you want the grain to look darker, use a dark-colored filler; if you're trying to de-emphasize the wood grain, making it more subtle, use a lighter-colored filler. Most woods will look better when the filler is a little darker than the wood itself, as this will enhance the grain rather than blend it in with the surrounding wood color.

Staining Before Filling

After stripping and sanding an open-grain wood, the next step is usually to fill the wood. There are some exceptions, however. When you're going to use a dye stain to color the wood, for example, you might want to stain the wood before filling it. The reason for staining before filling in this case is that dye stains must penetrate the wood to color it, and wood filler can hinder this penetration. This is not true when using pigmented stains, because they add color primarily on top of the wood.

One drawback to staining the wood before filling it is that you can cut through the stain color when you sand the wood filler, the last step in the filling process. Such cut-through areas can be difficult to blend in with the surrounding color. Using a water-soluble aniline dye can diminish this difficulty. Use the dye to stain the wood before filling it. You can then use the dye to restain the cut-through surface after you've completed the filling and sanding steps. A water-soluble stain will more easily blend the cut-through areas with the surrounding color.

Sealing Before Filling

Sealing the wood before filling may be necessary if you want to use a dark-colored filler, but you don't want to darken the overall wood color. Sealing the wood first prevents the filler from significantly darkening the wood surface while still allowing it to fill and add prominence to the wood grain.

If you decide to seal the wood surface before filling it, use a thinned coat of lacquer for spray sealing and a thinned coat of shellac for brush sealing. After the sealer coat dries, sand the surface lightly using extra-fine sandpaper (280-grit). After tacking the surface to remove sanding dust, proceed with the filling process.

Filling Open-Grain Wood

Difficulty Level:

TOOLS AND MATERIALS
- Paste wood filler
- Latex gloves
- Paintbrush
- Coarse rags
- 220-grit stearated sandpaper
- Rubber squeegee or plastic scraper
- #0000 steel wool or nylon abrasive pad

Because paste wood filler is so thick, you must thin it to a brushable consistency before applying it to wood. Use mineral spirits or naphtha to thin oil-based filler, and water to thin water-based filler.

1 Apply filler to the wood. Mix filler and thinner in a container until the solution has a thin, creamy consistency. If you're changing the filler color, add the necessary tint. Wearing latex gloves, apply the filler to the wood using a paintbrush (natural bristle for oil-based or synthetic for water-based). It's not important how you brush on the filler as long as you cover the entire wood surface, including cracks and crevices. Apply the filler to one small section of the piece at a time so that you'll have the opportunity to work it into the wood before it dries.

2 Remove excess filler. As soon as the filler begins to dry, use a coarse rag such as burlap to begin removing the excess. Wipe across the grain as much as possible so that you don't pull the filler out of the grain pores.

3 Pack the filler. After you've removed most of the excess filler, use the palms of your gloved hands to pack the filler down into the wood grain, rubbing in a circular or cross-grain motion.

4 Wipe across the grain. Using a clean rag, wipe over the wood surface to remove all excess filler. Wipe across the grain as much as possible to allow the filler to remain in the pores. Also at this point, clean excess filler from any corners, cracks, or crevices. You can use the point of a sharpened dowel to get at the filler, or use a screwdriver tip with a rag pulled over it. Be sure to get the wood surface as clean as possible without removing the filler from the wood grain.

5 Sand the surface. After the filler is completely dry, use 220-grit stearated paper to sand all flat wood surfaces. Sand in the direction of the grain. It's not necessary to sand heavily, only enough to smooth the surface. Rub out all turned or irregular areas with nylon abrasive pads or #0000 steel wool.

1 Use a brush to apply the paste wood filler to the wood. Make sure you cover the entire surface, including cracks and crevices.

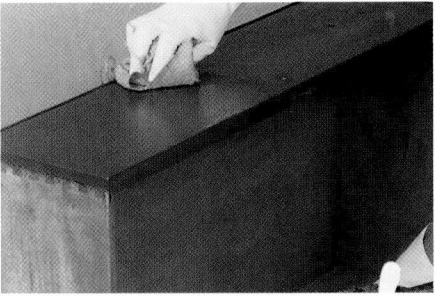

2 As the filler begins to dry and thicken, use a coarse rag to remove the excess by wiping across the wood grain.

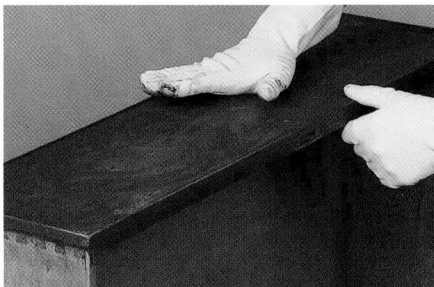

3 Pack the wood filler into the open grain by rubbing in a circular or cross-grain motion with the palm of your hand.

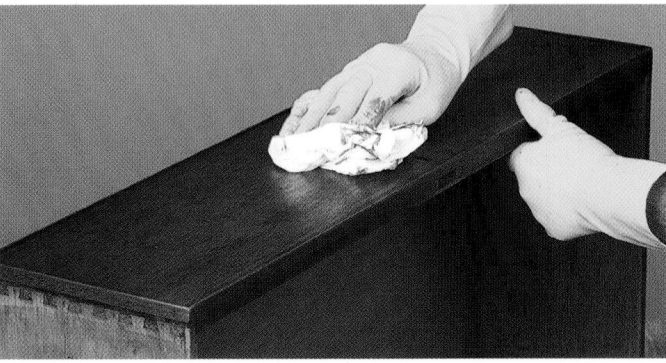

4 Use a clean rag to wipe the wood surface, removing any remaining excess filler. Remove filler from corners, cracks, and crevices.

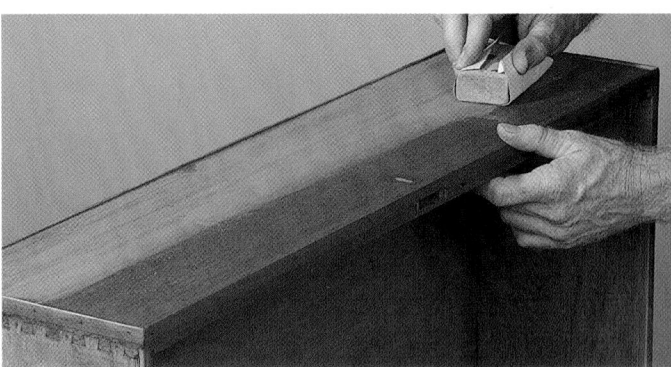

5 When the filler has dried completely, sand flat areas with 220-grit sandpaper to smooth the surface. Smooth out irregular surfaces with an abrasive pad.

STAINING WOOD

Just as mother always said, "the clothes make the man," so also can a finish make a piece of furniture. An otherwise unattractive piece can be greatly improved by an attractive finish. Conversely, a good-looking piece can be ruined by a bad finish.

Because wood color is such a crucial part of the final look of furniture, decisions concerning stain are important. Should the wood be stained in the first place? What type of stain should you use? If you do stain, what color will give you the look you're after?

Some of the answers to these questions can be a matter of personal preference, but others can make your work easier and allow you to get the best look for your particular piece.

Types of Stain

There are a number of stains available. Understanding a little more about them will help you make a choice.

Wood stains fall into two basic categories: dye stain and pigmented stain. Both types are usually thin and runny, making them difficult to work with; however, both are also available in gel form, making them almost foolproof. Manufacturers also offer stains combining both pigment and dye.

Dye Stain. There are three types of dye stain, each determined by its solvent: water soluble, alcohol soluble, and oil soluble. (See "Dye Stain," page 48.) Dye stains are particularly good for coloring wood evenly and enhancing otherwise subtle grain patterns in figured woods such as curly maple or fiddleback cherry. A disadvantage of dye stain is that it fades when exposed

Dye stains are excellent for enhancing otherwise subtle grain patterns, such as the pattern in this maple board.

to stain or not to stain?

Staining isn't always necessary. Some woods, such as walnut or mahogany, have a natural beauty that is revealed by simply applying a clear coat of finish. There are other naturally light woods, such as pine or maple, that you may want to keep that way. You should consider staining, however, if any of the following is true:

- **The wood is ugly and lifeless.** I've seen this happen many times when wood is stripped in preparation for refinishing. The right stain color can greatly enhance a piece in this condition.

- **The piece is constructed of inferior wood.** Many pieces of furniture have been constructed, either partially or totally, using plain-looking woods only to be stained and finished to look like more expensive woods. Prominent parts, such as tops and drawer fronts, often use attractive wood veneers, with a secondary wood used for the other parts. To achieve professional-looking results when refinishing this type of piece, you'll need to stain the secondary wood parts to match the better wood. To determine the natural color of the pri-

mary wood, wet it down with mineral spirits or put a coat of finish only on that part of the piece.

- **The piece is constructed of high-quality wood** but needs to be revitalized or enhanced. Sometimes even quality wood may have lost its vitality. An example of this is when walnut or mahogany has been bleached by sunlight. You might be able to revitalize the wood by staining it with a thinned reddish-colored stain. Other situations may require using stain at full strength to restore the original wood color.

- **The piece needs to match a special finish.** If you want to achieve a particular look you may need to stain the wood. If you're trying to match pieces, such as a desk chair to a desk, wipe the chair down with mineral spirits. This will give you an approximate idea of the stain to use on the chair to match the desk. Then in an inconspicuous area, such as the seat bottom, test the stain you choose for a color match. Compare the stain color while the stain is still wet, or let the stain dry and apply a coat of finish before comparing the color.

to sunlight. Some dye stains can be more difficult to use than pigmented stains, and they're usually harder to find when you try to buy them.

Pigmented Stain. Pigmented stains contain thick color pigments suspended in the stain solution. The amount of color left on the wood can usually be controlled by how the product is wiped after application. To remove more of the color, simply wipe the surface more thoroughly immediately after applying the stain. There are several reasons to choose a pigmented stain. A great variety of them are available, and manufacturers have designed them to be user-friendly. The directions are easy to follow and often yield optimal results.

Gel Stain. Gel stains can be classified under either pigmented or dye stains. (See Gel Stains," page 49.) Thicker in consistency than other kinds of stain, gel stains are easy to apply, produce no drips or runs, are easy to clean up, and provide even color. Just about anybody can use them with satisfactory results.

Pigment-Dye Stain. Some stains contain both pigment and dye. In these stains the dye portion colors the dense parts of wood that the pigment can't penetrate. You can tell whether a stain contains both pigment and dye if, after all the pigment has settled to the bottom of the container, the liquid part of the stain can still color a light piece of wood.

stain application

Although the differences in drying and penetration time for various stains can determine how quickly you must work or how large an area you can stain before wiping, the process itself is similar: saturate the wood with stain, and then wipe off the excess. Regardless of the stain you use, make sure you've prepared the surface properly—once stain is applied, it's difficult to deal with scratches and blemishes.

To check the wood for problems before staining, wet the piece down with mineral spirits and examine closely. Make sure all of the old finish or glue is removed and the wood is free from dust and dirt. Always wear gloves and a respirator while staining.

Washcoat. There is one more element to consider before you apply the stain: a washcoat. (Gel stains will not require this step.) A washcoat partially seals the wood to control stain penetration. Without a washcoat, stain can penetrate too deeply, causing certain areas to become too dark.

For an oil-based stain, you can apply a premixed wood conditioner as a washcoat. Another way to washcoat wood is to apply a coat of thinned shellac.

Applying Dye Stain
If you're using a water-based dye stain, first wet the raw wood with water to raise the grain. After the wood dries, light-sand the surface using 280- to 320-grit sandpaper and begin the staining procedure. If you're using alcohol- or oil-based stain, flood the wood surface with stain using a brush or rag, making sure the stain penetrates all areas well. Wipe off any excess stain with a clean rag.

To darken the color even further, you can mix a

To apply a dye stain, use a brush or rag to flood the wood surface, and then wipe off the excess with a clean, soft rag.

Apply gel stain by covering the wood surface and then wiping off any excess using a rag.

second, deeper color of dye stain and apply it right after the first application. To remove dye stain, use bleach. (See "Removing Stains or Color in the Wood," page 134.)

Applying Gel Stain
Because of gel stain's consistency, you apply it using a rag instead of a brush. It's a good idea to wear protective gloves. Apply the stain to cover the wood surface completely, and then wipe off any excess. Because gel stains add color more slowly and evenly than other types, you don't have to worry about lap marks and other inconsistencies.

Applying Pigmented Stain

Difficulty Level:

TOOLS AND MATERIALS
- Stain
- Respirator
- Cotton rags
- Latex gloves
- Paintbrush

These steps for stain application are general and subject to label instructions for the particular stain you are using.

1 Mix the stain. Stir stain thoroughly until the color pigment is distributed throughout the solvent. It's a good idea to wear protective gloves and a respirator, especially if you're working in less-than-ideal ventilation conditions.

2 Brush on the stain. Using a natural-bristle brush, flood the wood surface with stain, and let it penetrate into the wood for the prescribed amount of time. If necessary, stain one section at a time.

3 Wipe excess stain. Using a clean rag, wipe off the excess stain, going with the grain when possible. To allow the stain to add more color to the wood, use a lighter wiping action, smoothing out the color pigment on the wood surface using a soft rag.

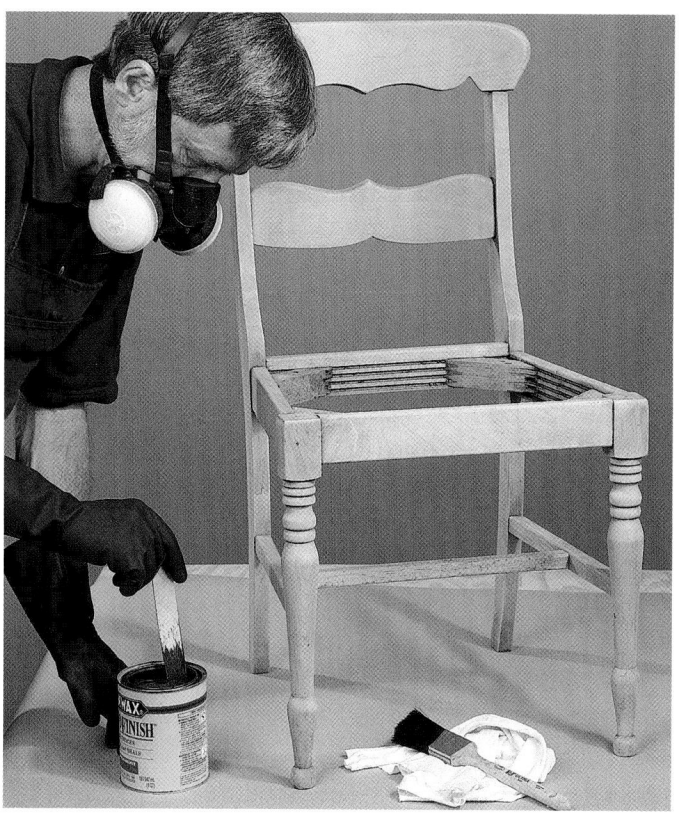

1 When using a pigmented stain, be sure to stir thoroughly to distribute the pigment through the solvent.

2 Use a natural-bristle brush to cover the wood surface completely with the stain.

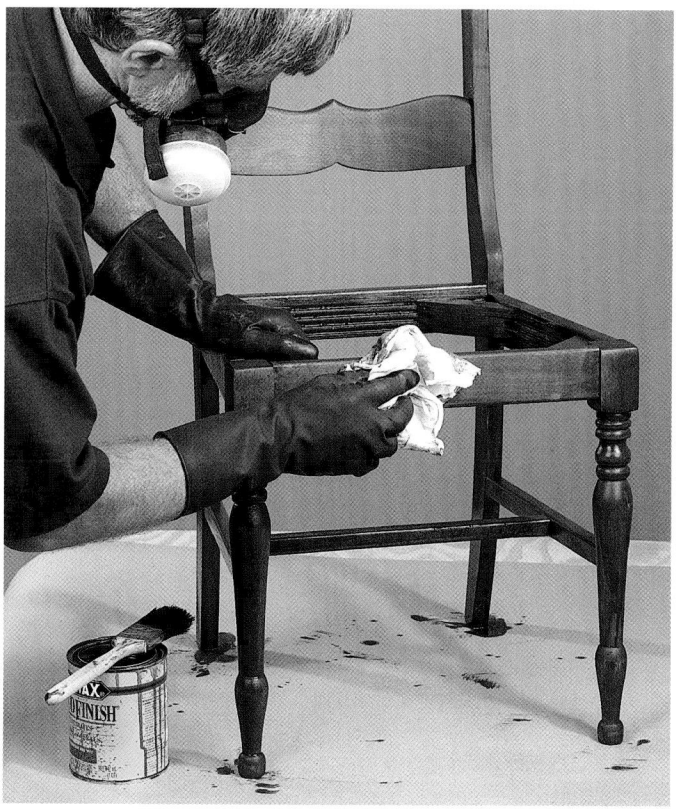

3 Use a clean, soft rag to wipe off any stain that hasn't penetrated the wood surface.

13
Applying a Finish

For someone restoring a piece of furniture, the refinishing process is usually the most rewarding phase. After all, the finish coat not only protects your investment, but can make all the difference in the appearance of a piece of wood. Even if you have spent hours stripping, sanding, filling, and staining, your project may still look dull and lifeless—until the moment the finish makes contact with the wood. Then, suddenly, the piece jumps to life, revealing its hidden beauty.

FINISH BASICS

The search for the ideal finish has continued for centuries, and although many finishes have been developed, none is perfect. Because no finish will suit every situation, you'll have to make compromises-mises when you choose one. Keep this fact in mind when you make your decision.

The finishes covered in this book are

- Shellac

- Lacquer and its variations

- Varnish and its variations

- Oil finishes

- Waterborne finishes

- Paint

- Wax

All these finishes have their strengths and weaknesses, as you will learn in this chapter. Some finishes are easy to apply and maintain but offer little protection; others give excellent protection but can be difficult to apply or keep up. Some finishes penetrate the wood more deeply than others. Some finishes can be wiped on; some can be brushed; and others are better sprayed.

Whatever finish and application method you use, you must make sure conditions are as favorable as possible for you to achieve good results. Minimize dust as much as you can. Use a tack cloth on the surface of the piece before applying, dust all surfaces, and thoroughly sweep or vacuum the floor. After cleaning, use a spray bottle of water to mist the floor if possible to help hold down any additional dust kicked up by movement. You can also reduce the possibility of airborne dust particles by waiting until the end of the day to apply your finish.

Next, make sure you have adequate ventilation. Also, try to establish a stable temperature and humidity level in the finish area. Most finishes work best at room temperature with a low relative humidity level. Although it may be hard to control temperature conditions totally, try to make conditions as favorable as possible.

Finally, set up your workspace lighting to allow light to fall across the surface of your project so you can see how the finish is going on. Put the piece you're finishing between you and the light. As the light reflects across the surface you're finishing, it will show clearly how the finish is going on and let you deal with any problems or missed areas.

Choosing a Finish

Even though you might not come up with a finish that meets all your demands, you can certainly find one that satisfies the most important ones. Ask yourself the following questions as you decide on the right finish for your piece:

• **What will the finish look like?** One of the main reasons you're finishing is to beautify the wood. Consider whether the type of finish you'd like to use is appropriate for your piece. A traditional-style piece, for example, may look better with a classic-looking film finish, such as shellac, lacquer, or varnish. Other pieces might lend themselves better to a penetrating finish such as tung oil or Danish oil. The bottom line is: will you be satisfied with how the finished product looks after all your work is done?

• **What kind of protection will the finish provide?** Do you need maximum protection, or is that a minimal consideration for the piece? To decide, consider where and how the piece will be used. If the piece will be placed in a room mainly for decoration and will receive little use, protection is not a primary consideration. Pieces such as cabinets or wall curios might fall into this category. But if the piece is used frequently, protection is vital. Table, chest, and dresser tops, for example, usually need a tough, durable water- and alcohol-resistant finish.

• **How difficult is it to apply?** Some finishes may require special skills and/or equipment. (See the application section for each type of finish.) Even though this question doesn't have anything to do with the purpose of a finish, it can be an important one to answer before beginning your project. Count the cost in terms of ability, time, and equipment before using a particular finish.

• **How repairable is the finish?** Oil and wax finishes are easy to fix, usually by just adding more finish, but film finishes are more tedious to repair. If there's a good possibility of damage or wear on your particular piece, then this is an important factor to consider when choosing a finish.

PAD-ON AND WIPE-ON FINISHES

French polishing involves applying shellac with a padded cloth, and is considered a *pad-on* finish. (See page 150.) The technique is tricky to master, but this finish is much more durable than wax or penetrating oil. But if you want the easiest finishing job and you're not concerned with protection and durability, use a *wipe-on* finish such as paste wax or one of the oil formulations.

applying a paste wax finish

You can apply a wax finish directly to raw, unfinished wood or wood that's been sealed with a thin coat of shellac. Good furniture paste waxes are available in clear and tinted forms. (See "Wax," page 57.) Depending on the look you want, you can use either kind.

Be sure the wood surface has been properly prepared. If you want to seal the wood before applying the wax, first put on a thin coat of shellac. After the sealer coat is dry, rub the surface down with #0000 steel wool to smooth it. Remove all steel-wool residue and dust using a tack rag, and then apply the wax. (See "Applying Paste Wax," page 112.)

Maintenance. You can usually repair a wax finish by simply applying another coat of wax. But to maintain a wax finish, it's a good idea to wash off the old wax every year or so and reapply the finish. This will prevent wax buildup and discoloration of the wax over time.

French Polishing

French polishing is the process of building up a finish by padding on many thin layers of shellac. This method originated hundreds of years ago and has produced some of the most beautiful furniture finishes ever seen. When done properly, the finish produces unusual depth and richness in the wood, almost impossible to create with other finishes. If enough steps are taken, you can build up a glass-like finish while maintaining a soft, natural luster. Because French polishing could almost be considered an art, it will take practice to perfect the skill before committing to try it out on a good piece of furniture.

For this padding technique, the shellac mixture—the polish—should be a 1- to 2½-pound mixture. The thinner the mixture, the easier the application, but the more coats it will require to build up the finish. While learning the padding method, start with a thin mixture (1-pound cut) until you get the hang of it; then you can progress to using the thicker cut.

Before you start, prepare the wood for finishing. When working on new wood, seal it with a coat of boiled linseed oil or tung oil. This isn't necessary when you're refinishing wood—you can begin by applying the shellac. The first shellac coat can be applied by pad or brush, as long as it's sufficiently thinned so it won't leave brush marks. Put the shellac mixture in a plastic squeeze bottle or a small-mouth jar so that you can control the amount dispensed onto the pad. While there are some variations in French polishing methods, you can follow the basic steps outlined here to achieve a fine finish.

alternative to French polish

A modern alternative to French polish is padding lacquer. Padding lacquer can be bought from finishing supply companies under a variety of names (Rapid Pad, Pad Lac, and Lacover, among others). Padding lacquer is actually a misnomer. It's really a premixed, shellac-based finish especially formulated as a pad-on finish. The material works well, is easy to use, and produces results similar to those of shellac. Padding lacquer can also be used to pad over existing finishes if you're recoating and touching up an area. Applied as you would French polish, padding lacquer dries and builds up quickly.

Difficulty Level:

TOOLS AND MATERIALS
- Cotton cloths
- Thinned shellac
- Latex gloves
- #0000 steel wool
- Mineral or linseed oil
- 320-grit stearated sandpaper
- Tack rag

1 Make the pad. The shellac is applied with a special pad made up of a wad of absorbent material (soft wool or cotton) wrapped in a lint-free, bleached, cotton cloth. The interior wadding can be of the same material, as long as it's absorbent. Ball up the wadding and wrap it inside the cotton cloth to form a pear-shaped pad about the size of a large egg. Pull the cloth tight around the wad to form a wrinkle-free surface.

When holding the pad, the loose ends of the cloth—which are pulled together around the absorbent wadding—should face up into your hand, while the smooth portion of the pad faces down. It needs to be clean, smooth, and wrinkle-free; otherwise defects will show up in your finish. When you're not using the pad, store it in an airtight container, such as a small jar with a screw-on lid. The pad will not dry out, and you'll be able to use it whenever you need it.

2 Disperse the finish. Before you actually apply the shellac, dampen the applicator with denatured alcohol and then with the shellac mixture. Disperse the mixture by tapping the pad several times into the palm of your other hand. (It may be a good idea to wear gloves to protect your hands).

3 Apply the finish. Pad the shellac onto the wood surface in the direction of the grain. The applicator should always be in motion when it comes in contact with the wood; otherwise it will leave print marks wherever it stops. The padding motion should resemble a pendulum, swinging down to the wood surface, making contact, moving across the surface, and lifting off the other side, all in one sweep. If the pad begins to get too dry, recharge it with the shellac.

Once you have covered the entire surface, begin the process again. Continue padding the shellac until the surface becomes tacky and the applicator pad begins to stick when it comes in contact with the surface. Seal the applicator pad in an airtight container, and let the finish dry for at least an hour.

After the finish is dry, use 320-grit stearated aluminum oxide paper to scuff-sand the surface. Scuff sanding means to sand lightly and only enough to smooth the surface. Follow the sandpaper by rubbing over the surface with #000 or #0000 steel wool or a fine nylon abrasive pad. Wipe the surface with a tack cloth, making sure it's free of dust and steel-wool particles. Then apply shellac as before by padding it on. As the pad begins to dry, change the direction of the padding motion from straight, pendulum-like strokes with the grain to small, circular strokes. Next go to figure-eight strokes and then back to straight-with-the-grain strokes. Changing the padding motion helps to spread out and level the finish, preventing it from forming ridges that you'll have to sand out later.

Continue adding shellac to the applicator pad and padding it onto the surface. Don't make the pad too wet or apply the finish with too much pressure, as this could begin to dissolve and cut through the previous shellac coat. The idea is to pad the shellac onto the sur-

face in such a way as to build up each coat on top of the previous one. As the finish begins to get tacky, stop and let it dry overnight.

At this point, the finish should be smooth enough to apply the next coat without sanding or rubbing. Apply the finish again, and allow it to dry overnight. Repeat as often as necessary to build up to the desired finish.

After the final application there may be some oil residue on the surface. To remove it, make a new applicator pad and slightly dampen it with denatured alcohol. Use light, straight, with-the-grain strokes to pick up the oil. If a satin sheen is desired, let the finish dry for several days and rub it down with the grain using #0000 steel wool pad followed by buffing using a soft, clean cloth.

1 The French polish pad is made up of a wad of absorbent material wrapped inside a cotton cloth.

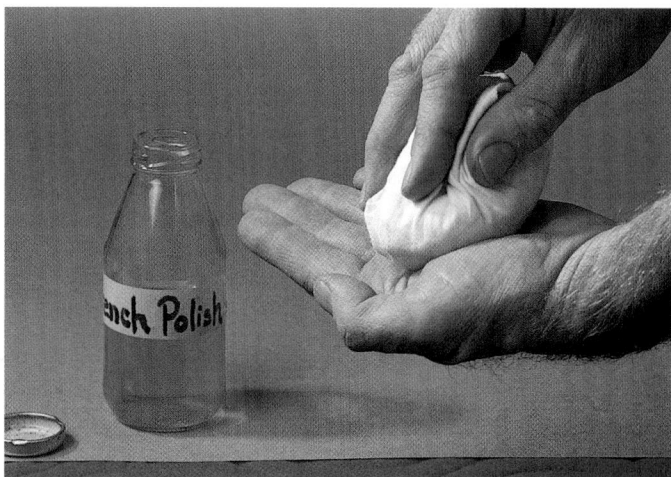

2 Dampen the pad with finish, and disperse it by tapping the pad into the palm of your hand.

3 Pad the shellac onto the surface by using a pendulum motion, keeping the pad constantly moving (above, left to right). Apply repeated coats until the finish is built up sufficiently. Scuff-sand between coats with 320-girt stearated sandpaper. Lastly, rub the surface down with #000 or #0000 steel wool dipped in paste wax followed by a good buffing with a soft, clean cloth.

Applying an Oil Finish

You can apply a number of different oil finishes by using the same basic procedure, which is detailed in the step-by-step instructions that follow. The main difference in applying these oil finishes is the drying time each requires; look for this specific information on the container label.

You can apply oil finishes using a brush, roller, or lint-free cloth. Some manufacturers even suggest using your hands to apply it. If the piece you're finishing is large, you may need to complete several of the finishing steps on one section before moving on to the next so you have plenty of time to work before the finish begins to dry. When finishing with oil, it's also helpful to warm the oil before application because warm oil penetrates wood better. To warm, place the container of oil in a pan of hot water for a few minutes.

Difficulty Level:

TOOLS AND MATERIALS
- Oil finish
- #0000 steel wool
- Cotton cloths
- Tack rag

1 Apply the oil. Be sure the wood is prepared for finishing, including staining if necessary, and that the surface has been dusted with a tack rag. Apply the oil liberally to the wood's surface, letting it penetrate for the prescribed amount of time (usually about 15 minutes). If the surface does not appear uniform after the oil begins to penetrate, apply more oil to dry areas.

2 Wipe the surface dry. Allow the oil to penetrate into the wood for a few minutes. Wipe away excess oil with a clean, soft cloth before the finish totally dries.

3 Rub the finish with steel wool. After allowing the oil to dry for the prescribed amount of time—usually 1 hour to overnight—rub the surface down using #0000 steel wool. The finish must be thoroughly dry before you begin this step.

4 Rub the finish with a tack cloth. Dust the surface with a tack rag, and repeat Steps 1, 2, and 3 as many times as necessary to get the look you want. Most problems in an oil finish (nicks, scratches, etc.) can be covered by simply applying another coat of oil finish. Oil finishes can be renewed about once a year or so by applying more of the same finish.

1 Use a cotton cloth to apply the oil finish liberally to the wood's surface.

2 After the oil has had time to penetrate into the wood, use a clean cloth to wipe away any excess.

3 When the oil has dried, use #0000 steel wool to rub the surface down.

4 Tack the surface, and repeat Steps 1, 2, and 3 until you are satisfied with the final look.

BRUSHED AND SPRAYED CLEAR FINISHES

Brushing Shellac

Brushing on a shellac finish is a simple method that can produce excellent results with a minimum of work and trouble. When applying shellac with a brush, work over one area at a time before moving on to the next. Use the brush to lay the shellac on the surface, overlapping the strokes and brushing with the direction of the wood grain when possible. Don't try to brush over areas once they have been coated because the finish usually will have already begun to dry.

Thin the first coat of shellac to about a 1-pound cut to act as a sealer coat; this means if you buy premixed shellac, you may have to thin it by adding denatured alcohol. To get a 1-pound cut of shellac from a 3-pound mixture, for example, you'll need to mix one part of the 3-pound shellac to 1⅓ parts of denatured alcohol. Most shellac containers provide mixing formulas.

It's not crucial that the first coat be a 1-pound cut mixture as long as you thin it to about half the thickness of successive coats. The thinner the mix, the easier it will be to work with, but more coats will be required.

Difficulty Level:

TOOLS AND MATERIALS
- Thinned shellac
- Latex gloves
- Tack rag
- 280- to 320-grit stearated sandpaper
- Cotton cloths
- #0000 steel wool
- Pure bristle brush

1 Brush on the shellac. Prepare the wood surface for finishing, and clean off all dust, tacking the surface. Apply the first coat of shellac with a brush after thinning it with denatured alcohol.

2 Sand the surface. After the first coat is dry— about ½ to 1 hour—scuff-sand the surface with very fine (280- to 320-grit) stearated sandpaper. If you've shellacked over a stained surface, be careful not to cut through the finish when sanding and remove the stain color. Wipe a tack cloth over the surface to remove dust, and then brush on a coat of unthinned shellac. Let the second coat dry for an hour or longer; then scuff-sand the surface with the same-grit sandpaper as before. Continue coating and sanding until the finish is sufficiently built up—this usually will mean a total of three or four coats. Allow more drying time between each succeeding coat (for example, first coat: ½ to 1 hour; second: 1 to 2 hours).

3 Finish the last coat. Rub the last coat down with #0000 steel wool for a satin sheen. If you want a semi-gloss sheen, wait one or two days for the finish to cure after the last coat, and apply paste wax with a #0000 steel-wool pad. Buff it with a soft cloth. For a gloss sheen, allow the wax to completely harden (about 1 hour), and polish the surface using a lamb's-wool pad.

1 Apply the shellac with a pure bristle brush. Brush in the direction of the wood grain whenever possible.

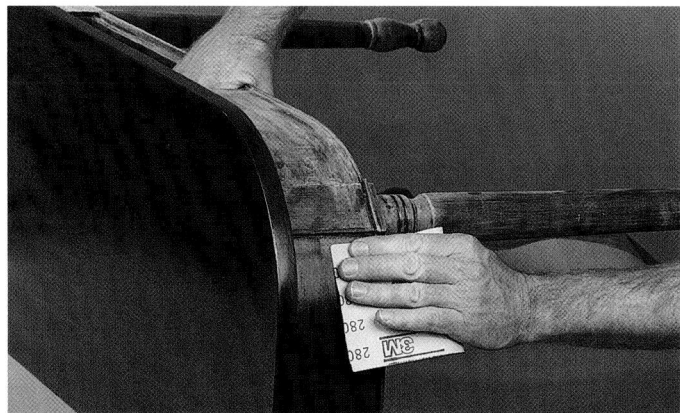

2 When the shellac is dry, use 280-grit stearated sandpaper to scuff-sand the surface.

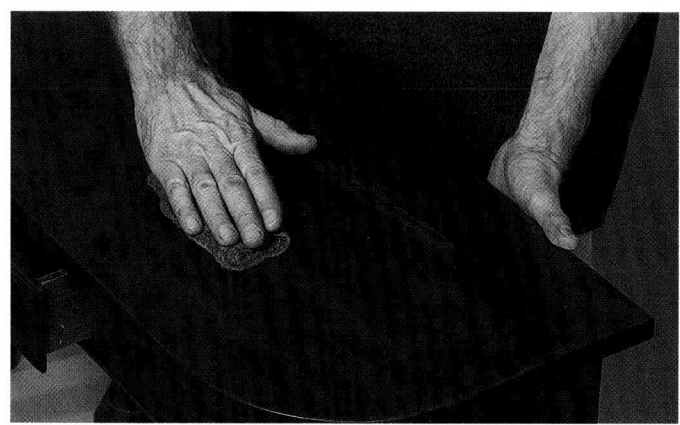

3 After applying the last coat, rub the surface down with #0000 steel wool for a satin sheen.

Applying a Lacquer Finish

Because lacquer is fast-drying, it's easier sprayed than brushed, and thus may not be the best choice for the do-it-yourselfer. This quick-drying characteristic can be a definite advantage, however, in that the finish will pick up few airborne dust particles before it dries, making for less work when trying to achieve smooth, profession-al-looking results. If you are willing to practice with lacquer to get the knack of applying it, you may find that you like using it better than other, slower-drying finishes. Since lacquer is available in various sheens, decide which is best for your piece before applying it.

Preparing to Spray Lacquer. If you plan to spray lacquer, remember that it's important to have the proper equipment, including a quality spray gun, an air compressor with hoses and air gauge, a safety-approved exhaust system with an explosion-proof fan and lights, and a good-quality, organic-cartridge respirator mask. Don't spray near open flames or sparks to avoid explosion or fire. When spraying, place the object between you and the exhaust fan, allowing you to spray in the direction

PRO TIP: controlling runs

Lacquer doesn't run easily because it dries quickly; however, runs are still possible. For example, if you stop moving the gun across the surface while depressing the trigger, too much finish could build in one spot and cause a run. Also, if you pass over the same spot too many times, such as on crosspieces or corners, the finish could run. You can control run problems by releasing the trigger whenever the gun is stopped or when it passes over previously sprayed areas.

When you begin spraying a piece of furniture, start with the less visible areas first, such as inside cabinets and drawers or under shelves. When spraying tops, spray the edges first. This strategy will keep any overspray to a minimum on the most visible parts of the furniture by coating them last. Before spraying lacquer, it might be necessary to add retarder solvent and a fisheye eliminator to prevent problems before they begin. (See "Lacquer," page 52.)

You should strain the finish through a paint strainer/filter before spraying it; these filters are available at paint stores. When you finish spraying, run some lacquer thinner through the gun to clean it. Occasionally, you may also have to take the gun apart to clean it.

of the fan. The spray gun should be aimed at the surface at a 90-degree angle from about 7 or 8 inches away. Keep the gun moving at a consistent speed while spraying, and keep it parallel with the surface being sprayed.

The spray gun will have several adjustment knobs; use them to adjust the spray (fan) pattern and the volume of fluid coming through the gun. For most finishing jobs, you'll need a rather wide fan pattern to cover the surface quickly. Test the fan pattern and the amount of finish being sprayed on, using scrap wood or a piece of cardboard. Make the adjustments so that the gun produces a full, wet coat when you're moving it across the work at moderate speed. This adjustment may require some trial and error to get it right.

The air cap on the nozzle of the gun can be turned to produce a vertical spray pattern for covering horizontal surfaces or a horizontal spray pattern for spraying vertical surfaces. When spraying lacquer, look closely at how the finish is going on the wood, and allow each pass to overlap the previous one by one-half. This will prevent any dry areas and ensure an even, wet coat of finish.

Spraying Lacquer. Prepare the wood for finishing. Tack the surface to remove dust particles, and spray a coat of lacquer sanding sealer on the piece. Allow the sealer to dry thoroughly; then sand the surface using 280- to 320-grit stearated silicone carbide paper. (If you're trying to get a slick, poreless lacquer finish, repeat this step to build up the sealer in the open grain until it's level with the surrounding surface. Sanding with 280- to 320-grit stearated paper after each sealer coat allows the sealer to build up in the open grain.) Tack the surface to remove dust; then spray a coat of lacquer onto the surface.

Allow the finish to dry at least 1 hour, and rub the piece down with #000 steel wool, smoothing the surface. Tack the piece again to remove all dust, and spray on another lacquer coat. After the finish dries for 1 to 2 hours, rub it down—if you desire—with #0000 steel wool, and then spray on another coat. After applying the final lacquer coat, allow the surface to dry overnight, and use #0000 steel wool to rub down the finish with the grain. For a waxed finish, allow the finish to dry for several days, and apply the wax with #0000 steel wool, rubbing with the grain, followed by a buffing with a clean, soft rag. To increase the shine, polish with a lamb's-wool attachment on an electric drill. (For other final finish treatments, see Chapter 14, "Finishing Touches," beginning on page 160, and follow specific instructions for desired sheens.)

Brushing Lacquer. Because the solvents in brushing lacquer are so strong that they can melt a synthetic-bristle brush, use a natural-bristle paintbrush for this application. The solvents can also have an adverse effect on pigmented wiping stains or oil-based fillers, causing them to partially dissolve, particularly as the lacquer is brushed on. They can also cause natural oils in some woods, such as rosewood or dark mahogany, to bleed. To prevent problems such as these, seal the wood surface with shellac before applying lacquer.

When applying multiple coats of brush lacquer, allow each coat enough time to dry completely before applying the next coat. Otherwise, each successive coat will have a tendency to soften and dissolve the previous one. The longer you let the previous coat dry, the less likely you are to experience this problem. One hour is usually sufficient unless the label instructs otherwise. Once you've sealed the surface, lightly scuff-sand it using 280- to 320-grit stearated silicone carbide paper, being careful not to cut through the shellac to the raw wood surface beneath.

After tacking the surface to remove dust, lay the piece to be finished horizontally if possible. Using a natural-bristle brush, apply a brush coat of lacquer with long, straight, slightly overlapping strokes. Don't try to brush the finish out as you would varnish or paint. Apply the finish by laying it on, working over one section at a time without rebrushing areas already coated. Allow the finish to dry at least for the amount of time prescribed by label directions, and then scuff-sand it with 280- to 320-grit stearated silicone carbide paper to remove any dust or rough areas.

Rub the surface down with a tack cloth; then apply another brush coat of lacquer and let it dry. If the finish is built up sufficiently at this point and it has dried overnight, use #0000 steel wool to rub it down in the direction of the wood grain to produce a satin sheen. To produce a gloss sheen, wait a few days, rub the surface down with paste wax on #0000 steel wool, and buff it using a soft, clean rag followed by a lamb's-wool attachment in an electric drill. If more finish is needed, brush on another coat before the final rubdown or waxing.

Applying a Varnish Finish

In the same way that lacquer can be considered a finish made for a spray gun, varnish is a finish made for a brush. Even though some modern varnishes such as polyurethane have considerably faster drying times than older formulations, they're still slow drying compared with lacquer. This slowness to dry allows the finisher ample working time during brush application. If you want a tough film finish and your only choice of applicator is a brush, consider a varnish finish. Varnish is a high-solids finish that will build on wood surfaces

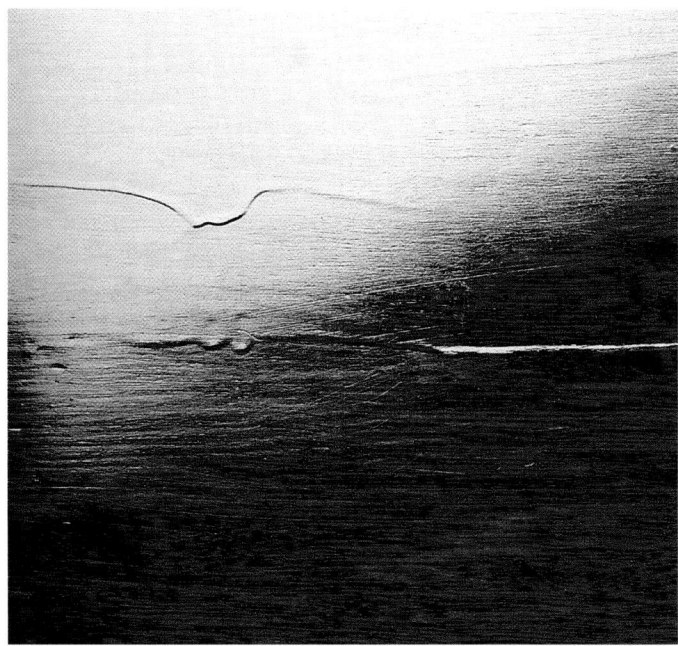

When working with varnish—or any slow-drying finish—view the surface in reflected light (above) so you can easily see any problems in the finish. Try to place the work horizontally to reduce the risk of runs, sags, and drips.

fairly quickly. But because it's slow drying, you'll have to deal with dust and debris that settles in the finish as it dries. To address this problem and guarantee good adhesion, you must sand between finish coats and sand, rub, or polish the final coat.

Although varnish, like lacquer, is available in various sheens, you can also control the sheen via the final rubbing or polishing process. (See "Finishing Touches," beginning on page 160.)

Preparation. If you're preparing to apply a varnish finish, it's important to have as dust-free an environment as possible. Turn off any blowers or fans, and don't work in an area where air is moving. Dust the entire work area, including the workbench and floor. Also, dust the piece you'll be finishing, and make sure that cracks, crevices, and even the wood grain are dust-free. If you have an air compressor with an air nozzle, you can get rid of dust from the area by blowing it out; if not, a vacuum cleaner with a brush attachment will work. You can also spray a mist of water on your bench and floor to hold the dust down.

After cleaning, give any airborne dust time to settle before you start finishing. A good time to apply a varnish finish is just before you leave the workroom for the day. This gives the finish time to dry without additional dust being kicked up by movement in your work area.

Lighting is also important when applying a varnish finish. Place the piece you're finishing between you and the light source so you can see the light reflecting across the finish surface. This will reveal how the finish is going on the piece. If possible, always place the work to be finished horizontally to reduce the possibility of runs, sags, or drips. Horizontal placement also gives the finish opportunity to flow out and level itself while drying; this may require partial disassembly, such as removing doors and drawers in order to lay them in a horizontal position.

When mixing varnish, stir it rather than shake it; shaking varnish can produce bubbles that will remain in the finish when it's applied to wood. The best brush to use is a good-quality china bristle brush; the finer the bristles, the less you'll have to contend with brush marks. Make sure the brush is clean and that it does not have old paint particles in it, which could ruin your finish. Make sure there are no loose bristles by flexing the brush on your hand a few times and then by vigorously brushing a clean surface with it.

PRO TIP: irregular surfaces

When applying varnish to irregular areas, use a fairly dry brush and follow these instructions:

■ **Turnings (round legs and spindles).** Apply the varnish by brushing across the turning and then by brushing lengthwise to smooth out the finish.

■ **Carvings.** Apply varnish to the carved area, making sure to get it into all cracks and crevices. Unload the brush of finish, and use it to brush out excess finish from the carving.

■ **Moldings.** Moldings can usually be finished by simply brushing the varnish lengthwise in the direction of the molding.

■ **Door panels.** Brush varnish first on the panel and then on the panel edge, the inside frame edge, the frame itself, and the outer edges.

■ **Inside corners and edges.** When finishing an inside corner on a panel, start the brush stroke in the corner and work outward. Avoid dragging the brush over panel edges, as this will cause drips and runs, and excess finish will form along the edge. Begin the brush stroke on the flat part of the panel away from the edge and brush toward it. Lift the brush just as it reaches the edge.

Soak the brush briefly in the correct finish solvent, and remove the excess from the brush before dipping it in the varnish. Soaking helps condition the bristles to accept the varnish and makes cleanup easier. When you load the brush with the finish, dip the bristles about one-third to one-half way into the finish, and then flex the brush on the inside of the can to work the varnish into the brush. Don't drag the brush across the rim, which can produce bubbles. Use a 2- to 2½-inch brush for large, flat areas and a smaller brush for detailed or irregular areas. To get rid of dust particles, hair, or lint from a freshly varnished surface that has not begun to dry, use a pointed artist's brush that has been made tacky with varnish. Lightly touch the particle with the brush's tip to remove it.

Application. Initially, apply the varnish to a prepared surface by brushing diagonally across the grain in short strokes to help spread the finish. Then, brushing with the grain, hold the brush almost perpendicular, and drag it lightly across the surface in the direction of the grain. Work over one area at a time until the entire surface is complete. Before the varnish begins to dry, unload the brush of varnish, and tip off the finish by again holding the brush at a right angle to the surface. Lightly drag the tip all the way across the surface in the direction of the grain. Begin your strokes in the air before lowering the brush onto the surface, and lift the brush off the surface immediately when reaching the other edge.

Allow the first varnish coat to dry, usually for 24 hours. Sanding varnish before it's dried sufficiently can damage

Paint can be a beautiful furniture finish for chairs, tabletops, and cabinets. It's a good idea to seal the wood and use a primer when applying paint.

PRO TIP: other paint primers

Thinned shellac can be used as an undercoat for any type of paint, and can accomplish several objectives. It seals the wood surface while slightly raising wood grain for a final preparatory sanding with fine sandpaper. Shellac also acts as a good barrier coat to prevent any contaminants or resins from wood knots, as in pine, from bleeding into the finish. Thinned shellac can provide a barrier coat if you're painting over another finish or paint that may not be compatible with the paint you are using. Finally, sealing the wood with shellac is also helpful if you think you may want to refinish the piece in a natural wood finish in the future; the shellac will prevent paint pigments from penetrating the wood grain, which could make it very difficult to remove later.

There are two other primer alternatives that work well. **Alkyd enamels** can be thinned like varnish and used as their own undercoating before applying the paint full strength. **Latex paint** can also act as a self-primer, as long as it isn't thinned. When the first coat is applied to raw wood, the grain will usually become raised, requiring a good sanding with fine paper before recoating.

the finish coat and may require refinishing. Scuff-sand the finish with 280-grit stearated silicone carbide paper to remove any roughness or dust and to provide inter-coat adhesion. Use a tack rag to remove all dust, and then apply a second coat of unthinned varnish.

After allowing the varnish to dry for 24 hours, again sand the finish with 280-grit paper. Use a felt sanding block on flat areas. Continue applying varnish for up to four coats, depending on the amount of film buildup you want. On the last coat, don't sand the varnish with 280-grit paper; instead, let it dry for 72 hours, and then sand the finish with 600-grit wet-or-dry sandpaper, using soapy water or mineral spirits as a lubricant. Give the surface a good rubdown with #0000 steel wool in the direction of the grain; then wipe the finish down with a clean, soft cloth. (Other final rubbing/polishing methods can also be used to produce a variety of effects; see Chapter 14, "Finishing Touches," beginning on page 160.)

PAINT FINISHES

Application methods for paint finishes vary, depending on the type of paint used. A variety of paints, including opaque lacquers, are suitable for painting furniture. Oil and latex paints can be applied by brush. Colored lacquers will usually need to be sprayed on.

No matter which paint you decide to use, preparing the wood surface before you begin is just as important as it is with transparent finishes. Although paint can hide many objectionable stains or unwanted color variations,

it cannot hide dents, nicks, gouges, or scratches that mar the wood surface. (See "Dents and Gouges," page 138.)

If you're painting a furniture piece with open-grain wood such as mahogany or oak, and you don't want open pores to show up in the final finish, use a paste wood filler. (See "Filling Open-Grain Wood," page 144.)

Most manufacturers of solvent-based paints also recommend using an undercoating, or primer, before applying the top color coat. A primer is an opaque version of the clear sealer used for transparent finishes. Primers are usually white but can be tinted to match the top-coat color more closely, making them easier to cover. Because primers are easy to sand, you can build them up in several coats, sanding the final coat to provide a smooth foundation for the top coats.

As with brushable transparent finishes, a paint finish is only as good as the brush with which it's applied, so be sure to use one of good quality. Use a synthetic-bristle brush to apply latex paints and a natural-bristle brush for solvent-based paints. Presoak the brush briefly in the appropriate solvent, and brush out the excess on clean paper or wood before dipping it into the paint.

Applying Alkyd Enamels

Difficulty Level:

TOOLS AND MATERIALS
- Thinned shellac
- Natural-bristle brush
- Tack cloth
- Primer
- Alkyd enamel
- #0000 steel wool
- Soft cotton cloth
- 280- to 320-grit sandpaper

1 Apply a shellac coat. Prepare the wood for finishing. (See "Preparing for Finish Sanding," page 141.) If you're painting over an existing finish or paint, use the deglosser solvent recommended on the paint label directions to wash the surface. Apply a thinned brush coat of shellac, and let it dry.

Sand the shellac-coated surface once it is dry. For best results use 280- to 320-grit stearated silicone carbide paper.

2 Apply primer. Dust the surface with a tack cloth, and brush on a coat of the recommended undercoating (primer) or a thinned coat of enamel. Allow the undercoating to dry fully.

3 Sand the surface. Sand the surface with 280- to 320-grit stearated silicone carbide paper, and remove all dust with a tack cloth. If you're using a primer or undercoating, brush on another coat, sanding after it dries with 280- to 320-grit stearated paper.

4 Apply a top coat. After the primer is dry, brush on a coat of enamel by first brushing across the grain and then with the grain, as with varnish. Continue the same brushing procedure as you would with varnish. (See "Applying a Varnish Finish," page 155.) Let enamel dry for about 30 hours. If the enamel covers the surface well and there appears to be a sufficient amount of top coat, go to the next step. If not, repeat Steps 4 and 5 to build up the top coat sufficiently.

5 Wet-sand the surface. Using 600-grit wet-or-dry sandpaper, wet-sand the surface using soapy water as a lubricant. Don't rub so vigorously that you'll cut through the paint surface. Also, be careful on ridges and edges so that you don't cut through the paint. For uneven areas, you may want to rub the painted finish with #000 or #0000 steel wool rather than sandpaper.

6 Rub down the surface with steel wool. When you've finished sanding, rub down the piece well with #0000 steel wool. Wipe the surface with a soft clean cloth. You should now have a smooth, glass-like finish, with no rough spots or brush marks apparent when you run your hand over it.

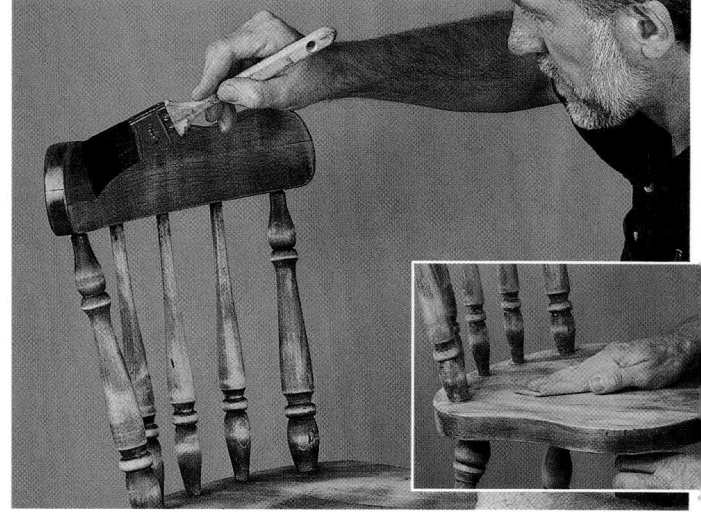

1 Apply a coat of shellac between an old finish or raw wood and the new paint. When dry, sand the surface (inset) using 280- to 320-grit stearated sandpaper.

3 Sand the surface with 280- to 320-grit stearated sandpaper. You can then apply another primer coat.

5 After the last top coat is dry, wet-sand the surface using 600-grit wet-or-dry paper and soapy water.

Kingdom Restorations Ltd.
323 Trevathan St.
Rocky Mount, NC 27804
800-344-9257
www.kingdomrestorations.com
Sells furniture restoration products such as applicators, fillers, finishes, and polishes.

Lee Valley Tools
P.O. Box 1780
Ogdensburg, NY 13669
800-871-8158
www.leevalley.com
Mail-order and retail supplier of woodworking tools and cabinet hardware.

Makita USA
14930 Northam St.
La Mirada, CA 90638
714-522-8088
www.makitausa.com
Manufacturers portable power tools, including saws, planers, drills, hammers, grinders, and sanders, as well as pneumatic tools and outdoor power equipment.

MLCS Router Bits and Woodworking Products
P.O. Box 165
Huntingdon Valley, PA 19006
800-533-9298
www.mlcswoodworking.com
Sells woodworking products and provides instructional videos on its Web site.

OVIS
110 Jack D. Burlingame Dr.
Millwood, WV 25262
800-326-6847
www.ovisonline.com
A wholesale distributor of industrial woodworking supplies and machinery.

Rockler
4365 Willow Dr.
Medina, MN 55340
800-279-4441
www.rockler.com
Sells wood products, tools, and hardware.

Ryobi North America
1424 Pearman Dairy Rd.
Anderson, SC 29625
800-525-2579
www.ryobitools.com
Produces portable and bench-top power tools for contractors and DIYers.

The Stanley Works
1000 Stanley Dr.
New Britain, CT 06053
860-225-5111
www.stanleyworks.com
Manufactures an extensive line of hand and power tools.

Tools Plus
153 Meadow St.
Waterbury, CT 06702
203-573-0750
www.tools-plus.com
Sells a large selection of tools and accessories from top manufacturers.

Upholstery Supplies
4885 S. Broadway
Englewood, CO 80113
866-528-4170
www.furniturerestorationtoolsandsupplies.com
Sells furniture repair and upholstery supplies.

Vermont American Tool Co.
1800 W. Central Rd.
Mount Prospect, IL 60056
224-232-2000
www.vermontamerican.com
Manufacturer of hand tools and power-tool accessories, including bits, gauges, cutters, blades, guides, and hard-to-find tools such as nut splitters.

Woodcraft
1177 Rosemar Rd.
P.O. Box 1686
Parkersburg, WV 26102
800-535-4482
www.woodcraft.com
Sells woodworking tools, plans, and supplies.

Wood Finishers Depot
5212 Sjolander Rd.
Baytown, TX 77521
866-883-3768
www.woodfinishersdepot.com
Sells touch-up and finishing supplies for wood.

Woodworker's Supply
5604 Alameda Pl. NE
Albuquerque NM 87113
800-645-9292
www.woodworker.com
Offers a selection of woodworking tools, hardware, abrasives, adhesives, wood clamps, and finishing supplies.

Glossary

Abrasive Any material used to wear away, smooth, or polish a surface; for example, sandpaper that is used to smooth wood.

Alligatored finish Any finished surface that shows numerous cracks caused by aging and drying.

Aluminum oxide A long-life grit for abrasive wheels and sandpapers.

Aniline dye A synthetic tinting medium made from coal-tar products, which can be dissolved in water or alcohol and used to change the color of wood.

Apron The board between the tops of a table's legs that supports the top or, in the case of a chair, the seat. Also called the *skirt*.

Backsaw A saw used for small work on the bench top. An extra-fine narrow backsaw is called a dovetail saw.

Block plane A small hand plane used on end grain.

Blotching A staining problem in which the stain is unevenly absorbed, causing light and dark areas. This is caused by a swirly grain or uneven density of a piece of wood.

Burn-in knife An electrically heated tool with a curved spoon-like tip that is used to melt lacquer or shellac sticks for repairing finish surfaces.

Burn-in stick A stick of filler material used to repair of surface damage to furniture. The filler must be melted onto the damaged surface and then trimmed smooth. Also called *lacquer stick* or *shellac stick*.

Butt joint A joint in which two pieces of wood are joined lengthwise without overlap or tongue.

C-clamp Used for small clamping work, these clamps get their name because of their shape.

Carcase The framework or body of a cabinet or piece of casegood furniture.

Carpenter's glue See *Polyvinyl glue.*

Casegood furniture Furniture such as bureaus and cabinets (casegoods) designed to contain things in drawers or behind doors as opposed to furniture that stands, such as tables and chairs.

Chamfer A square edge cut equally on one or both sides of a piece of wood so as to form a bevel.

Clamp A tool that holds pieces of wood or other items together, usually for gluing.

Clear finish Any of a number of wood finishes that allow the wood grain and color to be seen.

Closed-grain wood Wood such as maple and birch that has small, tight pores and a smooth surface when sanded.

Coarse-grain wood See *Open-grain wood.*

Contact cement A rubber-based liquid adhesive that bonds on contact; often used for applying veneers.

Crazing A mild form of alligatoring, characterized by small cracks in the finish.

Crosscut saw A saw used for cutting across the grain of wood.

Dado A type of groove that runs across the grain.

Danish oil See *Oil finish.*

Denatured alcohol A solvent used to thin shellac.

Distressing A finishing process that adds dents, scratches, burns, and other indications of wear and age to furniture for decorative purposes.

Dovetail joint A joint formed by one or more tapering projections (dovetails) on one board fitted tightly into mortises carved into another.

Dovetail saw See *Backsaw.*

Dowel A wood pin commonly used to join two pieces of wood. The dowel fits into holes drilled in each piece; this creates a dowel joint.

Dust mask A disposable device that covers the nose and mouth to prevent inhalation of dust or other material in the air. Compare with *respirator.*

Epoxy adhesive Adhesive based on an epoxy (or epoxide) resin or several such resins. Epoxy is of limited use in furniture-making, but it comes in handy for quick repairs.

Fasteners Nails, screws, brads, and other items that are used to join two components or secure hardware to furniture.

Fish eye Small craters in a new finish that are the result of an adverse reaction between the finish and substances such as wax or oil on the surface.

French polish A solution of shellac in alcohol used to give furniture a shiny finish. The alcohol evaporates to leave a thin coating of shellac on the piece.

Grain The direction and arrangement of wood fibers in a piece of wood. Grain reflects the growth-ring pattern in the tree. The grain will look different in different woods and as a result of different sawing techniques.

Grain filler See *Paste wood filler.*

Grit A measure of the roughness of an abrasive paper. The lower the figure given for the grit size, the coarser the paper.

Hardwood Wood that is cut from deciduous (leaf-shedding) trees. Although all such wood is designated as hardwood, some types are actually physically soft and easy to dent.

Hide glue The traditional glue used by cabinetmakers. It comes in toffee-like sheets, in pearls, or as a premixed liquid. Hide glue is reversible by applying heat and water.

Jack plane A general-purpose bench plane used to smooth rough stock. The bed is commonly 14 inches long with a 2-inch cutter.

Lac beetle An insect that secretes a fluid that is made into lac flakes, the basic ingredient in shellac.

Lacquer A clear or colored finish material that dries to a hard, glossy finish. Usually applied with a sprayer, lacquer dries too quickly for smooth application with a brush, unless it is specially formulated.

Lacquer stick See *Burn-in stick.*

Linseed oil A finishing oil made from pressed flax seeds. An ingredient used in paint (oil-based) and varnish.

Methylene chloride A chemical used as the active ingredient in most paint and varnish removers.

Mineral spirits Volatile solvent for oil-based finishes. Also called *turpentine* or *paint thinner.*

Miter joint A joint formed by cutting the

ends of two pieces of lumber at an equal angle—usually 45 degrees.

Mortise A (usually) rectangular slot or recess cut into a piece of wood and designed to receive a male part, or tenon.

Mortise-and-tenon joint A joint in which one piece has a square or rectangular projection (tenon) that fits snugly into a similarly shaped hole (mortise) in the second piece.

Mortise chisel A strong chisel designed specifically for cutting mortises.

Oil finish A clear finish produced by rubbing an oil, such as linseed or tung oil, on bare or stained wood. The oil is rubbed to a soft, glowing finish. Also called *Danish oil*.

Oilstone A fine-grained stone, lubricated with oil, which is used for sharpening cutting edges. Also called *sharpening stone*.

Open-grain wood Wood such as oak, mahogany, and walnut that has large, obvious pores. Also called *coarse-grain wood*.

Paint A pigmented opaque material that completely covers and hides the surface to which it is applied. Paint is available in oil-based and water-based formulas.

Paint thinner See *Mineral spirits*.

Paste wood filler Liquid or paste material designed to fill in holes or grain lines so that final finishes may be applied to a smooth surface. Also called *grain filler* or *pore filler*.

Patina The overall effect of the aging process on wood or a finish, generally characterized by a muting of the colors and a satin finish.

Polyurethane A varnish to which urethane resins have been added to improve durability.

Polyvinyl glue A frequently used wood glue that has as its base a synthetic resin called polyvinyl acetate. Also called *wood glue* (white) and *carpenter's glue* (yellow).

Pore filler See *Paste wood filler*.

Pumice A lava-rock abrasive ground into a powder as a polish.

Rabbet A notch-like cut made on the edge or end of a frame or board to receive a sheet of glass, a wooden panel, or another piece of wood to form a rabbet joint.

Rail The horizontal member of a frame or carcase.

Raising the grain A process of dampening the surface of wood with water to bring up or lift small fibers for final smooth sanding.

Rasp A rough-sided tool designed to dig into and wear away material such as wood.

Reamalgamated finish A previously alligatored or roughened finish that has been made level by rubbing the surface with solvent that melts the finish and allows it to dry smooth.

Respirator A filter device with a replaceable cartridge worn over the nose and mouth to remove irritants—dust and toxic pollutants—from inhaled air.

Rottenstone A fine powder abrasive made from crushing decomposed limestone. Rottenstone and oil are used as a fine finishing polish.

Router A wood-machining tool with a small vertical high-speed cutting blade.

Sanding block A padded wood block around which a piece of sandpaper is wrapped for hand-sanding a surface.

Sanding sealer A thinned shellac or other lightweight clear finish applied to wood to prevent the raising of wood grain by stain, filler, or final finish material.

Sandpaper A coated abrasive—usually flint, garnet, or aluminum oxide—glued to a paper, cloth, or plastic backing. It is used for smoothing or polishing woods.

Sawhorse A stand used to hold wood while it is being cut. Two sawhorses can hold plywood to form a work surface.

Sharpening guide A device used when sharpening the blades of chisels or planes. It holds the blade against the oilstone at exactly the correct angle.

Sharpening stone See *Oilstone*.

Shellac A clear finish material created by dissolving lac flakes in denatured alcohol. A 5-pound cut of shellac is made by dissolving 5 pounds of lac flakes in 1 gallon of denatured alcohol. A 1-pound cut is 1 pound of flakes in a gallon of alcohol.

Shellac stick See *Burn-in stick*.

Skirt See *Apron*.

Softwood Wood that comes from logs of cone-bearing (coniferous) trees.

Spline A thin piece of wood used as a wedge or as a joint reinforcement. A flat strip of wood may be glued into slots cut into two boards to be butt- or miter-joined. The spline increases the glue surface and the strength of the joint. In a worn joint, a spline may be inserted into the end of a cut dowel or tenon so that the section will fit more tightly into the joint hole or mortise.

Spontaneous combustion A fire caused by the heat generated by oxidizing oils in rags thrown in a pile.

Stain Any of various forms of water- or oil-based transparent or opaque coloring agents designed to penetrate the surface of the wood to color (stain) the material.

Stain controller Slow-evaporating petroleum-distillate solvent that is applied to hard-to-stain wood like pine as a washcoat. It works by filling up the pores and less-dense parts of the wood so the stain takes on a more even appearance. Also called *wood conditioner*.

Tack rag A piece of cheesecloth or other fabric treated with turpentine and varnish to create a sticky or tacky quality so that the rag will pick up and hold all the dust that it touches.

Tenon The male part of a mortise joint.

Toxic Poisonous.

Tung oil A water-resistant finishing oil or varnish ingredient made from crushed tung-tree seeds.

Turpentine See *Mineral spirits*.

Varnish A durable clear finish made of a mixture of resins, oil, and turpentine or other volatile spirits.

Veneer A thin sheet of wood applied to a piece of inferior wood or plywood. Fine wood veneer is used in furniture. This allows you to use rare and exotic woods, which either are not available in solid form or would be too expensive.

Vise A device, usually having a pair of jaws, designed to hold wood or other material while work is being done on it.

Warp The twisting of wood as it dries.

Washcoat Application of a wood conditioner, thinned linseed oil, or thinned shellac to wood prior to staining. You would apply a washcoat to wood that might blotch when stained with a liquid stain. See also *Stain controller*.

Wax stick A colored wax crayon that hides small defects in finished wood.

Wet-or-dry sandpaper A type of abrasive paper that can be used with lubrication. The grit is of silicon carbide, and the paper and glue are waterproof. Lubrication may be water or mineral spirits.

Wood conditioner See *Stain controller*.

Wood glue See *Polyvinyl glue*.

Wood putty A paste-like material used to fill holes and other defects in wood.

Index

Metric Equivalents

Length

1 inch	25.4mm
1 foot	0.3048m
1 yard	0.9144m
1 mile	1.61km

Area

1 square inch	645mm^2
1 square foot	0.0929m^2
1 square yard	0.8361m^2
1 acre	4046.86m^2
1 square mile	2.59km^2

Volume

1 cubic inch	16.3870cm^3
1 cubic foot	0.03m^3
1 cubic yard	0.77m^3

Common Lumber Equivalents

Sizes: Metric cross sections are so close to their U.S. sizes, as noted below, that for most purposes they may be considered equivalents.

Dimensional lumber	1 x 2	19 x 38mm
	1 x 4	19 x 89mm
	2 x 2	38 x 38mm
	2 x 4	38 x 89mm
	2 x 6	38 x 140mm
	2 x 8	38 x 184mm
	2 x 10	38 x 235mm
	2 x 12	38 x 286mm
Sheet sizes	4 x 8 ft.	1200 x 2400mm
	4 x 10 ft.	1200 x 3000mm
Sheet thicknesses	¼ in.	6mm
	⅜ in.	9mm
	½ in.	12mm
	¾ in.	19mm
Stud/joist spacing	16 in. o.c.	400mm o.c.
	24 in. o.c.	600mm o.c.

Capacity

1 fluid ounce	29.57mL
1 pint	473.18mL
1 quart	0.95L
1 gallon	3.79L

Weight

1 ounce	28.35g
1 pound	0.45kg

Temperature

Fahrenheit = Celsius x 1.8 + 32
Celsius = Fahrenheit - 32 x 5/9

Nail Size and Length

Penny Size	Nail Length
2d	1"
3d	1¼"
4d	1½"
5d	1¾"
6d	2"
7d	2¼"
8d	2½"
9d	2¾"
10d	3"
12d	3¼"
16d	3½"

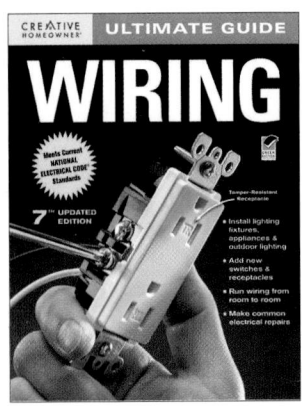
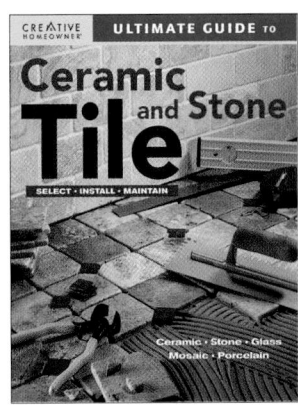

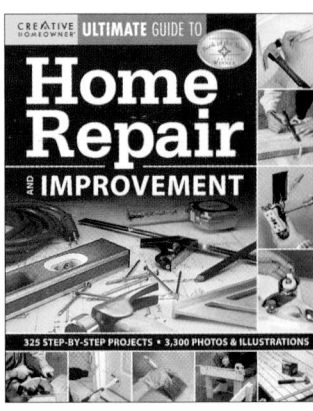

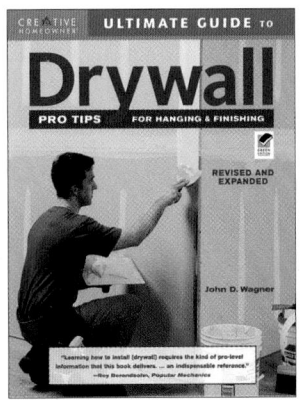

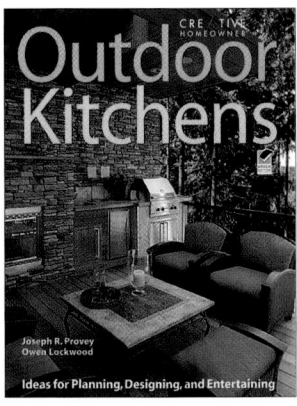

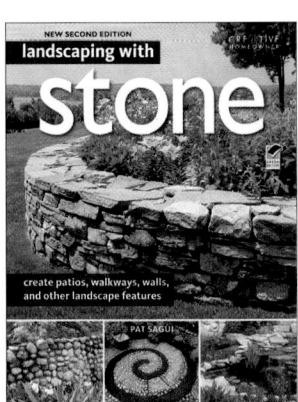